Index to Black American Writers
in Collective Biographies

Index to
BLACK AMERICAN WRITERS
in
Collective Biographies

DOROTHY W. CAMPBELL

1983   **LIBRARIES UNLIMITED, INC.**
Littleton, Colorado

LIBRARIES UNLIMITED, INC.
P.O. Box 263
Littleton, Colorado 80160

Library of Congress Cataloging in Publication Data

Campbell, Dorothy W., 1926-
    Index to Black American writers in collective
biographies.

    Includes index.
    1. Afro-American authors--Biography--Bibliography.
2. Afro-American authors--Biography--Indexes.
I. Title.
Z1229.N39C35   1983   016.81'09'896073   82-14940
[PS153.N5]
ISBN 0-87287-349-8

Libraries Unlimited books are bound with Type II nonwoven material that meets
and exceeds National Association of State Textbook Administrators' Type II
nonwoven material specifications Class A through E.

TABLE OF CONTENTS

Foreword

Since the 1960s, the period when more than 2,000 American colleges and universities established Afro-American studies programs to meet the demands of black students, there has been a growing interest in biographical information on black American writers. Because no one had analyzed collective biographies and other material in order to ferret out this information, librarians in all types of libraries have had to conduct long, extensive, and oftentimes fruitless searches for biographical information on black American writers.

Professor Dorothy W. Campbell has performed a yeoman's service by providing the world of scholarship this long-awaited *Index to Black American Writers in Collective Biographies*. She has painstakingly culled hundreds of literary sources to provide references to biographical information on approximately 1,900 black American writers. The names of some of these writers are not well known and are not found in the standard biographical dictionaries. The historical accident of race and color prevented many of these writers from having been included in other indices. The inclusion of the obscure as well as the very well known black writer in this index provides easy access to references that heretofore have not been readily available.

Students of black American culture are very often interested in gaining a greater understanding of an author by having access to critical material of biographical significance. The unique experience of black writers in America can be understood sometimes only by looking at the conditions that affected their lives. Helen E. Haines, in her memorable book *Living with Books*, said it best when she declared:

> Fine biography may thus be truly called by the old name, *Speculum vitae*. It gives to the reader a sense of sharing in actual human experience, yet of estimating and judging it at the same time; a sense of coming in touch with living persons, not with famous names, and at the same time a realization that each character, each destiny, is molded by influences of heredity, environment, and circumstances outside individual control.

With the publication of this reference book a searcher who would like to have "a sense of sharing in actual human experience" with a writer whose biographical sketch may be only in a collective biography now has access to this vital information. The inclusion of writers from many fields of endeavor makes this index indispensable as a reference tool. Moreover, the format and arrangement will make it very easy to use.

Professor Campbell's efforts have led to the unearthing of biographical information in collective biographies that will aid researchers, librarians, professors, and students in their quest for biographical material on black American writers.

E. J. Josey, Chief
Bureau of Specialist Library Services
New York State Education Department
Albany, New York

Introduction

The purpose of this index is to provide in a single volume references to biographical information on approximately 1,900 black American writers appearing in collective biographies. It is hoped that use of the volume will result in the provision of quick access to scattered information needed by persons such as those of the following categories: researchers, reference librarians, bibliographers; students and teachers involved in academic black studies courses; the casual reader seeking inspirational material; and the young reader who is beginning to study black American culture or may be seeking career-related material.

A broad concept of the term "writer" has been applied during the selection of biographies; therefore, in addition to creative writers, other contributors to resources in black American culture are included: biographers, autobiographers, historians, pioneer journalists, literary critics, illustrators of books, scholar/bibliographers, etc. Some writers who were born outside the United States but are well known for their activity in this country are included.

Two hundred sixty-seven titles with publication dates extending from 1837 to 1982 comprise the group of general biographical reference tools and specialized materials. Each work contains information about at least two black American writers. Included are many literary anthologies with biographical information appearing in introductory and appended sections, as well as some highly voluminous general works which were not exhaustively searched, as indicated by the minus sign in the list "Symbols and the Sources They Represent." Works prepared for children are marked by asterisks.

Information referred to in the index is considered to be 1) at least minimally substantive as regards some aspect of the writer's life, 2) suitable for indexing as individual biography, and 3) suitable for use by general users, even if it was prepared for a given clientele. The entries are arranged alphabetically by writer, with each name followed by date(s), one or more fields or activities, and variant names found in sources consulted. Variant names are enclosed in parentheses. Cross-references are provided as needed. For example:

Angelou, Maya (Marguerite Johnson), 1938-
Actress, poet, playwright

Johnson, Marguerite. *See* Angelou, Maya

Parentheses are also used to enclose the portions of names not shown in some publications. For example:

DuBois, W(illiam) E(dward) B(urghardt), 1868-1963

In this index, parenthetical portions have been disregarded during alphabetizing.

References that follow this personal data consist of symbols representing sources and, excepting those in audiovisual formats, indication of the specific location of biographical information within each source. It should be noted that symbols which represent reference sources are based on titles; those for non-reference sources are based on their main entries. Examples given here show both kinds:

Ency Blk Am   *Encyclopedia of Black America*

Noble. Beautiful   Noble, Jeanne L. *Beautiful, Also, Are*
                                the Souls of My Black Sisters

The list "Symbols and the Sources They Represent" provides explanation and bibliographic details for all titles included in the index.

Certain features of the works are shown in references. A particular edition may be indicated by inclusion of the last two digits of the year of publication. The symbols for three editions of a work shown below are accompanied by indication of publication dates.

Con Poets 70 *Contemporary Poets.* Published in 1970.
Con Poets 75 *Contemporary Poets.* 2nd ed. Published in 1975.
Con Poets 80 *Contemporary Poets.* 3rd ed. Published in 1980.

In most instances, when a time period of more than one year is shown in the title, the first year mentioned is indicated in the reference. Examples:

Who Blk Am 77 *Who's Who among Black Americans, 1977-1978.*
Writers Dr 82 *Writers Directory, 1982-1984.*

Appropriate abbreviations for illustrative material appear after the pagination for textual matter. Specific pagination for illustrative material is not given if such material is contained within the pagination for the textual material cited. Example:

Cur Biog Yrbk 76 p. 12-15 por

When appropriate, the number of a particular part of a volume is given. It appears after the volume number and is separated from it by a hyphen. The order of elements in references which include parts of volumes is shown in these examples:

Dict Am Biog Sup 58, 22-2: 345-47
(Symbol, year of publication, volume, part, pages)

Dict Lit Biog 7-1: 45-49 por
(Symbol, volume, part, pages, illustrative material)

It is hoped that the bibliographic details provided in this index will enable library users to independently identify biographical information about black American writers in collective sources considered for this project. Comments and reports of errors will be appreciated.

The use of holdings of many libraries is respectfully acknowledged. The collections consulted most frequently were those of the James E. Shepard Memorial Library and the School of Library Science at North Carolina Central University, Durham, North Carolina, and the Perkins Library at Duke University, Durham, North Carolina. Progress was made during brief visits to the Stanford L. Warren Branch of the Durham County (North Carolina) Library; the Peabody Collection at Hampton Institute, Hampton, Virginia; and the Moorland-Spingarn Research Center at Howard University, Washington, DC. The courtesy shown by librarians of these institutions was encouraging and is reflected in this index.

The compiler gratefully acknowledges the support of librarians, friends, and family which affected the development of this project. An expression of sincere appreciation is extended to E. J. Josey, Chief of the Bureau of Specialist Library Services of the State of New York, who suggested the idea, reviewed the plan, and provided invaluable assistance during the period of implementation; to Dr. Annette L. Phinazee, Dean of the School of Library Science at North Carolina Central University, who offered evaluative comments and advice; to Mary L. Brown, who helped with the identification of illustrators of children's books; to Deborah Cherry, Della Fulbright, Janice Hammett, Edna Lambeth, Audrey Miller, Patricia Perry, and Willa Thomas, who assisted with various preliminary tasks; to Deborah Cherry, Denise Gray, and Cora Sturgis for assistance with typing; to Cynthia for assisting in numerous ways and for the moving expression of concern in her poem "Mother, Do You Ever Sleep?" Deepest gratitude is due Joe, whose patience and general enthusiasm constituted a source of immeasurable support.

Dorothy W. Campbell
Assistant Professor
School of Library Science
North Carolina Central University
Durham, North Carolina

Abbreviations

*	Prepared especially for children
-	Search of contents was not exhaustive
ca.	about
ed.	edited, edition, editor
front.	frontispiece
il.	illustrated, illustration
jr.	junior
n.d.	no date
obit.	obituary
opp.	opposite
p.	page(s)
phot.	photography
por(s)	portrait(s)
pref.	preface
pseud.	pseudonym
pt.	part
rev.	revised
sup.	supplement
vol(s)	volume(s)

Symbols and Short Titles

Symbol	Short Title
ALA Yrbk	ALA Yearbook
Abdul. Enter	Famous Black Entertainers of Today
Adams. Auth	Afro-American Authors
Adoff. Blk on	Black on Black
*Adoff. Blk out	Black out Loud
*Adoff. Brothers	Brothers and Sisters
Adoff. Poet	Poetry of Black America
Afro-Am Art	Afro-American Artists
Afro-Am Ency	Afro-American Encyclopedia
Afro-Am Novel	Afro-American Novel, 1965-1975
*Alexander. Young	Young and Black in America
Alhamisi. Arts	Black Arts
-Alli Sup	A Supplement to Allibone's Critical Dictionary
Am Auth	American Authors, 1600-1900
Am Auth & Bks	American Authors and Books
Am Novel	American Novelists of Today
Am Wom Wr	American Women Writers
-AmSCAP	The ASCAP Biographical Dictionary
Anth Mag Verse	Anthology of Magazine Verse
Au Speaks	The Author Speaks
Auth & Ill	Authors and Illustrators of Children's Books
Auth Bk YP	Authors of Books for Young People
Auth News	Authors in the News
Barksdale. Writers	Black Writers of America
Barton. Witness	Witnesses for Freedom
Beasley. Trail	The Negro Trail Blazers of California

Symbol	Short Title
Beckles. Twenty	20 Black Women
Bennett. Pioneers	Pioneers in Protest
Bio Dict S Auth	Biographical Dictionary of Southern Authors
Bio Dr Am Cong	Biographical Directory of the American Congress
Bio Dr Librns	Biographical Directory of Librarians
Bio Dr Min	Biographical Directory of Negro Ministers
Bio Hist	Biographical History of Blacks in America
Blk Am Wr	Black American Writers
Blk Auth	Black Authors
Blk Lead	Black Leaders of the Twentieth Century
Blk Lit HS	Black Literature for High School Students
Blk Pioneers	Black Pioneers in American History
Blk Plots	Black Plots and Black Characters
Bone. Novel	The Negro Novel in America
Bontemps. American	American Negro Poetry
*Bontemps. Golden	Golden Slippers
Bontemps. Great	Great Slave Narratives
Bontemps. Harlem	The Harlem Renaissance Remembered
Books Are	Books Are by People
Bormann. Fore	Forerunners of Black Power
Boulware. Oratory	The Oratory of Negro Leaders
Brawley. Builders	Negro Builders and Heroes
Brawley. Early	Early Negro American Writers
Brawley. Lit	The Negro in Literature and Art
Broadside Auth	Broadside Authors and Artists
Brown. Caravan	The Negro Caravan
Brown. Homespun	Homespun Heroines
Bruce. Sketches	Short Biographical Sketches
Cele	Celebrations
Chamber	Chamber's Biographical Dictionary
Chapman. Blk V	Black Voices
Chapman. New	New Voices
Chester. Rising	Rising Tides
Childress. Scenes	Black Scenes
*Chittenden. Profiles	Profiles in Black and White

Symbol	Short Title
Christopher. Congress	America's Black Congressmen
Con Am Auth	Contemporary American Authors
-Con Auth	Contemporary Authors
-Con Auth ... R	Contemporary Authors First Revision
-Con Auth NR	Contemporary Authors New Revision Series
Con Auth P	Contemporary Authors Permanent Series
Con Drama	Contemporary Dramatists
Con Novel	Contemporary Novelists
Con Poets	Contemporary Poets
Coombs. Speak	We Speak as Liberators
Coombs. What	What We Must See
Cromwell. Read	Readings from Negro Authors
Crowell CAP	Crowell's Handbook of Contemporary American Poetry
Crowell CD	Crowell's Handbook of Contemporary Drama
Cullen. Carol	Caroling Dusk
Culp. Twen	Twentieth Century Negro Literature
Cuney. Linc	Lincoln University Poets
-Cur Biog Yrbk	Current Biography Yearbook
Dabney. Cin	Cincinnati's Colored Citizens
Daniel. Wom	Women Builders
Dannett. Profiles	Profiles of Negro Womanhood
David. Defiance	Black Defiance
David. Growing	Growing up Black
David. Living	Living Black in White America
David. Roots	Black Roots
David. Soldier	The Black Soldier
Davis. Cav	Cavalcade
Davis. Dark	From the Dark Tower
Davis. Mem	Memorable Negroes in Cleveland's Past
Davis. South	Southern Writing
Diamonstein. Open	Open Secrets
-Dict Am Biog	Dictionary of American Biography
-Dict Am Biog Sup	Dictionary of American Biography Supplement
Dict Lit Biog	Dictionary of Literary Biography
Dict Lit Biog Yrbk	Dictionary of Literary Biography Yearbook

Symbol	Short Title
-Dr Am Schol	Directory of American Scholars
Dr Perf Arts	Directory of Blacks in the Performing Arts
Dramatists	Dramatists
Dreer. Am Lit	American Literature
Drotning. Up	Up from the Ghetto
Ebony Success	The Ebony Success Library
Emanuel. Dark	Dark Symphony
Ency Am Biog	Encyclopedia of American Biography
Ency Blk Am	Encyclopedia of Black America
Exum. Keep	Keeping the Faith
Fauset. Freedom	For Freedom
Fax. Leaders	Contemporary Black Leaders
*Fleming. Pioneers	Pioneers in Print
Flynn. Achieve	Negroes of Achievement
Ford. Insights	Black Insights
Fourth Bk	Fourth Book of Junior Authors and Illustrators
Gayle. Bond	Bondage, Freedom and Beyond
Great Negroes	Great Negroes, Past and Present
Greene. Defenders	Black Defenders of America
Guide Am Lit	Guide to American Literature
Haley. Ency	Afro-American Encyclopedia
Haley. Spark	Sparkling Gems
Hammond. Van	In the Vanguard of a Race
Handbk Librns	Black Librarians as Creative Writers
Haskins. Profiles	Profiles in Black Power
Haslam. Forgot	Forgotten Pages of American Literature
Hayden. Kal	Kaleidoscope
Henderson. Under	Understanding the New Black Poetry
Hill. Anger	Anger and Beyond
Historical N Bio	Historical Negro Biographies
Hughes. Best	Best Short Stories by Negro Writers
Hughes. New	New Negro Poets, U.S.A.
Hughes. Poet	Poetry of the Negro, 1746-1949
Illus Bks YP	Illustrators of Books for Young People
Illus Ch Bks	Illustrators of Children's Books
Innis. Profiles	Profiles in Black

Symbol	Short Title
Int Auth & Wr	International Authors and Writers
Jenness. Twelve	Twelve Negro Americans
Johnson. Book	Book of American Negro Poetry
Jones. Fire	Black Fire
Jordan. Soul	Soulscript
Josey. Blk Librn	Black Librarian in America
Josey. What	What Black Librarians Are Saying
Katz. West	Black West
Kendricks. Voices	Afro-American Voices
Kerlin. Poets	Negro Poets and Their Poems
King. Drama	Black Drama Anthology
*King. Famous	Stories of Twenty-three Famous Negro Americans
King. Spirits	Black Spirits
King. Story	Black Short Story Anthology
Lerner. Wom	Black Women in White America
Lincoln Lib Arts	Lincoln Library of the Arts
Living BAA	Living Black American Authors
Locke. Four	Four Negro Poets
Loewenberg. Wom	Black Women in Nineteenth-Century American Life
Long. Writing	Afro-American Writing
Longman CT	Longman Companion to Twentieth Century Literature
Lyons. Leader	Black Leadership in American History
McGraw Ency WD	McGraw-Hill Encyclopedia of World Drama
Major. Poet	New Black Poetry
Majors. Wom	Noted American Negro Women
Margolies. Read	A Native Sons Reader
Metcalf. Profiles	Black Profiles
Metcalf. Up	Up from Within
Mezu. Leaders	Black Leaders of the Centuries
Miller. Dices	Dices or Black Bones
*Miller. Ten	Ten Slaves Who Became Famous
More Books	More Books by More People
More Jun Auth	More Junior Authors
Mott. Bio	Biographical Sketches

Symbol	Short Title
Mott. Nar	Narratives of Colored Americans
Murphy. Ebony	Ebony Rhythm
Murphy. N Voices	Negro Voices
Murphy. Today	Today's Negro Voices
NYT Obit	New York Times Obituaries Index
-Nat Cyclo	National Cyclopaedia of American Biography
Nat Play Dr	National Playwrights Directory
Negro Alm	Negro Almanac
Negro Handbk	Negro Handbook
Neyland. Flor	12 Black Floridians
Noble. Beautiful	Beautiful Also
North Car Auth	North Carolina Authors
Northrop. College	College of Life
Notable Am Wom	Notable American Women
Notable Am Wom Mod	Notable American Women: Modern Period
Notable Names	Notable Names in the American Theatre
Novelists	Novelists and Prose Writers
Ohio Auth	Ohio Authors and Their Books
Oliver. Drama	Contemporary Black Drama
O'Neill. Speeches	Speeches by Black Americans
Ovington. Portraits	Portraits in Color
Owen. Poet	Contemporary Poetry of North Carolina
Oxford Am	Oxford Companion to American Literature
Paths	Paths toward Freedom
Penguin Am Lit	Penguin Companion to American Literature
Penn. Press	Afro-American Press and Its Editors
*Peters. Ebony	Ebony Book of Black Achievement
Poets	Poets
Pol Profiles	Political Profiles
Profiles Blk Ach	Profiles of Black Achievement
Profiles Lit	Profiles in Literature
Reader's Adviser	Reader's Adviser: A Layman's Guide
Reader's Ency	Reader's Encyclopedia of American Literature
Richardson. Great	Great American Negroes Great Black Americans
Richmond. Bid	Bid the Vassal Soar

Symbol	Short Title
Robinson. Nommo	Nommo
Robinson. Poets	Early Black American Poets
Robinson. Prose	Early Black American Prose
Rogers. World	World's Great Men of Color
*Rollins. Enter	Famous Negro Entertainers
*Rollins. Famous	Famous American Negro Poets
*Rollins. They	They Showed the Way
Scally. Catholic	Negro Catholic Writers
Scruggs. Wom	Women of Distinction
Selected BAA	Selected Black American Authors
Sherman. Invisible	Invisible Poets
Shuman. Galaxy	Galaxy of Black Writing
Shuman. Nine	Nine Black Poets
*Sign Am Auth	Significant American Authors
*Sign Am Wom	Significant American Women
Simmons. Men	Men of Mark
Something ATA	Something about the Author
Southern Wr	Southern Writers
*Sterling. Fore	Black Foremothers
*Sterling. Four	Four Took Freedom
*Sterling. Lift	Lift Every Voice
Sterling. Speak	Speak out in Thunder Tones
*Sterne. Dream	I Have a Dream
Third Bk	Third Book of Junior Authors
Thorpe. Hist	Black Historians
Troup. Geor	Distinguished Negro Georgians
Turner. Voices	Voices from the Black Experience
Twen CA	Twentieth Century Authors
Twen CA Sup	Twentieth Century Authors, First Supplement
Twen CCW	Twentieth Century Children's Writers
Wagner. Poets	Black Poets of the United States
*Walser. Young	Young Readers' Picturebook of Tar Heel Authors
Watts Wr	From the Ashes
Webster Am Biog	Webster's American Biographies
White. Verse	Anthology of Verse by American Negroes
Whitlow. Lit	Black American Literature

Symbol	Short Title
-Who Am	Who's Who in America
Who Blk Am	Who's Who among Black Americans
Who Col Am	Who's Who in Colored America
Who Col Lo	Who's Who in Colored Louisiana
Who Col Race	Who's Who of the Colored Race
Who Theatre	Who's Who in the Theatre
Who Twen	Who's Who in Twentieth Century Literature
Who Was	Who Was Who in America
Who Was H	Who Was Who: Historical Volume
Who Was HR	Who Was Who: Historical, Revised Edition
Williams. Wom	American Black Women
Wom Am	Women in America: A Guide
Woodson. Orators	Negro Orators and Their Orations
Wor Auth	World Authors
Writers Dr	Writers Directory
Young. 1755	Major Black Religious Leaders, 1755-1940
Young. Since 1940	Major Black Religious Leaders since Nineteen Forty
*Young, M. Lead	Black American Leaders

Symbols and the Sources They Represent

ALA Yrbk
ALA Yearbook: A Review of Library Events. Vols. 1-6. Chicago: American Library Association, 1976-1981. Annual.

Abdul. Enter
Famous Black Entertainers of Today. By Raoul Abdul. New York: Mead (c1974). 159p.

Adams. Auth
Afro-American Authors. By William Adams. Boston: Houghton Mifflin (c1972). 165p.

Adoff. Blk on
Black on Black: Commentaries by Negro Americans. Compiled and edited by Arnold Adoff. New York: Macmillan (1968). 236p.

*Adoff. Blk out
Black out Loud: An Anthology of Modern Poems by Black Americans. Edited by Arnold Adoff; drawings by Alvin Hollingsworth. New York: Macmillan, 1970. 86p. il.

*Adoff. Brothers
Brothers and Sisters: Modern Stories by Black Americans. Edited by Arnold Adoff. New York: Macmillan, 1970. 237p.

Adoff. Poet
Poetry of Black America. Edited by Arnold Adoff. New York: Harper & Row, 1973. 552p.

Afro-Am Art
Afro-American Artists: A Bio-Bibliographical Directory. Compiled and edited by Theressa D. Cederholm. Boston: Trustees of the Boston Public Library, 1973. 348p.

Afro-Am Ency
Afro-American Encyclopedia. 10 vols. Miami, FL: Educational Book Publishers, 1974. il.

Afro-Am Novel
The Afro-American Novel, 1965-1975: A Descriptive Bibliography of Primary and Secondary Material. By Helen R. Houston. Troy, NY: Whitston, 1977. 214p.

*Alexander. Young
Young and Black in America. Compiled by Rae Pace Alexander. Introductory notes by Julius Lester. New York: Random House (c1970). 143p.

Alhamisi. Arts
Black Arts: An Anthology of Black Creations. Edited by Ahmed Alhamisi and Harun Kofi Wangara. Detroit: Black Arts Publications, 1969. 158p.

-Alli Sup
A Supplement to Allibone's Critical Dictionary of English Literature and British and American Authors. 2 vols. By John F. Kirk. Lippincott, 1891. Detroit: Gale Research Co., 1965.

Am Auth
American Authors, 1600-1900: A Biographical Dictionary of American Literature. Edited by Stanley J. Kunitz and Howard Haycraft. New York: H. W. Wilson, 1938. 846p.

Am Auth & Bks
American Authors and Books, 1964 to the Present Day. 3rd revised edition. By W. J. Burke and Will D. Howe. Revised by Irving Weiss and Anne Weiss. New York: Crown, 1972. 719p.

Am Novel
American Novelists of Today. By Harry R. Warfel. New York: American Book Co., 1951. Reprint. Westport, CT: Greenwood Press, 1976. 478p.

Am Women Wr
American Women Writers: A Critical Guide from Colonial Times to the Present. Vols. 1-3. Edited by Lina Mainiero. New York: Frederick Ungar, 1979-1981.

-AmSCAP

-AmSCAP 66
The ASCAP Biographical Dictionary of Composers, Authors and Publishers. 1966 edition. Compiled and edited by the Lynn Farnol Group, Inc. New York: The American Society of Composers, Authors and Publishers (c1966). 845p.

-AmSCAP 80
ASCAP Biographical Dictionary. 4th edition. Compiled for the American Society of Composers, Authors and Publishers by Jaques Cattell Press. New York: R. R. Bowker Co., 1980. 589p.

Anth Mag Verse
Anthology of Magazine Verse for 1926 and Yearbook of American Poetry (Sequi-Centennial Edition). Edited by William Stanley Braithwaite. Boston: B. J. Brimmer, 1926.

Au Speaks
The Author Speaks: Selected "PW" Interviews, 1967-1976. By Publishers Weekly editors and contributors. New York: R. R. Bowker Co., 1977.

Auth & Ill
Authors and Illustrators of Children's Books: Writings on Their Lives and Works. By Miriam Hoffman and Eva Samuels. New York: Bowker, 1972. 471p.

Auth Bk YP

Auth Bk YP 67
Authors of Books for Young People. 1st Supplement. By Martha E. Ward and Dorothy A. Marquardt. Metuchen, NJ: Scarecrow, 1967. 289p.

Auth Bk YP 71
Authors of Books for Young People. 2nd edition. By Martha E. Ward and Dorothy A. Marquardt. Metuchen, NJ: Scarecrow, 1971. 579p.

Auth Bk YP Sup 79
Authors of Books for Young People. Supplement to the 2nd edition. By Martha E. Ward and Dorothy A. Marquardt. Metuchen, NJ: Scarecrow, 1979. 302p.

Auth News
Authors in the News. Vols. 1 and 2. Edited by Barbara Nykoruk. Detroit: Gale Research Co., 1976, 1977.

Barksdale. Writers
Black Writers of America: A Comprehensive Anthology. Edited by Richard Barksdale and Keneth Kinnamon. New York: Macmillan, 1972. 917p.

Barton. Witness
Witnesses for Freedom: Negro Americans in Autobiography. By Rebecca C. Barton. New York: Harper, 1948.

Beasley. Trail
The Negro Trail Blazers of California. By Delilah L. Beasley. Los Angeles, 1919. 317p. il.

Beckles. Twenty
20 Black Women: A Profile of Contemporary Black Maryland Women. By Frances N. Beckles. Baltimore: Gateway Press, 1978. 146p. pors.

Bennett. Pioneers
Pioneers in Protest. By Lerone Bennett, Jr. Chicago: Johnson Publishing Co., 1968. 267p.

Bio Dict S Auth
Biographical Dictionary of Southern Authors. By Lucian L. Knight. Originally published as *Library of Southern Literature, vol. 15: Biographical Dictionary of Authors.* Atlanta, GA: Martin & Hoyt, 1929. Reprint. Detroit: Gale Research Co., 1978. 487p.

Bio Dr Am Cong
Biographical Directory of the American Congress, 1774-1961. Washington, DC: Government Printing Office. 1961. 1863p.

Bio Dr Librns
A Biographical Directory of Librarians in the United States and Canada. 5th edition. Lee Ash, editor; B. A. Uhlendorf, associate editor. Chicago: American Library Association, 1970. 1250p.

Bio Dr Min

Bio Dr Min 65
Biographical Directory of Negro Ministers. By Ethel L. Williams. New York: Scarecrow, 1965. 421p.

Bio Dr Min 75
Biographical Directory of Negro Ministers. 3rd edition. By Ethel L. Williams. Boston: G. K. Hall, 1975. 584p.

Bio Hist
Biographical History of Blacks in America since 1528. By Edgar A. Toppin. New York: David McKay, 1971. 499p.

Blk Am Wr
Black American Writers Past and Present: A Biographical and Bio-Bibliographical Dictionary. 2 vols. By Theressa Gunnels Rush, Carol Fairbanks Myers and Esther Spring Arata. Metuchen, NJ: Scarecrow, 1975.

Blk Auth
Black Authors. (Filmstrips) New York: Brunswick Productions; New York: Miller-Brody Productions, 1976.

Blk Lead
Black Leaders of the Twentieth Century. (Filmstrips, cassettes) Miami, FL: International Book Corp., 1969.

Blk Lit HS
Black Literature for High School Students. By Barbara Stanford and Karima Amin. Urbana, IL: National Council of Teachers of English, 1978. 273p.

Blk Pioneers
Black Pioneers in American History. Edited by Jonathan Katz. New York: Caedmon.

Vol. 1, 19th Century. Performance by Eartha Kitt and Moses Gunn. (1 record, TC 1252 or 1 cassette, CDL 51252)

Vol. 2, 19th-20th Centuries. Performance by Diana Sands and Moses Gunn. (1 record, TC 1299 or 1 cassette, CDL 51299)

Blk Plots
Black Plots and Black Characters: A Handbook for Afro-American Literature.
By Robert L. Southgate. Syracuse, NY: Gaylord Professional Publications, 1979.
456p.

Bone. Novel
The Negro Novel in America. Revised edition. By Robert A. Bone. New Haven,
CT: Yale University Press, 1965. 289p.

Bontemps. American

Bontemps. American 63
American Negro Poetry. Edited by Arna Bontemps. New York: Hill and Wang
(1963). 197p.

Bontemps. American 74
American Negro Poetry. Edited and with an introduction by Arna Bontemps.
Revised edition. New York: Hill and Wang (1974). 231p.

*Bontemps. Golden
Golden Slippers: An Anthology of Negro Poetry for Young Readers. Compiled
by Arna Bontemps. New York: Harper & Row, 1941. 220p.

Bontemps. Great
Great Slave Narratives. Selected and introduced by Arna Bontemps. Boston:
Beacon (c1969). 331p.

Bontemps. Harlem
The Harlem Renaissance Remembered. Essays edited with a memoir by Arna
Bontemps. New York: Dodd, Mead (c1972). 310p. il.

Books Are
*Books Are by People: Interviews with 104 Authors and Illustrators of Books for
Young Children.* Edited by Lee Bennett Hopkins. New York: Citation Press,
1969. 349p. il.

Bormann. Fore
Forerunners of Black Power: The Rhetoric of Abolition. Edited by Ernest G.
Bormann. Englewood Cliffs, NJ: Prentice-Hall, 1971. 248p.

Boulware. Oratory
The Oratory of Negro Leaders: 1900-1968. By Marcus H. Boulware. Westport,
CT: Negro Universities Press, 1969. 312p.

Brawley. Builders
Negro Builders and Heroes. By Benjamin Brawley. Chapel Hill: University of
North Carolina, 1937. 315p.

Brawley. Early
Early Negro American Writers. Selections with biographical and critical introductions. By Benjamin Brawley. Chapel Hill: University of North Carolina Press, 1935. 305p.

Brawley. Lit
The Negro in Literature and Art in the United States. By Benjamin Brawley. New York: Duffield, 1930. Reprint. St. Clair Shores, MI: Scholarly Press, 1972. 231p.

Broadside Auth
Broadside Authors and Artists: An Illustrated Biographical Dictionary. Compiled and edited by Leaonead Bailey. Detroit: Broadside Press, 1974. 125p. il.

Brown. Caravan
The Negro Caravan: Writings by American Negroes. Edited by Sterling A. Brown, Arthur P. Davis, and Ulysses Lee. New York: Dryden Press, 1941. 1082p.

Brown. Homespun
Homespun Heroines and Other Women of Distinction. Compiled and edited by Hallie Q. Brown; foreword by Mrs. Josephine Turpin Washington. Xenia, OH: Aldine Pub. Co. (c1926). 248p. pors.

Bruce. Sketches
Short Biographical Sketches of Eminent Negro Men and Women in Europe and the United States. Compiled by John E. Bruce. Yonkers, NY: Gazette Press, 1910. 103p.

Cele
Celebrations: A New Anthology of Black American Poetry. Compiled and edited by Arnold Adoff. Introduced by Quincy Troupe. Chicago: Follett, 1977. 285p.

Chamber
Chamber's Biographical Dictionary. Revised edition. Edited by J. O. Thorne. London: W. & R. Chambers, 1969. 1432p.

Chapman. Blk V
Black Voices: An Anthology of Afro-American Literature. Compiled by Abraham Chapman. New York: New American Library, 1968. 718p.

Chapman. New
New Black Voices: An Anthology of Contemporary Afro-American Literature. Edited by Abraham Chapman. New York: New American Library (c1972). 606p.

Chester. Rising
Rising Tides: 20th Century American Poets. Edited by Laura Chester and Sharon Barba. New York: Washington Square Press, 1973. 410p.

Childress. Scenes
Black Scenes. Edited by Alice Childress. Garden City, New York: Doubleday, 1971. 154p.

*Chittenden. Profiles
Profiles in Black and White: Stories of Men and Women Who Fought against Slavery. By Elizabeth F. Chittenden. Illustrated with photographs and engravings. New York: Scribner's Sons, 1973. 182p. il.

Christopher. Congress
America's Black Congressmen. By Maurine Christopher. New York: Thomas Y. Crowell (1971). 283p. il.

Con Am Auth
Contemporary American Authors: A Critical Survey and 219 Bio-Bibliographies. By Fred Benjamin Millett. New York: Harcourt, 1940. 716p.

-Con Auth
Contemporary Authors: A Bio-Bibliographical Guide to Current Authors and Their Works. Vols. 1-103. Detroit: Gale Research Co., 1962-1982.

-Con Auth ... R
Contemporary Authors First Revision. Vols. 17-44. Detroit: Gale Research Co., 1965-1979.

-Con Auth NR
Contemporary Authors New Revision Series. Vols. 1-4. Detroit: Gale Research Co., 1962-1981.

Con Auth P
Contemporary Authors Permanent Series. Vols. 1 and 2. Detroit: Gale Research Co., 1975, 1978.

Con Drama

Con Drama 73
Contemporary Dramatists. Edited by James Vinson. New York: St. Martin's Press (c1973). 926p.

Con Drama 77
Contemporary Dramatists. 2nd edition. Edited by James Vinson and D. L. Kirpatrick. New York: St. Martin's Press, 1977. 1088p.

Con Novel

Con Novel 72
Contemporary Novelists. Edited by James Vinson. New York: St. Martin's Press (c1972). 1442p.

Con Novel 76
Contemporary Novelists. 2nd edition. Edited by James Vinson and D. L. Kirpatrick. New York: St. Martin's Press (c1976). 1636p.

Con Poets

Con Poets 70
Contemporary Poets. Editor, Rosalie Murphy; series editor, James Vinson. New York: St. Martin's Press, 1970. 1243p.

Con Poets 75
Contemporary Poets. 2nd edition. James Vinson, editor; D. L. Kirpatrick, associate editor. New York: St. Martin's Press, 1975. 1849p.

Con Poets 80
Contemporary Poets. 3rd edition. James Vinson and Daniel Kirpatrick, eds. New York: St. Martin's Press, 1980. 1900p.

Coombs. Speak
We Speak as Liberators: Young Black Poets. Edited by Orde Coombs. New York: Dodd, Mead, 1970. 252p.

Coombs. What
What We Must See: Young Black Storytellers, an Anthology. Compiled by Orde Coombs. New York: Dodd, Mead, 1971. 210p.

Cromwell. Read
Readings from Negro Authors for Schools and Colleges. By Otelia Cromwell. New York: Harcourt, Brace, 1931. 388p.

Crowell CAP
Crowell's Handbook of Contemporary American Poetry. By Karl Malkoff. New York: Thomas Y. Crowell (c1973). 338p.

Crowell CD
Crowell's Handbook of Contemporary Drama. By Michael Anderson, Jacques Guicharnaud, Kristin Morrison, Jack D. Zipes, and others. New York: Thomas Y. Crowell (c1971). 505p.

Cullen. Carol
Caroling Dusk: An Anthology of Verse by Negro Poets. Edited by Countee Cullen. Decorations by Aaron Douglas. New York: Harper, 1927. 237p. il.

Culp. Twen
Twentieth Century Negro Literature; or a Cyclopedia of Thought. Edited by Daniel Wallace Culp. Toronto, 1902. Reprint. New York: Arno Press, 1969. 472p.

Cuney. Linc
Lincoln University Poets: Centennial Anthology, 1854-1954. Edited by Waring Cuney, Langston Hughes, and Bruce McM. Wright. Foreword by Horace Mann Bond; introduction by J. Saunders Redding. New York: Fine Editions Press, 1954. 72p.

-Cur Biog Yrbk
Current Biography Yearbook. New York: H. W. Wilson Co., 1940-1980.

Dabney. Cin
Cincinnati's Colored Citizens; Historical, Sociological and Biographical. By Wendell P. Dabney. New York: Negro Universities Press, 1926. 440p. pors.

Daniel. Wom
Women Builders. By Sadie I. Daniel. Washington: Associated Publishers, 1970. 308p. Reprint of 1931 edition.

Dannett. Profiles
Profiles of Negro Womanhood. 2 vols. By Sylvia G. L. Dannett. Yonkers, NY: Educational Heritage, 1964, 1966. il. pors.

David. Defiance
Black Defiance: Black Profiles in Courage. Edited by Jay David. New York: William Morrow, 1972. 240p.

David. Growing
Growing up Black. Edited by Jay David. New York: William Morrow, 1968. 256p.

David. Living
Living Black in White America. Edited by Jay David and Elaine Crane; foreword by David Lewis. New York: William Morrow, 1971. 317p.

David. Roots
Black Roots. Edited by Jay David and Catherine Green. Evanston, IL: McDougal-Littell (c1976). 224p.

David. Soldier
The Black Soldier from the American Revolution to Vietnam. Edited by Jay David and Elaine Crane. New York: William Morrow, 1971. 248p.

Davis. Cav
Cavalcade: Negro American Writing from 1760 to the Present. Arthur P. Davis and Saunders Redding, editors. Boston: Houghton Mifflin, 1971. 905p.

Davis. Dark
From the Dark Tower; Afro-American Writers, 1900 to 1960. By Arthur P. Davis. Washington, DC: Howard University Press, 1974. 302p. il.

Davis. Mem
Memorable Negroes in Cleveland's Past. By Russell H. Davis. Cleveland: The Western Reserve Historical Society, 1969. 58p. il.

Davis. South
Southern Writing, 1585-1920. Edited by Richard Beale Davis, C. Hugh Holman, and Louis D. Rubin, Jr. New York: Odyssey, 1970. 994p.

Diamonstein. Open
Open Secrets: Ninety-four Women in Touch with Our Time. By Barbaralee Diamonstein. New York: Viking, 1972. 474p.

-Dict Am Biog
Dictionary of American Biography. Prepared under the auspices of the American Council of Learned Societies. New York: Scribner's Sons.
    Original edition, vols. 1-20, 1928-1937
    Subscription edition, vols. 1-11, 1944-1958

-Dict Am Biog Sup
Dictionary of American Biography Supplement. Vols. 1-5. New York: Scribner's Sons, 1944-1977.

Dict Lit Biog
Dictionary of Literary Biography. Vols. 1-8. Detroit: Gale Research Co., 1978-1981.

Dict Lit Biog Yrbk
Dictionary of Literary Biography Yearbook: 1980. Detroit: Gale Research Co. (c1981).

-Dr Am Schol
Directory of American Scholars. New York: R. R. Bowker Co., 1969, 1974, 1978.

Dr Perf Arts
Directory of Blacks in the Performing Arts. By Edward Mapp. Metuchen, NJ: Scarecrow Press, 1978. 428p.

Dramatist
Dramatists. James Vinson, editor; D. L. Kirpatrick, associate editor. New York: St. Martin's Press, 1979. 648p. (Great Writers of the English Language)

Dreer. Am Lit
American Literature by Negro Authors. By Herman Dreer. New York: Macmillan, 1950. 334p. il.

Drotning. Up
Up from the Ghetto. 1st edition. By Phillip T. Drotning and Wesley W. South. New York: Cowles, 1970. 207p.

Ebony Success
The Ebony Success Library. 3 vols. By the editors of Ebony. Nashville, TN: Southwestern Co., by arrangement with Johnson Publishing Co., 1973. il.
    Vol. 1, *1000 Successful Blacks*
    Vol. 2, *Famous Blacks Give Secrets of Success*
    Vol. 3, *Career Guide*

Emanuel. Dark
Dark Symphony: Negro Literature in America. Edited by James A. Emanuel and Theodore Goss. New York: Free Press, 1968. 604p.

Ency Am Biog
Encyclopedia of American Biography. Edited by John A. Garraty. New York: Harper & Row, 1974. 1241p.

Ency Blk Am
Encyclopedia of Black America. Edited by W. Augustus Low and Virgil A. Clift. New York: McGraw-Hill, 1981. 921p. il.

Exum. Keep
Keeping the Faith: Writings by Contemporary Black American Women. Edited by Pat Crutchfield Exum. Greenwich, CT: Fawcett Publications (c1974). 288p.

Fauset. Freedom
For Freedom: A Biographical Story of the American Negro. By Arthur Huff Fauset. Drawings by Mabel Betsy Hill. Philadelphia: Franklin Publishing and Supply Co., 1927. 200p. il.

Fax. Leaders
Contemporary Black Leaders. By Elton C. Fax. New York: Dodd, Mead, 1970. 243p. il.

*Fleming. Pioneers
Pioneers in Print: Adventures in Courage. By Alice Fleming. Chicago: Reilly & Lee Books, 1971. 130p.

Flynn. Achieve
Negroes of Achievement in Modern America. By James J. Flynn. Introduction by Roy E. Wilkins; illustrated with photographs. New York: Dodd, Mead, 1970. 272p. il.

Ford. Insights
Black Insights: Significant Literature by Black Americans—1760 to the Present. Edited by Nick Aaron Ford. Waltham, MA: Ginn, 1971. 373p.

Fourth Bk
Fourth Book of Junior Authors and Illustrators. Edited by Doris De Montreville and Elizabeth D. Crawford. New York: H. W. Wilson, 1978. 369p.

Gayle. Bond
Bondage, Freedom and Beyond: The Prose of Black Americans. Edited by Addison Gayle, Jr. Garden City, NY: Doubleday, 1971. 154p.

Great Negroes
Great Negroes Past and Present. 3rd edition. By Russell L. Adams. Chicago: Afro-American Publishing Co., 1969. 212p.

Greene. Defenders
Black Defenders of America, 1775-1973. By Robert Ewell Greene. Chicago: Johnson Publishing Co., 1974. 416p.

Guide Am Lit
Guide to American Literature from Emily Dickinson to the Present. By James T. Callow and Robert J. Reilly. New York: Barnes & Noble, 1977. 272p.

Haley. Ency
Afro-American Encyclopedia. Compiled by James T. Haley. Nashville, TN: Haley and Florida, 1895. 640p.

Haley. Spark
Sparkling Gems of Race Knowledge Worth Reading. Compiled by James T. Haley. Nashville, TN: J. T. Haley & Co., 1897. 200p. il.

Hammond. Van
In the Vanguard of a Race. By L. H. Hammond. New York: Council of Women for Home Missionaries and the Missionary Education Movement of the United States and Canada, 1922. 176p. il.

Handbk Librns
"Black Librarians as Creative Writers," by Ann A. Shockley. In *Handbook of Black Librarianship*, compiled and edited by E. J. Josey and Ann A. Shockley. Littleton, CO: Libraries Unlimited, 1977. p. 160-66.

Haskins. Profiles
Profiles in Black Power. By James Haskins. Garden City, NY: Doubleday, 1972, 259p.

Haslam. Forgot
Forgotten Pages of American Literature. By Gerald W. Haslam. New York: Houghton Mifflin, 1970. 398p.

Hayden. Kal
Kaleidoscope: Poems by American Negro Poets. Edited by Robert Hayden. New York: Harcourt, Brace & World, 1967. 231p.

Henderson, Under
Understanding the New Black Poetry: Black Poetry, Black Speech and Black Music as Poetic Reference. Compiled by Stephen E. Henderson. New York: William Morrow, 1973. 394p.

Hill. Anger
Anger and Beyond: The Negro Writer in the United States. 1st edition. Edited by Herbert Hill. New York: Harper & Row, 1966. 227p.

Historical N Bio
Historical Negro Biographies. By Wilhelmena S. Robinson. New York: Publishers Co., 1967. 291p. por. (International Library of Negro Life and History)

Hughes. Best
The Best Short Stories by Negro Writers: An Anthology from 1899 to the Present. Edited and with an introduction by Langston Hughes. Boston: Little, Brown, 1967. 508p.

Hughes. New
The New Negro Poets, U.S.A. By Langston Hughes. Foreword by Gwendolyn Brooks. Bloomington: Indiana University Press, 1964. 127p.

Hughes. Poet
The Poetry of the Negro, 1746-1970: An Anthology. Edited by Langston Hughes and Arna W. Bontemps. Garden City, NY: Doubleday (c1970). 645p.

Illus Bks YP

Illus Bks YP 70
Illustrators of Books for Young People. By Martha E. Ward and Dorothy A. Marquardt. Metuchen, NJ: Scarecroww Press, 1970. 166p.

Illus Bks YP 75
Illustrators of Books for Young People. 2nd edition. By Martha E. Ward and Dorothy A. Marquardt. Metuchen, NJ: Scarecrow Press, 1975. 223p.

Illus Ch Bks

Illus Ch Bks 57
Illustrators of Children's Books, 1957-1966. Compiled by Lee Kingman, Joanna Foster and Ruth Giles Lontoft. Boston: Horn Book, 1968. 295p. il.

Ill Ch Bks 67
Illustrators of Children's Books, 1967-1976. Compiled by Lee Kingman, Grace Allen Hogarth and Harriet Quimby. Boston: Horn Book, 1978. 290p. il.

Innis. Profiles
Profiles in Black: Biographical Sketches of 100 Living Black Unsung Heroes. 1st edition. Edited by Doris Funnye Innis and Julian Wu; consulting editor: Joyce Duren. New York: CORE Publications, a Division of the Congress of Racial Equality, 1976. 240p. il.

Int Auth & Wr
International Authors and Writers Who's Who. 8th edition. Edited by Adrian Gaster. Cambridge, England: International Biographical Centre, 1977.

Jenness. Twelve
Twelve Negro Americans. By Mary Jenness. New York: Friendship Press, 1936. 180p.

Johnson. Book
The Book of American Negro Poetry. Edited by James Weldon Johnson. New York: Harcourt, Brace, 1931. 300p.

Jones. Fire
Black Fire: An Anthology of Afro-American Writing. By LeRoi Jones and Larry Neal. New York: William Morrow, 1968. 670p.

Jordan. Soul
Soulscript: Afro-American Poetry. Edited by June Jordan. Garden City, NJ: Zenith Books, Doubleday (c1970). 146p.

Josey. Blk Librn
The Black Librarian in America. Edited, with an introduction by E. J. Josey. Metuchen, NJ: Scarecrow Press, 1970. 336p.

Josey. What
What Black Librarians Are Saying. Edited by E. J. Josey. Metuchen, NJ: Scarecrow Press, 1972, 317p.

Katz. West
The Black West. By William Leon Katz. Revised edition. Garden City, NY: Doubleday, 1973. 336p. il.

Kendricks. Voices
Afro-American Voices, 1960's-1970's. By Ralph Kendricks and Claudette Levitt. New York: Oxford Book Co., 1970.

Kerlin. Poets
Kerlin. Poets 23
Negro Poets and Their Poems. By Robert T. Kerlin. Washington, DC: Associated Publishers (c1923). 285p. il.

Kerlin. Poets 35
Negro Poets and Their Poems. 3rd edition. Revised and enlarged; illustrated. By Robert T. Kerlin. Washington, DC: Associated Publishers (c1935). 354p.

King. Drama
Black Drama Anthology. Edited by Woodie King and Ron Miller. New York: Columbia University Press (c1972). 671p.

*King. Famous
Stories of Twenty-three Famous Negro Americans. By John T. King and Marcet H. King. Austin, TX: Steck-Vaughn, 1967. 120p.

King. Spirits
Black Spirits: A Festival of New Black Poets in America. Edited by Woodie King. New York: Random House, 1972. 252p.

King. Story
Black Short Story Anthology. Edited by Woodie King. New York: Columbia University Press, 1972. 381p.

Lerner. Wom
Black Women in White America: A Documentary History. Edited by Gerda Lerner. New York: Pantheon Books, 1972. 629p.

Lincoln Lib Arts
The Lincoln Library of the Arts, II. Columbus, OH: The Frontier Press Company, 1973. 846p.

Living BAA
Living Black American Authors: A Biographical Dictionary. By Ann Allen Shockley and Sue P. Chandler. New York and London: R. R. Bowker, 1973. 220p.

Locke. Four
Four Negro Poets. Edited by Alain Locke. New York: Simon & Schuster, 1927. 31p.

Loewenberg. Wom
Black Women in Nineteenth-Century American Life. Edited by Bert James Loewenberg and Ruth Bogin. University Park: Pennsylvania State University Press, 1976. 355p.

Long. Writing
Afro-American Writing: An Anthology of Prose and Poetry. 2 vols. Edited by Richard A. Long and Eugenia W. Collier. New York: New York University Press, 1972.

Longman CT
Longman Companion to Twentieth Century Literature. By Alfred C. Ward. London: Longman Group (c1970). 593p.

Lyons. Leader
Black Leadership in American History. By Thomas T. Lyons. Menlo Park, CA: Addison-Wesley (c1971). 246p.

McGraw Ency WD
McGraw-Hill Encyclopedia of World Drama. 4 vols. New York: McGraw-Hill, 1972.

Major. Poet
The New Black Poetry. Edited by Clarence Major. New York: International Publishers, 1969. 156p.

Majors. Wom
Noted American Negro Women, Their Triumphs and Activities. By M. A. Majors. Chicago: Donohue and Heneberry, 1893. 365p. il.

Margolies. Read
A Native Sons Reader. Edited by Edward Margolies. New York: J. B. Lippincott, 1970. 360p.

Metcalf. Profiles
Black Profiles. Expanded edition. By George R. Metcalf. New York: McGraw-Hill, 1970. 405p.

Metcalf. Up
Up from Within: Today's New Black Leaders. By George R. Metcalf. New York: McGraw-Hill, 1971.

Mezu. Leaders
Black Leaders of the Centuries. By S. Okechukwu Mezu and Ram Desai. Buffalo, NY: Black Academy Press (n.d.). 301p.

Miller, Dices
Dices or Black Bones. Edited by Adam D. Miller. Illustrated by Glenn Myles. Boston: Houghton Mifflin, 1970.

*Miller. Ten
Ten Slaves Who Became Famous. By Basil Miller. Grand Rapids, MI: Zondervan Publishing House, 1951. 72p. il.

More Books
More Books by More People: Interviews with Sixty-five Authors of Books for Children. By Lee Bennett Hopkins. New York: Citation Press, 1974. 410p.

More Jun Auth
More Junior Authors. Edited by Muriel Fuller. New York: H. W. Wilson, 1963.

Mott. Bio
Biographical Sketches and Interesting Anecdotes of Persons of Color. 2nd edition. Compiled by Abigail F. Mott. New York: Mahlon Day, 1837. 260p.

Mott. Nar
Narratives of Colored Americans. Compiled by Abigail F. Mott and M. S. Wood. New York: W. Wood, 1877. 276p.

Murphy. Ebony
Ebony Rhythm: An Anthology of Contemporary Negro Verse. Edited by Beatrice M. Murphy. Freeport, NY: Books for Libraries (1968, c1948). 162p.

Murphy. N Voices
Negro Voices: An Anthology of Contemporary Verse. Edited by Beatrice M. Murphy. Illustrations by Clifton Thompson Hill. New York: Henry Harrison (c1938). 173p. il.

Murphy. Today
Today's Negro Voices: An Anthology by Young Negro Poets. Edited by Beatrice M. Murphy. New York: J. Messmer (1970). 141p.

NYT Obit
The New York Times Obituaries Index, 1969-1978. Vol. 2. New York: The New York Times, 1980.

-Nat Cyclo
National Cyclopaedia of American Biography. New York and Clifton, NJ: James T. White, 1891- .
    Permanent series, vols. 1-60, 1891-1981
    Current series, A-L, 1924-1972

Nat Play Dr
National Playwrights Directory. Edited by Phyllis J. Kaye. Waterford, CT: The O'Neill Theater Center, 1977. 374p.

Negro Alm

Negro Alm 71
The Negro Almanac. 2nd edition. Compiled and edited by Harry A. Ploski and Ernest Kaiser. New York: Bellwether (c1971). 1110p. il.

Negro Alm 76
The Negro Almanac: A Reference Work on Afro-Americans. 1776 Bicentennial Edition, 1976. Compiled and edited by Harry A. Ploski and Warren Marr, II. New York: Bellwether (c1976). 1206p. il.

Negro Handbk
The Negro Handbook. Compiled by the editors of Ebony. Chicago: Johnson Publishing Co., 1966. 535p.

Neyland. Flor
12 Black Floridians. By Leedel W. Neyland. Tallahassee: Florida Agricultural and Mechanical University Foundation, 1970. 98p.

Noble. Beautiful
Beautiful Also, Are the Souls of My Black Sisters: A History of the Black Woman in America. By Jeanne L. Noble. Englewood Cliffs, NJ: Prentice-Hall, 1978. 353p.

North Car Auth
North Carolina Authors: A Selective Handbook. Prepared by a Joint Committee of the North Carolina English Teachers Association and the North Carolina Library Association. Chapel Hill: University of North Carolina Library, 1952. 136p.

Northrop. College
The College of Life; or Practical Self-Educator. A Manual of Self-Improvement for the Colored Race. By Henry D. Northrop. Originally published in 1895. Miami, FL: Menemosyne, 1969. 656p. il.

Notable Am Wom
Notable American Women, 1607-1950: A Biographical Dictionary. 3 vols. Edward T. James, editor; Janet Wilson James, associate editor; Paul S. Boyer, assistant editor. Cambridge, MA: Belknap Press of Harvard University Press, 1971.

Notable Am Wom Mod
Notable American Women: The Modern Period; A Biographical Dictionary. Edited by Barbara Sicherman (and others). Cambridge, MA: Belknap, 1980. 773p.

Notable Names
Notable Names in the American Theatre. Clifton, NJ: James T. White, 1976. 1250p.

Novelists
Novelists and Prose Writers. James Vinson, editor; D. L. Kirpatrick, associate editor. New York: St. Martin's Press, 1979. 1367p. (Great Writers of the English Language)

Ohio Auth
Ohio Authors and Their Books ..., 1796-1950. By William Coyle. Cleveland, OH: World, 1962.

Oliver, Drama
Contemporary Black Drama. Selected and edited with introductions by Clinton F. Oliver and Stephanie Sills. New York: Charles Scribner's Sons, 1971. 451p.

O'Neill. Speeches
Speeches by Black Americans. Compiled and edited by Daniel J. O'Neill. Encino, CA: Dickenson Publishing Co. (c1971). 274p.

Ovington. Portraits
Portraits in Color. By Mary White Ovington. New York: Viking, 1927. 241p.

Owen. Poet
Contemporary Poetry of North Carolina. Edited by Guy Owen and Mary C. Williams. Winston-Salem, NC: John F. Blair, 1977. 171p.

Oxford Am
Oxford Companion to American Literature. 4th edition. New York: Oxford University Press, 1965. 991p.

Paths
Paths toward Freedom: A Biographical History of Blacks and Indians in North Carolina by Blacks and Indians. Illustrations by James and Ernestine Huff. Raleigh: North Carolina State University Center for Urban Affairs (c1976). 240p. il.

Penguin Am Lit
Penguin Companion to American Literature. Edited by Malcolm Bradbury, Eric Mottram and Jean Franco. New York: McGraw-Hill (c1971). 384p.

Penn. Press
The Afro-American Press and Its Editors. By Irvin Garland Penn. Springfield, MA: Willey, 1891. 565 (11)p. pors.

*Peters. Ebony
The Ebony Book of Black Achievement. By Margaret Peters. Chicago: Johnson Publishing Co., 1970. 90p. il.

Poets
Poets. Edited by James Vinson; D. L. Kirpatrick, associate editor. New York: St. Martin's Press, 1979. 1141p. (Great Writers of the English Language)

Pol Profiles
Political Profiles. 5 vols. Edited by Nelson Lichtenstein; associate editor, Eleanora W. Schoenbaum. New York: Facts on File, Inc., 1976-1979.

Profiles Blk Ach
Profiles of Black Achievement. (Filmstrip, record or cassette) Guidance Associates, 1973-1976.

Profiles Lit
Profiles in Literature: Tom and Muriel Feelings. (Reel-to-reel videotape) Philadelphia: Temple University, College of Education, Dept. of Educational Media, 1971.

Reader's Adviser
The Reader's Adviser: A Layman's Guide to Literature. 12th edition. Vol. 1: *The Best in American and British Fiction, Poetry, Essays, Literary Biography, Bibliography, and Reference.* Edited by Sarah L. Prakken. New York: R. R. Bowker, 1974. 808p.

Reader's Ency
The Reader's Encyclopedia of American Literature. By Max J. Herzberg and the staff of the Thomas Y. Crowell Company. New York: Thomas Y. Crowell Co. (c1962). 1280p.

Richardson. Great

Richardson. Great 56
Great American Negros. By Ben Richardson. Revised by William A. Fahey; illustrated by Robert Hallock. New York: Thomas Y. Crowell (c1956). 339p. il.

Richardson. Great 76
Great Black Americans. 2nd revised edition. Formerly titled *Great American Negroes.* By Ben Richardson and William A. Fahey. New York: Thomas Y. Crowell (c1976). 344p. pors.

Richmond. Bid
Bid the Vassal Soar: Interpretive Essays on the Life and Poetry of Phillis Wheatley (ca. 1753-1784) and Moses Horton (ca. 1797-1883). By M. A. Richmond. Washington, DC: Howard University Press, 1974. 216p.

Robinson. Nommo
Nommo: An Anthology of Modern Black African and Black American Literature. Edited by William H. Robinson. New York: Macmillan (c1972). 501p.

Robinson. Poets
Early Black American Poets: Selections with Biographical and Critical Introductions. By William H. Robinson, Jr. Dubuque, IA: Wm. C. Brown (c1971). 309p.

Robinson. Prose
Early Black American Prose: Selections with Biographical and Introductions. By William H. Robinson, Jr. Dubuque, IA: Wm. C. Brown (c1971). 274p.

Rogers. World
World's Great Men of Color. Vol. 2. By J. A. Rogers. New York: Collier Books, Macmillan (c1972). (Original edition, c1947).

*Rollins. Enter
Famous Negro Entertainers of Stage, Screen, and TV. By Charlemae H. Rollins. New York: Dodd, Mead, 1967. 122p. pors.

*Rollins. Famous
Famous American Negro Poets. By Charlemae H. Rollins. New York: Dodd, Mead & Company (c1965). 96p. il.

*Rollins. They
They Showed the Way; Forty American Negro Leaders. By Charlemae H. Rollins. New York: Crowell, 1964. 165p.

Scally. Catholic
Negro Catholic Writers, 1900-1943: A Bio-Bibliography. By Sister Mary Anthony Scally. Detroit: Walter Romig, 1945. 152p.

Scruggs. Wom
Women of Distinction: Remarkable in Works and Invincible in Character. By Lawson A. Scruggs. Raleigh, NC: L. A. Scruggs, 1893.

Selected BAA
Selected Black American Authors: An Illustrated Bio-Bibliography. Compiled by James A. Page. Boston: G. K. Hall, 1977. 398p. il.

Sherman. Invisible
Invisible Poets: Afro-Americans of the Nineteenth Century. By Joan A. Sherman. Urbana: University of Illinois Press, 1974. 270p.

Shuman. Galaxy
A Galaxy of Black Writing. Edited by R. Baird Shuman. Durham, NC: Moore Publishing, 1968. 441p.

Shuman. Nine
Nine Black Poets. Edited and with an introduction by R. Baird Shuman. Durham, NC: Moore Publishing, 1968. 236p.

*Sign Am Auth
Significant American Authors, Poets, and Playwrights. Chicago: Children's Press, 1975. 78p.

*Sign Am Wom
Significant American Women. Chicago: Children's Press, 1975. 78p. il.

Simmons. Men
Men of Mark. By William J. Simmons. Geo. M. Rewell, 1887. Reprint. Chicago: Johnson Publishing Co., 1970. 829p.

Something ATA
Something about the Author: Facts and Pictures about Contemporary Authors and Illustrators of Books for Young People. Vols. 1-25. Detroit: Gale Research Co. (c1971-1981).

Southern Wr
Southern Writers: A Biographical Dictionary. Edited by Robert Bain, Joseph M. Flora and Louis D. Rubin, Jr. Baton Rouge: Louisiana State University Press, 1979. 515p.

*Sterling. Fore
Black Foremothers: Three Lives. By Dorothy Sterling. Old Westbury, NY: Feminist Press (c1979). 167p.

*Sterling. Four
Four Took Freedom. By Philip Sterling and Rayford Logan. Illustrated by Charles White. Garden City, NY: Doubleday (c1967). 116p. il.

*Sterling. Lift
Lift Every Voice. By Dorothy Sterling and Benjamin Quarles. Illustrated by Ernest Crichlow. Garden City, NY: Doubleday, Zenith Books, 1965. 116p. il.

Sterling. Speak
Speak out in Thunder Tones: Letters and Other Writings by Black Northerners, 1787-1867. Edited by Dorothy Sterling. Garden City, NY: Doubleday, 1973. 396p. il.

*Sterne. Dream
I Have a Dream. By Emma Sterne. New York: Alfred A. Knopf (c1965). 229p.

Third Bk
Third Book of Junior Authors. Edited by Doris De Montreville and Donna Hill. New York: H. W. Wilson, 1972. 320p.

Thorpe. Hist
Black Historians, a Critique. By Earl E. Thorpe. New York: Morrow, 1969. 260p.

Troup. Geor
Distinguished Negro Georgians. By Cornelius V. Thorpe. Dallas: Royal (1962). 203p.

Turner. Voices
Voices from the Black Experience: African and Afro-American Literature. Edited by Darwin T. Turner and others. Lexington, MA: Ginn, 1972. 280p.

Twen CA
Twentieth Century Authors: A Biographical Dictionary of Modern Literature. Edited by Stanley J. Kunitz and Howard Haycraft. New York: H. W. Wilson, 1942. 1577p.

Twen CA Sup
Twentieth Century Authors, First Supplement: A Biographical Dictionary of Modern Literature. Edited by Stanley J. Kunitz and Vineta Colby. New York: H. W. Wilson, 1955. 1123p.

Twen CCW
Twentieth Century Children's Writers. Editor, D. L. Kirpatrick. New York: St. Martin's Press (c1978). 1507p.

Wagner. Poets
Black Poets of the United States from Paul Lawrence Dunbar to Langston Hughes. By Jean Wagner. Translated by Kenneth Douglas. Urbana: University of Illinois Press, 1973.

*Walser. Young
Young Readers' Picturebook of Tar Heel Authors. 5th edition, revised. By Richard Walser and Mary Reynolds Peacock. Raleigh: North Carolina Department of Cultural Resources, Division of Archives and History (c1981). 74p. il.

Watts Wr
From the Ashes; Voices of Watts. Watts Writers' Workshop. Edited by Budd Schulberg. New York: New American Library (c1967). 277p.

Webster Am Biog
Webster's American Biographies. Charles Van Doren, editor; Robert McHenry, associate editor. Springfield, MA: Merriam, 1979. 1233p.

White. Verse
An Anthology of Verse by American Negroes. By Newman Ivey White. Durham, NC: Trinity College Press, 1924. 259p.

Whitlow. Lit
Black American Literature: A Critical History. By Roger Whitlow. Chicago: Nelson Hill, 1973.

-Who Am
Who's Who in America. Vols. 1-41. Chicago: Marquis, 1899- . Biennial.

Who Blk Am
Who's Who among Black Americans. 2nd edition, 1977-1978. Northbrook, IL: Who's Who among Black Americans, Inc., 1978.

Who Col Am
Who's Who in Colored America: A Biographical Dictionary of Notable Living Persons of Negro Descent in America. New York: Who's Who in Colored America Corp., 1927-1950. pors.
    Who Col Am 27   Vol. 1 (c1927)
    Who Col Am 29   2nd edition, 1928-1929 (c1929)
    Who Col Am 33   3rd edition, 1930-1932 (c1933)
    Who Col Am 37   4th edition, 1933-1937 (c1937)
    Who Col Am 40   5th edition, 1938-1940 (c1940)
    Who Col Am 42   6th edition, 1941-1944 (c1942)
    Who Col Am 50   7th edition, 1940 (c1950)

Who Col Lo
Who's Who in Colored Louisiana, with Brief Sketches of History and Romance. Edited and prepared by A. E. Perkins. Batin Rouge: Louisiana State University Press, 1930. 153p. il.

Who Col Race
Who's Who of the Colored Race: A General Biographical Dictionary of Men and Women of African Descent. Edited by Frank Lincoln Mather. Chicago, 1915. Detroit: Gale Research Co., 1976. 296p.

Who Theatre
Who's Who in the Theatre: A Biographical Record of the Contemporary Stage. 16th edition. Edited by Ian Herbert. Detroit: Gale Research Co., 1977. 1389p.

Who Twen
Who's Who in Twentieth Century Literature. By Martin Seymour-Smith. New York: Holt, Rinehart and Winston, 1976. 414p.

Who Was
Who Was Who in America. Vols. 1-6. Chicago: Marquis, 1942-1976.

Who Was H
Who Was Who: Historical Volume, 1607-1896. Chicago: Marquis (c1963).

Who Was HR
Who Was Who: Historical Volume, 1607-1896. Revised edition, 1967. Chicago: Marquis (c1967).

Williams. Wom
American Black Women in the Arts and Social Sciences: A Bibliographic Survey. By Ora Williams. Revised and expanded edition. Metuchen, NJ: Scarecrow Press, 1978. 197p. il.

Wom Am
Women in America: A Guide to Books, 1963-1975. By Barbara Haber. Boston: G. K. Hall, 1978. 202p.

Woodson. Orators
Negro Orators and Their Orations. By Carter Goodwin Woodson. Washington: Associated Publishers, 1925. 711p.

Wor Auth

Wor Auth 50-70
World Authors, 1950-1970: A Companion Volume to Twentieth Century Authors. Edited by John Wakeman. New York: H. W. Wilson, 1975. 1594p.

Wor Auth 70-75
World Authors, 1970-1975: A Companion Volume to Twentieth Century Authors. Edited by John Wakeman. New York: H. W. Wilson, 1980. 894p.

Writers Dr

Writers Dr 76
The Writers Directory, 1976-1978. New York: St. Martin's Press, 1976. 1500p.

Writers Dr 80
The Writers Directory, 1980-1982. New York: St. Martin's Press, 1979. 1389p.

Writers Dr 82
The Writers Directory, 1982-1984. New York: St. Martin's Press, 1350p.

Young. 1755
Major Black Religious Leaders, 1755-1940. By Henry J. Young. Nashville, TN: Abingdon (c1977). 173p.

Young. Since 1940
Major Black Religious Leaders since Nineteen Forty. By Henry J. Young. Nashville, TN: Abingdon, 1979. 160p.

*Young, M. Lead
Black American Leaders. By Margaret B. Young. Illustrated with photography. New York: Franklin Watts, 1969. 120p. il.

Index to Black American Writers in Collective Biographies

Aaron, (Hank) Henry Louis, 1934-
  Professional athlete, autobiographer
    Afro-Am Ency 1: 1-2 / Cur Biog Yrbk
    58 p. 2-4 / Ebony Success 1: 2 por /
    Ency Blk Am p. 1 / Negro Alm 76
    p. 692 il / Who Am 80, 1: 1 / Who
    Blk Am 77 p. 1
Abajian, James Detarr, 1914-
  Author, curator
    Con Auth 65-68: 9 / Who Blk Am 77
    p. [1]
Abbott, Robert Sengstacke, 1870-1940
  Publisher, editor, writer
    Afro-Am Ency 1: 3 il / Who Col Am
    40 p. 15 / Who Was 2: 15
Abdul, Raoul, 1929-
  Opera singer, music critic, author
    Con Auth 29-32R: 10-11 / Dr Perf Arts
    p. 1 / Selected BAA p. 1 / Something
    ATA 12: 12-por, il / Who Blk Am 77 p. 1
Abner, David, Jr., 1860-
  Educator, lecturer, editor
    Simmons. Men p. 809-11 il / Who Col
    Race p. 1
Abrams, Robert J., 1924-
  Poet
    Blk Am Wr 1: 20 / Hughes. New p. 117
Abrams, Theresa Williams, 1903-
  Poet
    Blk Am Wr 1: 19-20
Adams, Alger Leroy (Philip B. Kaye), 1910-
  Clergyman, novelist, editor
    Ency Blk Am p. 2 / Who Blk Am 77 p. 3
Adams, Elizabeth Laura, 1909-
  Convert, poet, book reviewer, autobiographer
    Barton. Witness p. 123-34 / David. Grow-
    ing p. 60-70 / Scally. Catholic p. 19-23

Adams, Jeanette
  Teacher, poet
    Exum. Keep p. 282
Adams, Lucinda Bragg
  Musician, writer
    Majors. Wom p. 215
Adams, Russell L(ee), 1930-
  Educator, author
    Bontemps. American 74 p. 215 / Con
    Auth 53-56: 12-13 / Living BAA p. 1 /
    Who Blk Am 77 p. 5
Adams, William, 1913-
  Essayist
    Scally. Catholic p. 23-24
Adams, William, 1940-
  Teacher of English, author
    Adams. Auth p. [v]
Addison, Lloyd, 1937-
  Poet, editor
    Blk Am Wr 1: 21 / Broadside Auth
    p. 17 / Con Auth 45-48: 13
Afton, Effie. See Harper, Frances E(llen)
  W(atkins)
Akhnaton, Askia. See Eckels, Jon B.
Alba, Nanina, 1917-1968
  Poet, teacher
    Adoff. Poet p. 517 / Blk Am Wr 1:
    22-23 / Broadside Auth p. 17 / Hughes.
    Poet p. 517 / Selected BAA p. 2
Albert, Octavia Victoria Rogers, 1853-1889
    Majors. Wom p. 219
Alexander, Lewis Grandison, 1900-1945
  Poet
    Adoff. Poet p. 517 / Blk Am Wr 1:
    23-24 / Cromwell. Read p. 363 / Cullen.
    Carol p. 122 / Hughes. Poet p. 591 /
    Murphy. N Voices p. 9

Alexander, Margaret W. *See* Walker (Alexander), Margaret Abigail

Alford, Thomas E., 1935-
Librarian, administrator
Bio Dr Librns 70 p. 12 / Josey. Blk
Librn p. 130-36 / Josey. What p. 303 /
Who Blk Am 77 p. 11

Alhamisi, Ahmed Akinwale, 1940-
Artist, poet
Alhamisi. Arts p. 109 / Blk Am Wr 1:
34 / Broadside Auth p. 18 / Jones.
Fire p. 657

Alhamisi, Ahmed Legraham
Editor, journalist
Jones. Fire p. 657

Allen, Ernest. *See* Mkalimoto, Ernie

Allen, George Leonard, 1905-1935
Poet
Brown. Caravan p. 363 / Cullen. Carol
p. 203 / Kerlin. Poets 35 p. 333

Allen, James Egert, 1896-1980
Educator
Con Auth 97-100 p. 13 / Living BAA
p. 1 / Who Blk Am 77 p. 13

Allen, Junius Mordecai, 1875-1906
Poet
Blk Am Wr 1: 24-25 / Kerlin. Poets
23 p. 269 / Kerlin. Poets 35 p. 333 /
Robinson. Poets p. 263 / Robinson. Prose
p. 177 / Wagner. Poets p. 141-45 / White.
Verse p. 116

Allen, Richard, 1760-1831
Bishop, orator
Bennett. Pioneers p. 42-45 por / Bio
Hist p. 247-48 / Blk Am Wr 1: 25 /
Brawley. Builders p. 30-34 / Brawley.
Early p. 87-89 / David. Defiance p. 3-15 /
Dict Am Biog 28, 1: 204-205 / Ency
Am Biog p. 29-30 / Great Negroes 69
p. 100 il / Historical N. Bio p. 5 por /
King. Famous p. 64-69 / Nat Cyclo
13: 200-201 / Northrop. College p. 28-29
por / Rollins. They p. 12-16 / Simmons.
Men p. 329-34 il / Sterling. Speak p. 371 /
Webster Am Biog p. 24 / Young. 1755
p. 25-40

Allen, Robert L., 1942-
Educator, editor
Living BAA p. 2 / Who Blk Am 77 p. 14

Allen, Samuel (Paul Vesey), 1917-
Attorney, poet
Adams. Auth p. 162 / Adoff. Poet
p. 517 / Afro-Am Ency 1: 120 / Blk
Am Wr 1: 27 / Blk Plots p. 189 /
Bontemps. American 63 p. 187 /

Allen, Samuel (Paul Vesey) (cont'd) ...
Bontemps. American 74 p. 215 / Broadside Auth p. 18-19 / Cele p. 251 / Con
Auth 49-52: 17-18 / Davis. Cav p. 615 /
Dr Am Schol 78 E p. 10 / Ency Blk Am
p. 99-100 / Hayden. Kal p. 146 / Hughes.
New p. 117 / Hughes. Poet p. 591 /
Living BAA p. 2 / Robinson. Nommo
p. 485 / Something ATA 9: 6 por / Who
Am 80, 1: 51 / Who Blk Am 77 p. 14

Allen, William G.
Journalist, author
Cromwell. Read p. 363

Alonzo, Cecil
Playwright, director
Dr Perf Arts 78 p. 7-8

Aman, Mohammed M., 1940-
Educator, librarian
Bio Dr Librns 70 p. 16 / Con Auth
49-52: 20-21 / Living BAA p. 3 / Who
Blk Am 77 p. 16

Amin, Karima
Educator, author
Blk Lit HS p. 273

Amini, Johari M. *See* Latimore, Jewel C.

Amis, Lola Elizabeth Jones, 1930-
Educator, playwright
Blk Am Wr 1: 31-32 / Living BAA p. 3-4

Amungo, Sonebeyatta. *See* Hagan, Roosevelt

Anderson, Alice D.
Poet
Murphy. Ebony p. 1

Anderson, Bernard E., 1936-
Educator
Con Auth 53-56: 19 / Who Blk Am 77
p. 17

Anderson, Garland, 1886-1939
Playwright
Dr Perf Arts 78 p. 9 / Johnson. Book
p. 202-205

Anderson, Henry L. N., 1934-
Novelist, teacher
Blk Am Wr 1: 33

Anderson, James Harvey, 1848-
Minister
Culp. Twen p. 322-23 il / Who Col Race
p. 8

Anderson, Marian, 1902-
Singer, autobiographer
Afro-Am Ency 1: 143-44 il / Bio Hist
p. 248 / Cur Biog Yrbk 50 p. 8-10 por /
Dannett. Profiles 2: 158-71 por / Ency Am
Biog p. 32 / Flynn. Achieve p. 249-55 /
Great Negroes 69 p. 188 il / Historical
N Bio p. 157-58 por / Negro Handbk 66

Aubert, Alvin Bernard, 1930-
Poet, educator, editor
Blk Am Wr 1: 40 / Broadside Auth p. 23 /
Cele p. 251 / Con Auth 81-84:
21-22 / Con Poets 75 p. 39-40 / Con
Poets 80 p. 50-52 / Who Blk Am 77
p. 29 / Writers Dr 76 p. 38 / Writers
Dr 80 p. 46
Ausby, Ellsworth, 1942-
Painter, illustrator
Afro-Am Art p. 11
Austin, Lettie J(ane), 1925-
Educator, editor, essayist
Con Auth 65-68: 36 / Living BAA p. 6-7
Axam, John A., 1930-
Librarian
Bio Dr Librns p. 37 / Josey. What p.
303 / Who Blk Am 77 p. 30
Ayer, Jacqueline B(randford), 1930-
Author, illustrator
Con Auth 69-72: 40 / Illus Bks YP 75
p. 14 / Illus Ch Bks 57 p. 75 / Some-
thing ATA 13: 6-7 por, il / Third Bk
p. 23-24 por
Ayers, Vivian
Poet, playwright
Blk Am Wr 1: 42 / Hughes. New p. 117-18

Bacote, Clarence Albert, 1906-
Historian
Con Auth P-2: 36-37 / Ency Blk Am
p. 147
Bailey, Leonead Pack (Leaonead Pack Drain),
1906-
Librarian, compiler of biographical directory
Broadside Auth p. 23-24
Bailey, M(innie Elizabeth) Thomas, ca. 1922-
Historian, educator
Con Auth 57-60: 35-36 / Ency Blk Am
p. 148
Bailey, Pearl (Mae), 1918-
Entertainer, autobiographer
Afro-Am Ency 1: 179 / AmSCAP 66
p. 28 / AmSCAP 80 p. 21 / Con Auth
41-44: 40-41 / Cur Biog Yrbk 55 p.
34-36 por / Cur Biog Yrbk 69 p. 23-25
por / Ebony Success 1: 17 por / Living
BAA p. 7 / Notable Names p. 532 /
Selected BAA p. 17 por / Who Blk Am 77
p. 34 / Who Theatre 77 / Writers Dr
80 p. 54
Bailey, Solomon. *See* Bayley, Solomon

Bailey, William Edgar
Poet
Kerlin. Poets 23 p. 269 / Kerlin. Poets
35 p. 333
Baker, Augusta (Alexander), 1911-
Librarian, children's author, folklorist
ALA Wor Ency p. 70-71 / ALA Yrbk 76
p. 101 por / Bio Dr Librns 70 p. 44 /
Blk Am Wr 1: 42 / Con Auth 1: 20-21 /
Flynn. Achieve p. 93-108 / Josey. Blk
Librn p. 117-23 / Living BAA 7-8 /
Selected BAA p. 8 por / Something ATA
3: 16-17 por
Baker, Houston A., Jr., 1943-
Professor of English, essayist, lecturer
Blk Am Wr 1: 43 / Con Auth 41-44R:
39-40 / Living BAA p. 8 / Selected BAA
p. 8 por / Who Blk Am 77 p. 35 /
Writers Dr 80 p. 56
Baldridge, Cyrus Leroy, 1889-
Illustrator
Afro-Am Art p. 14 / Illus Bks YP 70
p. 9-10 / Illus Bks YP 75 p. 16
Baldwin, James, 1924-
Novelist, short story writer, essayist,
playwright
Adams. Auth p. 97 / Adoff. Blk on p.
227 / Afro-Am Ency 1: 185 il / Afro-Am
Novel p. 8 / Am Auth & Bks 72 p. 34 /
Barksdale. Writers p. 722-25 / Bio Hist
p. 250-51 / Blk Am Wr 1: 44 / Blk Auth /
Blk Plots p. 194 / Bone. Novel
p. 216-17 / Chapman. New p. 409 /
Con Auth 1-4R: 44-45 / Con Drama 73
p. 66-69 / Con Novel 72 P. 72-75 /
Con Novel 76 p. 82-83 / Crowell CD
p. 38-39 / Cur Biog Yrbk 59 p. 21-22
por / David. Defiance p. 210-15 / David.
Living p. 46-73 / David. Roots p. 110 /
Dict Lit Biog 2: 15-22 por / Dict Lit
Biog 7-1: 45-49 por / Ebony Success
1: 17 por / Emanual. Dark p. 296-97 /
Ency Am Biog p. 52-54 / Ency Blk Am
p. 149-50 il / Ford. Insights p. 192-93 /
Haslam. Forgot p. 332 / Historical N Bio
p. 160 por / Hughes. Best p. 497 / Int
Auth & Wr 77 p. 49 / Kendricks. Voices
p. 290 / King. Story p. 277 / Living
BAA p. 8 / Long. Writing 2: 619-20 /
Longman CT p. 46 / Margolies. Read
p. 353 / McGraw Ency WD 1: 125 por /
Notable Names 76 p. 535-36 / Novelists
79 p. 67-69 / Oliver. Drama p. 235-36 /

Baldwin, James (cont'd) ...
Pol Profiles: Johnson p. 31 / Pol Pro-
files: Kennedy p. 19-20 / Reader's Adviser
74, 1: 626-27 / Selected BAA p. 9-10
por / Sign Am Auth p. 64 / Something
ATA 9: 15 / Turner. Voices p. 258 /
Webster Am Biog p. 58 / Whitlow. Lit
p. 127-30 / Who Am 74, 1: 141 / Who
Am 80, 1: 159 / Who Blk Am 77 p. 35 /
Who Twen p. 27-28 / Wor Auth 50-70
p. 107-109 / Writers Dr 76 p. 50 /
Writers Dr 80 p. 58

Baldwin, Maria Louise, 1856-1922
Educator, lecturer
Brawley. Builders p. 277-79 / Daniel.
Wom p. 240-62 / Lerner. Wom p. 294 /
Notable Am Wom 1: 86-88

Ball, Charles, 1781-1850
David. Living p. 87-105

Bambara, Toni Cade (Toni Cade), 1939-
Writer, poet, lecturer
Blk Am Wr 1: 49 / Blk Plots p.
194-95 / Con Auth 29-32R: 39-40 / Ency
Blk Am p. 150 / Living BAA p. 9 /
Who Blk Am 77 p. 36-37

Banks, Barbara
Exum. Keep p. 282-83

Banks, Brenda C., 1947-
Short story writer
Blk Am Wr 1: 49-50

Banks, Ernest (Ernie), 1931-
Baseball coach, author
Ebony Success 1: 18 por

Banks, Irma Louise
Teacher, novelist
Selected BAA p. 11

Banks, Janette E., 1934-
Artist, writer
Afro-Am Art p. 14-15

Banneker, Benjamin, 1731-1806
Mathematician, author
Afro-Am Ency 1: 194-98 il / Barksdale.
Writers p. 48-50 / Bennett. Pioneers p.
12-26 il / Bio Hist p. 251-52 / Brawley.
Builders p. 25-29 / Brawley. Early p.
75-79 / Dict Am Auth p. 17-18 / Ency Am
Biog p. 56-57 / Fauset. Freedon
p. 36-46 il / Great Negroes 69 p. 18 il /.
Historical N Bio p. 9 por / Ken-
dricks. Voices p. 44 / King. Famous
p. 11-16 / Mott. Nar p. 60-61 / Robin-
son. Prose p. 11-12 / Rollins. They
p. 20-23 / Selected BAA p. 11-12 /
Sterling. Speak p. 372 / Webster Am
Biog p. 62

Banner, William Augustus, 1915-
Educator, author
Con Auth 45-48: 34-35 / Who Am 80, 1:
163 / Who Blk Am 77 p. 40

Bannister, Annie Bethel Scales. *See* Spencer,
Anne

Baraka, Imamu Amiri. *See* Jones, (Everette)
Le Roi

Barber, John
Short story writer
Coombs. What p. 205

Barbour, Floyd
Playwright
Childress. Scenes p. 147

Barksdale, Richard K(enneth), 1915-
Professor of English, critic, short story
writer, author
Blk Am Wr 1: 57 / Con Auth 49-52:
46 / Living BAA p. 9-10 / Who Am 74,
1: 159 / Who Am 80, 1: 178 / Who Blk
Am 77 p. 43

Barlow, George, 1948-
Poet
Blk Am Wr 1: 58-59 por / Broadside
Auth p. 25-26 / Cele p. 251 / Shuman.
Galaxy p. 250

Barnett, Ida Bell. *See* Wells (Barnett), Ida
B(ell)

Barrax, Gerald W(illiam), 1933-
Poet, teacher
Adoff. Poet p. 518 / Afro-Am Ency 1:
206 / Blk Am Wr 1: 59-60 / Blk Plots
p. 195-96 / Cele p. 252 / Chapman.
New p. 210 / Con Auth 65-68: 40 /
Hayden. Kal p. 198 / Living BAA p. 10 /
Owen. Poet p. 143 / Selected BAA p. 13

Barrett, Nathan N(oble), 1933-
Novelist
Con Auth 17-20R: 55

Bass, Kingsley B., Jr. *See* Bullins, Ed

Bates, Arthenia Jackson. *See* Millican,
Arthenia Bates

Bates, Daisy Lee Gaston, 1922-
Journalist, autobiographer
Afro-Am Ency 1: 211-12 il / Alexander.
Young p. 38-56 por / Dannett. Profiles
2: 294-304 / David. Growing p. 22-38,
203-206 / David. Living p. 262-81 /
Historical N Bio p. 162-63 por / Lerner.
Wom p. 306 / Negro Alm 71 p. 871 /
Negro Alm 76 p. 1000 / Pol Profiles:
Eisenhower p. 28-29 / Sign Am Wom
p. 57 il / Sterne. Dream p. 116-43

Bates, Myrtle
Poet
Exum. Keep p. 283

Battle, Soloman Oden, 1934-
Editor, screenplay writer, photographer
Blk Am Wr 1: 63 / Con Auth 25-28R:
53 / Who Am 78 p. 199 / Who Blk Am
77 p. 49 / Writers Dr 80 p. 75
Bayley, Solomon (Solomon Bailey)
Narrator of experiences
Bruce. Sketches p. 15-18 / Mott. Bio
p. 31-53, 46-74 / Mott. Nar p. 133-43
Bayton, James A., 1912-
Educator
Living BAA p. 11
Beadle, Samuel Alfred
Poet, essayist
Blk Am Wr 1: 64
Bearden, Romare H(oward), 1912?-
Artist, author
Afro-Am Art p. 19-21 / AmSCAP 66
p. 41 / Cur Biog Yrbk 72 p. 28-30 por /
Ebony Success 1: 22 por / Ency Blk Am
p. 169 / Lincoln Lib Arts 2: 450 / Who
Am 78, 1: 212
Beasley, Delilah Leontium, 1871-1934
Historian, journalist
Dannett. Profiles 1: 224-25 il / Ency Blk
Am p. 169-70
Beasley, Edward, Jr., 1932-
Educator
Living BAA p. 11
Beck, Robert (Iceberg Slim), 1918-
Novelist, autobiographer
Blk Am Wr 1: 66 / Robinson. Nommo
p. 475
Beckham, Barry Earl, 1944-
Novelist, biographer
Afro-Am Novel p. 25 / Blk Am Wr 1:
66 / Con Auth 29-32R: 52-53 / Con Novel
76 p. 119 / Living BAA p. 12
Beckwourth, James P., 1798-1867
Explorer, narrator
Alli Sup 1: 118 / Bio Hist p. 253-54 /
Ency Blk Am p. 436 por / Great Negroes
69 p. 38 il / Historical N Bio p. 49-50
il / Oxford Am 65 p. 66 / Peters. Ebony
p. 29-30 / Who Was H: 49 / Reader's
Ency 62 p. 71 / Rollins. They p. 27-31
Bell, James Madison, 1826-1902
Abolitionist, poet
Afro-Am Ency 1: 230 / Blk Am Wr 1:
67 / Brawley. Early p. 279 / Dict Am
Biog 29, 2: 156 / Ency Blk Am p. 171 /
Historical N Bio p. 51 / Kerlin. Poets
23 p. 269 il / Robinson. Poets p. 82-83 /
Selected BAA p. 14 por / Sherman.

Bell, James Madison (cont'd) ...
Invisible p. 80-83 / White. Verse p.
37-38 / Who was 5: 119
Bell, Philip A., ca. 1808-1889
Editor, journalist
Ency Blk Am p. 171 / Sterling. Speak
p. 372
Beman, Amos G., 1803-1874
Minister, teacher, essayist, lecturer
Sterling. Speak p. 372
Benford, Lawrence, 1946-
Poet
Afro-Am Ency 1: 233 / Blk Am Wr 1:
68 / Major. Poet p. 145
Benitez, Lillie Kate Walker
Dancer, painter, poet
Henderson, Under p. 380
Benjamin, Robert Charles O'Hana, 1855-
Editor
Afro-Am Ency 2: 242 / Penn Press p.
320-34 / Simmons. Men p. 711-12
Bennett, Bob, 1947-
Poet
Jones. Fire p. 658
Bennett, George Harold (Hal Bennett), 1930-
Blk Am Wr 1: 69-70 / Con Auth 97-
100: 40-41 / Living BAA p. 12 / Selected
BAA p. 14
Bennett, Gwendolyn B., 1902-
Artist, literary critic, poet
Adoff. Poet p. 518 / Afro-Am Ency 1:
243 / Am Women Wr 1: 140-42 / Blk Am
Wr 1: 69 / Bontemps. American 63 p.
187 / Bontemps. American 74 p. 215 /
Cullen. Carol p. 153-55 / Hughes. Poet
p. 592 / Johnson. Book p. 243 / Living
BAA p. 12
Bennett, Hal. *See* Bennett, George Harold
Bennett, Lerone, Jr., 1928-
Journalist, historian, educator, poet
Adoff. Blk on p. 227 / Cele p. 252 /
Con Auth 45-48: 47 / Ebony Success 1:
25 por; 2: 10-15 il / Ency Blk Am
p. 172 / Who Am 74 p. 225 / Who Blk
Am 77 p. 61
Berkley, Constance Elaine, 1931-
Poet, educator, lecturer
Blk Am Wr 1: 72-73 / Living BAA
p. 13 / Who Blk Am 77 p. 63
Berry, C(hantal) S(andre), 1948-
Broadside Auth p. 26
Berry, Faith Daryl, 1939-
Journalist, editor
Blk Am Wr 1: 73 / Who Blk Am 77 p. 64

Bolton, Shirley L., 1945-
Painter, illustrator
Afro-Am Art p. 29
Bond, Frederick W.
Journalist, playwright, poet
Dreer. Am Lit p. 75
Bond, Horace Mann, 1904-1972
Educator, social scientist
Brown. Caravan p. 1027 / Con Auth 1-R:
32 / Cur Biog Yrbk 54 p. 107-109 por /
Ency Blk Am p. 185 / Metcalf. Up
p. 149-92 / Selected BAA p. 18
Bond, Jean Carey
Author of books for children and young
adults
Auth Bk YP Sup 79 p. 28-29
Bond, (Horace) Julian, 1940-
State legislator, civil rights leader, poet
Afro-Am Ency 2: 355 phot / Blk Am Wr
1: 78 / Bontemps. American 63 p. 187 /
Bontemps. American 74 p. 215 / Cele
p. 252 / Con Auth 49-52: 70-21 / Ebony
Success 1: 32 por / Ency Blk Am p. 186
por / Hughes. New p. 118 / Hughes. Poet
p. 592-93 / Living BAA p. 16-17 /
Negro Alm 76 p. 360 phot / Pol Pro-
files: Johnson p. 54 / Selected BAA
p. 17 por / Webter Am Biog p. 116 /
Who Am 80, 1: 351 / Who Blk Am 77
p. 78-79
Bonner, Marita, 1905-
Playwright, poet, short story writer
Blk Plots p. 323
Bontemps, Arna Wendell, 1902-1973
Librarian, poet, novelist, playwright, critic,
short story writer
Adams. Auth p. 72 / Adoff. Poet p.
518-19 / Afro-Am Ency 2: 356-57 il / Am
Auth & Bks 72 p. 65 / Anth Mag Verse
26, pt. 4 p. 6 / Auth Bk YP 64 p. 26 /
Auth Bk YP 71 p. 54 / Barksdale.
Writers p. 628-30 / Blk Am Wr 1: 79 /
Blk Plots p. 202 / Bone. Novel p. 120 /
Bontemps. American 63 p. 187 / Bon-
temps. American 74 p. 215-16 / Brawley.
Caravan p. 254 / Broadside Auth p.
27-28 / Chapman Blk V p. 87 / Con
Auth 1: 33 / Con Auth 41-44R: 80 /
Con Poets 70 p. 117-18 / Cullen. Carol
p. 162 / Cur Biog Yrbk 73 p. 450 /
Davis. Cav p. 332 / Davis. Dark
p. 83-84 / Dreer. Am Lit p. 269 /
Ebony Success 1: 33 por / Emanuel.
Dark p. 477-78 / Ency Blk Am p. 186,

Bontemps, Arna Wendell (cont'd) ...
il p. 521 / Ford. Insights p. 80-81 /
Gayle. Bond p. 148 / Great Negroes 69
p. 159 / Handbk Librns p. 161-62 /
Hill. Anger p. 214 / Historical N Bio
p. 164-65 por / Hayden. Kal p. 78 /
Hughes. Best p. 498 / Hughes. Poet
p. 593 / Johnson. Book p. 262 / Kerlin.
Poets 35 p. 334 / Long. Writing 2:
439-40 / More Books p. 48-53 por /
Negro Handbk 66 p. 396 / Profiles Blk
Ach 402-287 / Rollins. Famous p. 61-68 /
Selected BAA p. 19 por / Something
ATA 2: 32-34 il / Wagner. Poets p. 183 /
Whitlow. Lit p. 100-101
Booker, Simeon Saunders, 1918-
Journalist, author
Con Auth 11-12: 52 / Ebony Success
1: 34 por / Living BAA p. 17 / Selected
BAA p. 20 / Who Blk Am 77 p. 81
Booker, Sue, 1946-
Journalist, poet, filmstrip writer, editor
Ebony Success 1: 34 por / Who Am 78
p. 343 / Who Blk Am 77 p. 81
Booth, Charles Edward, 1947-
Clergyman
Bio Dr Min 75 p. 37 / Who Blk Am
77 p. 82
Booth, Lavaughn Venchael, 1919-
Clergyman, educator
Ebony Success 1: 35 por / Who Am 78
p. 345 / Who Blk Am 77 p. 82
Borde, Percival Sebastian, 1922-
Educator, author
Who Blk Am 77 p. 82
Borders, William Holmes, 1905-
Clergyman, poet, author
Bio Dr Min 65 p. 40 / Troup. Geor p.
33-34 / Who Blk Am 77 p. 83
Boulden, Jesse Freeman
Legislator, editor, poet
Simmons. Men p. 490-94 il
Boulware, Marcus H(anna), 1907-
Educator, author, editor
Con Auth 45-48: 66 / Con Auth R-1:
63-64 / Living BAA p. 17
Bourke, Sharon
Poet
Cele p. 253 / Henderson. Under p. 381
Bowen, Ariel Serina Hodges
Teacher of music, writer
Afro-Am Ency 2: 366 / Culp. Twen p.
264-65 / Dannett. Profiles 1: 226-27 il

Bowen, John Wesley E(dward), 1855-1933
Educator, theologian
Afro-Am Ency 2: 366-67 / Bio Dict S
Auth p. 45 / Culp. Twen p. 28-29 por /
Dict Am Auth p. 458 / Historical N
Bio p. 54 / Who Col Am 29 p. 43
por / Who Col Am 33 p. 49, por
p. 51 / Who Col Lo p. 77 / Who Col
Race p. 32 / Who Was 4: 105
Bowen, Robert T., 1936-
Poet
Broadside Auth p. 28
Bowles, Eva D.
Social worker
Lerner Wom p. 330
Bowman, John Walter, 1908-
U.S. Army captain, clergyman, essayist
Scally, Catholic p. 30-31
Bowser, J. Dallas, 1846-
Editor, teacher, politician
Penn. Press p. 230-32 / Simmons. Men
p. 488-89
Bowser, Rosa Dixon, 1885-1931
Educator, orator
Afro-Am Ency 2: 369 / Culp. Twen p.
176-77 por
Boyd, Francis A., 1844-
Poet
Blk Am Wr 1: 85 / Robinson, Poets
p. 76-77
Boyd, Melba Joyce, 1950-
Poet
Blk Am Wr 1: 85 / Broadside Auth
p. 28-29
Boyd, Richard Henry, 1843-1922
Minister, publisher, writer
Dict Am Biog 29, 2: 528 / Dict Am Biog
64, 1-2: 528 / Historical N Bio p. 54-55
por
Boyd, Samuel E.
Poet
Murphy. Ebony p. 7
Boyer, Jill Witherspoon, 1947
Poet
Blk Am Wr 1: 86
Broadside Auth p. 29
Cele p. 253
Boze, Arthur Phillip, 1945-
Free-lance writer
Blk Am Wr 1: 86-87 / Broadside Auth
p. 29-30 / Con Auth 57-60: 78
Bracey, John Henry, Jr., 1941-
Lecturer, educator
Con Auth 29-32: 73-74 / Living BAA p.
18 / Who Blk Am 77 p. 88

Bradford, Walter Louis, 1937-
Poet, essayist
Broadside Auth p. 30
Bragg, George Freeman, Jr., 1863-
Minister, author
Culp. Twen p. 356-57 / Ency Blk Am
p. 189 / Who Col Am 37 p. 74 /
Who Col Am 42 p. 70-71 / Who Col
Race p. 34
Bragg, Linda Brown
Poet
Cele p. 253
Braithwaite, William, 1878-1962
Editor, poet, novelist, biographer,
autobiographer
Am Auth & Bks 72 p. 74 / Barton.
Witness p. 93-100 / Blk Am Wr 1: 87 /
Brawley. Lit p. 89-96 / Brown. Caravan
p. 318-19 / Dreer. Am Lit p. 42 /
Ency Blk Am p. 189-90 por / Kerlin.
Poets 35 p. 334 / Long. Writing 1: 267 /
Negro Alm 71 p. 666-67 / Negro Alm 76
p. 716 / Oxford Am 65 p. 103 / Reader's
Ency 62 p. 105 / Rollins. Famous
p. 53-55 / Twen CA p. 179 / Who Col
Am 37 p. 75 / Who Col Am 40
p. 74 / Who Col Am 42 p. 71 / Who
Was 4: 111
Branch, William Blackwell, 1927-
Playwright
Blk Am Wr 1: 91 / Blk Plots p. 203-204 /
Childress. Scenes p. 147 / Con Auth
81-84: 64-65 / Dr Perf Arts 78 p.
36-37 / Ency Blk Am p. 190 / King.
Drama p. 439 / Living BAA p. 18 /
Selected BAA p. 21 / Who Blk Am 77
p. 92
Brandon, Brumsic, Jr., 1927-
Graphic artist, cartoonist
Afro-Am Art p. 33 / Con Auth 61-64:
80-81 / Something ATA 9: 25 / Who Blk
Am 77 p. 93
Brawley, Benjamin (Griffith), 1882-1939
Clergyman, teacher, literary historian, biog-
grapher, writer of short stories
Afro-Am Ency 2: 377 / Am Auth & Bks
72 p. 75 / Blk Am Wr 1: 93 / Blk
Plots p. 204 / Cromwell. Read p. 364 /
Ency Blk Am p. 191 / Hughes. Poet
p. 594 / Nat Cyclo 37: 159 / Negro
Alm 71 p. 667 / Negro Alm 76 p.
716-17 / Reader's Ency 62 p. 107 /
Selected BAA p. 22 por / Southern Wr
p. 45-46 / Thorpe. Hist p. 55-59 / Twen

Brawley, Benjamin (cont'd) ...
CA 42 p. 184-85 / White. Verse p. 156 /
Who Col Am 40 p. 77 / Who Col Race
p. 36
Brawley, Edward M(acKnight), 1851-1923
Minister, editor, educator
Afro-Am Emcy 2: 372 / Brawley. Builders
p. 201 / Culp. Twen p. 254-55 il /
Simmons. Men p. 644-47 il
Braxton, Jodi
Poet
Cele p. 253
Braxton, William Ernest, 1878-1932
Painter, illustrator
Afro-Am Art p. 33
Brazeal, Brailsford Reese, 1905-
Economist, educator
Troup. Georg p. 38-40 / Who Am 78,
1: 388 / Who Blk Am 77 p. 94
Breathett, George, 1925-
Educator, historian
Con Auth 13-14: 60 / Ency Blk Am p. 191
Brewer, J(ohn) Mason, 1896-1975
Folklorist, author
Con Auth P-2: 84 / Living BAA p. 19 /
Selected BAA p. 24 por
Brewer, William Miles, 1889-1970
Educator, historian, editor, reviewer
Ency Blk Am p. 192 / Thorpe. Hist p. 182
Brewster, Townsend T.
Poet
Afro-Am Ency 2: 392
Brimmer, Andrew Felton, 1926-
Economist, author
Bio Hist p. 256-57 / Cur Biog Yrbk
68 p. 66-68 por / Ency Blk Am p. 192 /
Metcalf. Up p. 261-93 / Negro Alm 76 p.
345-46 / Selected BAA p. 25 por / Who
Blk Am 77 p. 97-98 / Young, M. Lead
p. 58-60 il
Brisbane, Robert Hughes, 1913-
Political scientist, author
Con Auth 77-80: 62-63 / Ency Blk Am
p. 192 / Living BAA p. 20
Brister, Iola Montrose
Poet
Murphy. Ebony p. 13 / Murphy. N
Voices p. 16
Britton, Mary E.
Journalist
Majors. Wom p. 216-17 / Penn. Press
p. 415-19

Brooke, Edward W., Jr., 1919-
Politician, author
Afro-Am Ency 2: 399-402 il / Bio Hist
p. 257-58 / Christopher, Congress p.
228-36 / Ebony Success 2: 16-21 il /
Flynn. Achieve p. 138-43 / Great Negroes
69 p. 130 il / Metcalf. Profiles p.
279-305 / Selected BAA p. 25-26 por /
Young, M. Lead p. 98-100 por
Brooks, Blanche V. H.
Majors. Wom p. 30-31
Brooks, Charlotte Kendrick
Writer for young people
Living BAA p. 20-21 / Something ATA
24: 56 / Who Blk Am 77 p. 101
Brooks, Edwin, 1928-
Poet
Major. Poet p. 146
Brooks, Gwendolyn, 1917-
Poet
Adams. Auth p. 76 / Adoff. Blk out
p. 77 / Adoff. Poet p. 519 / Afro-Am
Ency 2: 403 il / Am Women Wr 1:
241-43 / Bio Hist p. 258-59 / Blk Am
Wr 1: 114 / Blk Auth / Blk Lead / Broad-
side Auth p. 31-32 / Chapman. Blk V p.
460-61 / Chapman. New p. 201 / Con
Auth NR-1: 74-75 / Con Poets 75
p. 180-82 / Con Poets 80 p. 176-78 /
Cullen. Carol p. 153-55 / Cur Biog
Yrbk 50 p. 72-74 por / Cur Biog Yrbk
77 p. 83-86 por / Dannett. Profiles 2:
254-63 por / Davis. Cav p. 57-58 /
Davis. Dark p. 186 / Dict Lit Biog 5-1:
100-106 / Dreer. Am Lit p. 89 / Drotning.
Up p. 170-76 / Ebony Success 1: 42 por /
Ebony Success 2: 22-27 il / Emanuel.
Dark p. 498-99 / Ency Am Biog p.
139-40 / Ency Blk Am p. 193, il p.
522 / Ford. Insights p. 223-24 / Great
Negroes 69 p. 158 il / Guide Am Lit
p. 103 / Haslam. Forgot p. 328 / Hayden.
Kal p. 150 / Historical N Bio p. 167 por /
Hughes. Best p. 498 / Hughes. Poet
p. 594-95 / King. Famous p. 32-34 /
Living BAA p. 21 / Long. Writing 2:
575-76 / Margolies. Read p. 353 /
Negro Alm 71 p. 667 por / Negro Alm
76 p. 717 por / Noble. Beautiful p.
179-82 / Poets p. 145-46 / Robinson.
Nommo p. 475-76 / Rollins. Famous
87-91 por / Selected BAA p. 26-27 por /
Sign Am Wom p. 58 il / Something ATA

Brooks, Gwendolyn (cont'd) ...
  6: 33 / Turner. Voices p. 259 / Twen
  CA Sup p. 128-29 por / Webster Am
  Biog p. 140 / Whitlow. Lit p. 130 /
  Who Am 80, 1: 433 / Who Blk Am 77 p.
  101 / Writers Dr 76 p. 130-31 / Writers
  Dr 80 p. 155 / Writers Dr 82 p. 118
Brooks, Helen Morgan
  Poet
    Blk Am Wr 1: 102 / Hughes. New p.
    118 / Hughes. Poet p. 595
Brooks, Jonathan Henderson, 1904-1945
  Clergyman, poet, short story writer
    Afro-Am Ency 2: 403 / Blk Am Wr 1:
    102 / Bontemps. American 63 p. 188 /
    Brown. Caravan p. 364 / Cullen. Carol
    p. 192-93 / Hughes. Poet p. 595
Brooks, Rosa Paul
  Poet
    Dreer. Am Lit p. 90
Brooks, Stella B.
  Folklorist
    Living BAA p. 20
Brooks, Walter Henderson, 1851-
  Minister
    Culp. Twen p. 314-15 / Who Col Am
    40 p. 81-82 / Who Col Race p. 39
Brooks, William F.
  Poet
    Cuney. Linc p. 67
Brown, A. L. Milner
  Poet, educator, journalist
    Afro-Am Ency 2: 406
Brown, Benjamin A.
  Short story writer, novelist, editor
    Afro-Am Ency 2: 407
Brown, Cecil M., 1942-
  Critic, playwright, teacher
    Con Auth 73-76: 88
    Selected BAA p. 28
    Who Blk Am 77 p. 105
Brown, Charlotte Hawkins, 1882-1961
  Educator, orator, author
    Boulware. Oratory p. 105-107 / Brawley.
    Builders p. 283-84 / Daniel. Wom 70
    p. 137-67 il, por / Dannett. Profiles 2:
    58-63 por / Lerner. Wom p. 124-25 /
    Notable Am Wom Mod p. 111-13 / Paths
    p. 138 / Who Col Am 37 p. 81 / Who
    Col Am 40 p. 82-83 / Who Col Am
    42 p. 79-80, por p. [81]
Brown, Claude, 1937-
  Novelist
    Afro-Am Ency 2: 409 / Blk Am Wr 1:

Brown, Claude (cont'd) ...
    104 / Con Auth 73-76: 88-89 / Cur
    Biog Yrbk 67 p. 43-45 por / David.
    Growing p. 207-214 / Ency Blk Am p.
    194 / Ford. Insights p. 310 / Lincoln
    Lib Arts 2: 475-76 / Negro Alm 71 p.
    667-68 por / Negro Alm 76 p. 717, por
    p. 718 / Selected BAA p. 28 il / Who
    Am 74, 1: 392 / Who Blk Am 77 p. 105
Brown, David Scott, 1931-
  Painter, illustrator
    Afro-Am Art p. 36
Brown, Elmer W., 1909-
  Educator, cartoonist, illustrator
    Afro-Am Art p. 36
Brown, Fannie Carole, 1942-
  Poet, editor
    Watts Wr p. [179]
Brown, Frank London, 1927-1962
  Novelist, short story writer, poet, maga-
  zine editor
    Afro-Am Ency 2: 411 / Blk Am Wr 1:
    105-106 / Blk Plots p. 205 / Chapman.
    Blk V p. 201-202 / Hughes. Best p. 498 /
    Hughes. Poet p. 595-96 / Margolies. Read
    p. 354 / Selected BAA p. 28 por
Brown, H(ubert) Rap, 1943-
    Am Auth & Bks 72 p. 83 / Pol profiles:
    Johnson p. 71-72 / Robinson. Nommo
    p. 476
Brown, Hallie Quinn, 1860-1949
  Poet, teacher, lecturer
    Afro-Am Ency 2: 412-13 / Daniel. Wom
    p. 289-308 por / Dannett. Profiles 1:
    234-35 il / Haley. Ency p. 581-83 por /
    Haley. Spark p. 91-94 / Historical N Bio
    p. 168-69 il / Negro Alm 71 p. 873 /
    Negro Alm 76 p. 1002 / Ohio Auth
    p. 81 / Notable Am Wom 1: 253-54 /
    Scruggs. Wom p. 14-23
Brown, Henry "Box," 1816-
  Narrator of personal experiences
    Afro-Am Ency 2: 413-18 il / Blk Am
    Wr 1: 106 / Ency Blk Am il p. 787
Brown, Isabella Maria, 1917-
  Teacher, poet
    Afro-Am Ency 2: 419 / Blk Am Wr 1:
    107 / Hughes. New p. 118-19 / Hughes.
    Poet p. 596
Brown, Jim(my), 1936-
  Athlete, actor, autobiographer
    Alexander. Young p. 70-82 por / Who Blk
    Am 77 p. 109

Brown, Joe C.
Poet
    Murphy. Ebony p. 15
Brown, Joseph Clifton, 1908-
Educator, author, poet
    Broadside Auth p. 32 / Who Blk Am
    77 p. 109
Brown, Lennox (John), 1934-
Playwright, poet, lecturer
    Blk Am Wr 1: 108-109 / Con Auth
    93-96: 72 / Nat Play Dr p. 32 por
Brown, Letitia Woods, 1915-1976
Educator, historian
    Con Auth 69-72: 100 / Con Auth 73-76:
    90 / Ency Blk Am p. 195
Brown, Margery Wheeler (Mrs. Richard E.
 Brown), 1920-
Art teacher, illustrator, writer for children
    Con Auth 25-28R: 104 / Selected BAA
    p. 29 / Something ATA 5: 32-33 /
    Something ATA 10: 3
Brown, Oscar, Jr., 1926-
Playwright, entertainer, actor, writer
    Negro Alm 76 p. 872 / Who Am 78, 1:
    433 / Who Am 80, 1: 450 / Who Blk Am
    77 p. 111
Brown, Roscoe C., Jr., 1922-
Editor, author
    Ebony Success 1: 46 por / Ency Blk Am
    p. 196 / Negro Alm 76 p. 1022 por /
    Selected BAA p. 46 por / Who Am 80,
    1: 435 / Who Blk Am 77 p. 113
Brown, S. Joe. See Brown, Sue M. (Wilson)
Brown, Sterling Allen, 1901-
Poet, critic, editor, short story writer
    Adams. Auth p. 128 / Adoff. Poet p.
    519 / Afro-Am Ency 2: 440 / Am Auth
    & Bks 72 p. 83 / Barksdale. Writers
    p. 632-33 / Bontemps. American 63
    p. 188 / Bontemps. American 74 p. 216 /
    Broadside Auth p. 32-33 / Brown. Cara-
    van p. 381 / Cele p. 254 / Chapman.
    Blk V p. 403-404 / Cromwell. Read
    p. 364 / Cullen. Carol p. 129-30 / Davis.
    Cav p. 400 / Davis. Dark p. 126 / Dreer.
    Am Lit p. 60-61 / Emanuel. Dark p.
    137-38 / Ency Blk Am p. 196, il p. 522 /
    Ford. Insights p. 66 / Hayden. Kal
    p. 68-69 / Hughes. Poet p. 596 / Johnson.
    Book p. 247-48 / Living BAA p. 22 /
    Long. Writing 2: 467 / Negro Alm 71
    p. 668 / Negro Alm 76 p. 718 / Poets
    p. 146-47 / Profiles Blk Ach 402-303 /
    Reader's Ency 62 p. 116 / Selected BAA

Brown, Sterling Allen (cont'd) ...
    p. 30 por / Turner. Voices p. 259 /
    Wagner. Poets p. 476 / Who Blk Am
    77 p. 114
Brown, Sterling Nelson, 1857-
Minister, educator
    Culp. Twen p. 68 / Who Col Race p. 45
Brown, Sue M. (Wilson), 1877-1941
Civic worker, author
    Afro-Am Ency 2: 440-41 / Dannett. Pro-
    files 1: 236-37 il / Who Col Am 40 p. 89
Brown, Virginia Suggs, 1924-
Educational director
    Blk Am Wr 1: 114 / Living BAA p. 22
Brown, Wesley, 1945-
Poet
    Blk Am Wr 1: 114
Brown, William B.
Poet
    Murphy. N Voices p. 18
Brown, William Wells, 1814-1884
Novelist, dramatist, autobiographer,
historian
    Afro-Am Ency 2: 442-44 il / Am Auth
    & Bks 72 p. 84 / Barksdale. Writers
    p. 180-81 / Blk Am Wr 1: 114 / Brawley.
    Early p. 168-70 / Cromwell. Read p. 364 /
    David. Defiance p. 34-46 / Davis. Cav
    p. 57-58 / Davis. South p. 411 / Dict
    Am Biog 29, 3: 161 / Dict Am Biog
    58, 2-1: 161 / Dict Lit Biog 3: 27-29 por /
    Ency Am Biog p. 139-40 / Historical
    N Bio p. 56 il / Kendricks. Voices p. 84 /
    Lincoln Lib Arts 2: 476 / Long. Writing
    1: 47 / Negro Alm 71 p. 668 / Negro
    Alm 76 p. 718 / Novelists 79 p. 174-75 /
    Robinson, Prose p. 193-94 / Sign Am
    Auth p. 10 / Southern Wr p. 49-50 /
    Sterling. Speak p. 372 / Thorpe. Hist
    p. 38-39
Browne, George B.
Poet
    Murphy. Ebony p. 16
Browne, Patricia Wilkins, 1950-
Playwright
    Blk Am Wr 1: 118
Browne, Roscoe Lee
Poet
    Who Am 80, 1: 439
Browne, Theodore, 1910-
Playwright
    Childress. Scenes p. 147-48
Bruce, Blanche K(elso), 1841-1898
Public official, writer, lecturer
    Afro-Am Ency 2: 450 il / Bio Dr Am

Bruce, Blanche K(elso) (cont'd) ...
Cong 61 p. 614 / Bio Hist p. 259-60 /
Brawley. Builders p. 127-32 por / Chris-
topher. Congress p. 15-24 / Dict Am Biog
29, 3: 180-81 / Dict Am Biog 59,
2-1: 180-81 / Ency Am Biog p. 140-41 /
Ency Blk Am p. 197 / Fauset. Freedom
p. 80-85 / Great Negroes 69 p. 43 il /
Historical N Bio p. 56-57 il / Negro Alm
71 p. 309 / Negro Alm 76 p. 319-20
por / Peters. Ebony p. 51-52 / Simmons.
Men p. 483-87 / Sterling. Four p. 98-111 /
Webster Am Biog p. 145 / Who Col Am
27 p. 29 / Who Col Am 29 p. 56 /
Who Was H: 81 / Who Was HR: 149 /
Woodson. Orators p. 267 / Young,
M. Lead p. 93-94 por

Bruce, Grit. *See* Bruce, John E(dward)

Bruce, John E(dward) (Grit; Grit Bruce),
1856-1924
Public official, journalist, novelist, poet
Afro-Am Ency 2: 450 por / Blk Am Wr 1:
119-20 / Penn. Press p. 344-47 / Thorpe.
Hist p. 149 / Who Col Race 1: 47

Bruce, Richard, 1906-
Poet
Cullen. Carol p. 205-206

Bruno, Joann
Playwright, writer of stories for children
Blk Am Wr 1: 120-21

Bryant, Frederick James, Jr., 1942-
Poet
Adoff. Poet p. 519 / Blk Am Wr 1:
121 / Cele p. 254 / Chapman. New p.
215 / Jones, Fire p. 659 / Selected BAA
p. 31

Bryant, Hazel J(oan), 1939-
Producer, director, playwright
Dr Perf Arts 78 p. 45-46 / Who Blk Am
77 p. 119

Bryant, L. A., 1927-
Living BAA p. 23

Bryant, Lawrence Chesterfield, 1916-
Educator, minister
Who Blk Am 77 p. 120

Buchanan, Alexander. *See* Parks, Gordon

Buford, Naomi E.
Poet
Murphy. Ebony p. 16

Buggs, George Edward, 1947-
Broadside Auth p. 33-34

Bullins, Ed (Kingley B. Bass, Jr.), 1935-
Playwright, poet, novelist, short story writer
Afro-Am Novel p. 34 / Alhamisi. Arts

Bullins, Ed (Kingley B. Bass, Jr.) (cont'd) ...
p. 45 / Blk Am Wr 1: 122-25 por /
Blk Plots p. 206-207 / Childress. Scenes
p. 148 / Con Auth 49-52: 89-91 / Con
Drama 73 p. 124-25 / Crowell CD p.
76-77 / Cur Biog Yrbk 77 p. 90-92
por / Ebony Success 1: 50 por / Dict
Lit Biog 7: 100-111 / Dr Perf Arts 78
p. 47-48 / Dramatists 79 p. 96-98 /
Ency Blk Am p. 198 / Haslam. Forgot
p. 352 / Jones. Fire p. 659 / King.
Story p. 59 / Lincoln Lib Arts 2:
480 / Living BAA p. 23 / Major. Poet
p. 146 / Negro Alm 71 p. 670 / Negro
Alm 76 p. 718-19 por / Notable Names
p. 600 / Oliver. Drama p. 367-68 /
Robinson. Nommo p. 475-76 / Selected
BAA p. 32 / Shuman. Galaxy p. 58 /
Who Blk Am 77 p. 123 / Who Theatre
77 p. 449 / Wor Auth 70-75 p. 134-37
por / Writers Dr 76 p. 144 / Writers
Dr 80 p. 170 / Writers Dr 82 p. 131

Bullock, Etta Stanton
Librarian
Josey. What p. 303

Bullock, Henry Allen, 1906-1973
Educator
Afro-Am Ency 2: 456 / Con Auth 41-
44R: 107 / Living BAA p. 23-24

Bunche, Ralph J(ohnson), 1904-1972
Diplomat, educator, author
Afro-Am Ency 2: 457-59 por / Bio Hist
p. 260-61 / Brown. Caravan p. 924 /
Con Auth 33-36R: 155 / Cur Bio Yrbk
48 p. 77-79 por / Ency Am Biog p.
147-48 / Flynn. Achieve p. 1-17 / Great
Negroes 69 p. 127 / Historical N Bio
p. 170 por / Nat Cyclo H: 32 / Nat
Cyclo 57: 304-305 por / Negro Alm 71
p. 338-39 / Negro Alm 76 p. 346 / Negro
Handbk 66 p. 397 / NYT Obit 2: 4-6 il /
Reader's Ency 62 p. 122 / Richardson.
Great 56 p. 213-25 il / Richardson.
Great 76 p. 206-17 por / Selected BAA
p. 33-34 por / Webster Am Biog
p. 151-52 / Who Col Am 50 p. 74-75
por / Who Was 5: 99 / Young, M. Lead
p. 76-78 por

Bunton, Frederica Katheryne
Poet
Murphy. Ebony p. 17

Burbridge, Edward Dejoie
Sports editor, poet
Blk Am Wr 1: 126 / Murphy. N Voices
p. 22

Burgan, Issac Medford, 1848-
Educator, clergyman
Simmons. Men p. 784-89 por / Who Col
Race p. 50

Burgie, Irving (Lord Burgess), 1924-
Songwriter, playwright
Afro-Am Ency 2: 461 / AmSCAP 66
p. 91 / Who Blk Am 77 p. 125

Burnett, Paula Denise (Alexander), 1951-
Broadside Auth p. 34

Burrell, Berkeley Graham, 1919-1979
Business executive
Con Auth 33-36R: 161 / Ebony Success
1: 53 por / Ency Blk Am p. 200 /
Who Am 78, 1: 480 / Who Blk Am 77
p. 127

Burrell, Evelyn Patterson
Poet, teacher of English
Con Auth 53-56: 77-78 / Selected BAA
p. 34-35

Burrell, Walter P., Jr., 1944-
Journalist, playwright, poet
Dr Perf Arts 78 p. 51 / Ebony Success
1: 53 por / Selected BAA p. 35 / Who
Blk Am 77 p. 128

Burroughs, Margaret Taylor Goss, 1917-
Artist, illustrator, poet, writer
Afro-Am Art p. 52-53 / Blk Am Wr 1:
127-28 por p. 126 / Con Auth 21-24R:
135 / Ebony Success 1: 54 por / Innis.
Profiles p. 110-111 por / Living BAA
p. 24 / Negro Alm 76 p. 770 / Selected
BAA p. 34-35 por

Burroughs, Nannie Helen, 1882-1961
Educator, orator
Boulware. Orators p. 103-105 / Daniel.
Wom p. 111-36 / Hammond. Van p.
47-62 por / Lerner. Wom p. 132-33 /
Negro Alm 71 p. 873 / Negro Alm 76 p.
1002-1003 / Notable Am Wom 4: 125-27 /
Who Col Am 42 p. 95 / Williams. Wom
p. 176

Burton, John W.
Poet
Murphy. Ebony p. 18 / Murphy. N
Voices p. 25

Bush, Joseph Bevans, ?-1968
Poet, essayist
Alhamisi. Arts p. 128 / Coombs. Speak
p. 239 / Shuman. Galaxy p. 63

Butcher, James W., Jr., 1909-
Educator, playwright
Brown. Caravan p. 520

Butcher, Margaret Just, 1913-
Teacher of English, author
Afro-Am Ency 5: 1497 / Living BAA p.
24 / Selected BAA p. 36

Butcher, (Charles) Philip, 1918-
Professor of English, social critic, essayist
Afro-Am Ency 2: 497 / Blk Am Wr 1:
129 / Con Auth 1-4: 56 / Con Auth 1-4R:
141 / Con Auth NR-4: 102-103 / Ebony
Success 1: 54 por / Emanuel. Dark
p. 527-28 / Ency Blk Am p. 210 /
Living BAA p. 24 / Negro Alm 71 p.
670 / Negro Alm 76 p. 719 / Selected
BAA p. 36-37 / Who Am 78, 1: 488 /
Who Blk Am 77 p. 130

Butler, (James) Alpheus, 1905-
Editor, poet
Murphy. Ebony p. 20 / Murphy. N Voices
p. 26-27

Butler, Anna M(abel) Land, 1901-
Teacher, poet, author, editor
Blk Am Wr 2: 131-32 por / Who Blk
Am 77 p. 130

Butler, Hood C.
Poet
Murphy. Ebony p. 22

Butler, Octavia E(stelle), 1947-
Novelist, science fiction writer
Con Auth 73-76: 103-104

Byam, Milton S.
Library administrator
Bio Dr Librns 70 p. 151 / Josey. Blk
Librn p. 50-68 / Who Blk Am 77
p. 134

Cade, Toni. *See* Bambara, Toni Cade

Cain, George, 1943-
Novelist
Afro-Am Novel p. 38 / Selected BAA
p. 37

Cain, Richard Harvey, 1825-1887
Clergyman, congressman, orator
Bio Dr Am Cong 61 p. 646 / Christopher.
Congress p. 87-96 / Dict Am Biog 29,
3: 403-404 / Dict Am Biog 58, 2-1:
403-404 / Negro Alm 76 p. 320 / Who
Was H: 147 / Who Was HR: 159 /
Woodson. Orators p. 328

Caines, Jeannette
Writer for young people
Blk Am Wr 1: 134

Caldwell, Ben
Artist, essayist, playwright, editor, short
story writer, poet
Blk Am Wr 1: 134-35 / Dr Perf Arts 78
p. 54 / Jones. Fire p. 659 / King.
Drama p. 389 / Robinson. Nommo p. 476
Caldwell, Lewis A. H. (Abe Noel), 1905-
Novelist
Blk Am Wr 1: 134 / Who Blk Am 77
p. 137
Calhoun, Eugene Clayton, 1912-
Clergyman, educator, writer
Ency Blk Am p. 212
Caliver, Ambrose, 1894-1964
Educator, writer on education
Ency Blk Am p. 212 / Historical N
Bio p. 171 / Who Col Am 29 p. 67 /
Who Col Am 40 p. 101 / Who Col
Am 42 p. 98, 101 / Who Col Am 50
p. 83-84 / Who Was 4: 147-48
Calloway, Cab, 1907-
Composer, conductor, author
AmSCAP 66 p. 102 / AmSCAP 80 p.
73 / Negro Alm 76 p. 821
Cambridge, Godfrey, 1933-
Comedian, actor, author
Lincoln Lib Arts 2: 487 / Negro Alm
76 p. 821-22 il
Campanella, Roy, 1921-
Professional baseball player, autobiographer
Cur Biog Yrbk 53 p. 105-108 por / David.
Roots p. 104-109 / Negro Alm 71 p. 649 /
Negro Alm 76 p. 695 / Who Am 74,
1: 478 / Who Am 78, 1: 511
Campbell, Beatrice Murphy. *See* Murphy
(Campbell), Beatrice
Campbell, Elmer Simms, 1906-1971
Cartoonist, illustrator
Afro-Am Ency 2: 518 / Brown. Caravan
p. 982 / Con Auth 93-96: 80 / Who Col
Am 50 p. 592
Campbell, James Edwin, 1867-1895
Poet, educator, editor
Afro-Am Ency 2: 518-19 / Barksdale.
Writers p. 450-51 / Blk Am Wr 1:
135-36 / Brown. Caravan p. 316 / His-
torical N Bio p. 59-61 il / Johnson.
Book p. 64-65 / Long. Writing 1: 231 /
Ohio Auth p. 97 / Sherman. Invisible
p. 186-87 / Wagner. Poets p. 129-30
Campbell, Thomas Monroe, 1883-
Educator, autobiographer
Jenness. Twelve p. 3-19
Cannon, C. E.
Poet
Broadside Auth p. 37-38

Cannon, David Wadsworth, Jr., 1911-1938
Poet
Blk Am Wr 1: 136-37 / Hughes. Poet
p. 596-97 / Murphy. Ebony p. 23
Cannon, Steve, 1935-
Novelist, poet, publisher
Blk Am Wr 1: 137
Carey, Archibald James, Jr., 1867-1931
Clergy, lawyer, orator
Boulware. Oratory p. 165 / Who Col Am
33 p. 80, 83; por p. 81 / Who Col
Am 50 p. 86-87 / Who Was 1: 191
Carmichael, Stokely, 1941-
Civil rights activist, essayist
Adoff. Blk on p. 227-28 / Afro-Am Ency
2: 533-34 il / Am Auth p. 101 / Bio
Hist p. 263-64 / Con Auth 57-60: 107 /
Cur Bio Yrbk 70 p. 66-69 por / Haskins.
Profiles p. 185-201 / Negro Alm 71
p. 299-31 por / Negro Alm 76 p. 311
por / Pol Profiles: Johnson p. 91-92 /
Selected BAA p. 38
Carmichael, Waverly Turner
Poet
Blk Am Wr 1: 138 / Johnson. Book
p. 162 / Kerlin. Poets 23 p. 269-70
Carpenter, Howard
Poet
Murphy. Ebony p. 27
Carr, Clarence F., 1880-
Educator, poet
Blk Am Wr 1: 138
Carrington, Harold, 1938-1964
Poet
Broadside Auth p. 38
Carroll, Vinnette
Actress, poet, playwright
Blk Am Wr 1: 138-39 / Who Blk Am
77 p. 146
Carson, Lular, 1921-
Novelist
Living BAA p. 25
Carter, Herman J. D.
Poet
Murphy. Ebony p. 27
Carter, Karl W., 1944-
Lawyer, poet
Blk Am Wr 1: 140
Carter, Randall Albert, 1867-1954
Clergyman, author
Who Col Am 40 p. 111 / Who Col
Am 42 p. 108 / Who Was 3: 143
Carter, Steve, 1929-
Playwright
Blk Am Wr 1: 140 / Childress. Scenes
p. 148 / Nat Play Dr p. 40 por

Clarke, Carl, 1932-
Poet
  Blk Am Wr 1: 152 / Broadside Auth p. 38
Clarke, Helen F.
Poet
  Murphy. Ebony p. 40
Clarke, John Henrik, 1915-
Columnist, poet, biographer, writer of short
stories
  Adoff. Poet p. 519 / Afro-Am Ency 3:
  619-20 / Auth News 1: 106 por / Cele
  p. 254 / Chapman. Blk V p. 631-32 /
  Con Auth 53-56: 107 / Ebony Success 1:
  69 por / Ency Blk Am p. 273 / Living
  BAA p. 29 / Murphy. Ebony p. 42 /
  Selected BAA p. 45 por / Turner. Voices
  p. 260-61
Clarke, Milton, 1817-?
Autobiographer
  Brown. Caravan p. 703
Clarke, Thomas H(enry) R(eginald), 1874-
Writer on politics
  Who Col Am 40 p. 121-22
Claxton, Richard. *See* Gregory, Dick
Clay, Buriel, II, 1943-
Poet, playwright
  Blk Am Wr 1: 155-56
Clayton, Mayme
Historian
  Williams. Wom p. 177
Cleage, Albert B., Jr., 1911-
Clergyman, author
  Con Auth 65-58: 124 / Ebony Success 1:
  70 por / Haskins. Profiles p. 61-74 /
  Who Blk Am 77 p. 170 / Young. Since
  1940 p. 82, 86-87
Cleage, Pearl Michelle. *See* Lomax, Pearl
Michelle Cleage
Cleaver, (Leroy) Eldridge, 1935-
Political activist, writer
  Adams. Auth p. 143 / Afro-Am Ency 3:
  622-23 il / Am Auth 72 p. 123 / Barks-
  dale. Writers p. 882-84 / Blk Am Wr 1:
  157 / Blk Lit HS p. 58 / Chapman.
  New p. 474 / Con Auth 21-24R: 177-79 /
  Cur Biog Yrbk 70 p. 85-88 por / David.
  Defiance p. 184-99 / Ford. Insights p.
  346 / Haskins. Profiles p. 141-59 / Ken-
  dricks. Voices p. 331 / Living BAA p.
  30 / Long. Writing 2: 699-700 / Margo-
  lies. Read p. 354 / Metcalf. Profiles
  p. 369-400 / O'Neill. Speeches p. 228 /
  Pol Profiles: Johnson p. 114-15 / Pol
  Profiles: Nixon p. 130-31 / Robinson.
  Nommo p. 476 / Turner. Voices p. 261

Cleaves, Mary Wilkerson
Poet
  Murphy. Ebony p. 45
Clem, Charles Douglas, 1876-1934
Poet, editor, lecturer
  Blk Am Wr 1: 158 / Ency Blk Am
  p. 274-75 / Sherman. Invisible p.
  199-201 / Who Col Race p. 68-69 / Wood-
  son. Orators p. 628
Clement, George Clinton, 1871-1934
Bishop, editor
  Who Col Race p. 68-69 / Who Was 1:
  230 / Woodson. Orators p. 628
Clemmons, Carole Gregory, 1945-
Teacher, poet
  Adoff. Poet p. 520 / Blk Am Wr 1:
  159 / Broadside Auth p. 39 / Cele p.
  254 / Major. Poet p. 148 / Shuman.
  Galaxy p. 68 / Shuman. Nine p. 80
Clemmons, Francois, 1945-
Poet, editor, actor, singer
  Con Auth 41-44R: 142 / Shuman. Galaxy
  p. 272
Clemons, Lulamae, 1917-
Living BAA p. 30-31
Cleveland, Edward Earl, 1921-
Clergyman, writer
  Bio Dr Min p. 92 / Who Blk Am
  77 p. 171
Clifford, Carrie Williams
Poet
  Blk Am Wr 1: 159 / Kerlin. Poets 23
  p. 270 / Kerlin. Poets 35 p. 334
Clift, Virgil A(lfred), 1912-
Educator, editor, author
  Con Auth 9R: 90 / Ency Blk Am
  p. 275 / Living BAA p. 31
Clifton, Lucille (Thelma), 1936-
Writer of fiction for children and young
people, poet
  Adoff. Poet p. 520 / Beasley. Trail p.
  36-41 / Blk Am Wr 1: 159 / Chester.
  Rising p. 253 / Con Auth 49-52: 116 /
  Con Poets 75 p. 258-59 / Con Poets
  80 p. 256-57 / Dict Lit Biog 5-1:
  132-36 por / Miller. Dices p. 139 /
  Something ATA 20: 20 / Twen CCW p.
  279-81 / Who Am 80 1: 622 / Who Blk
  Am 77 p. 172 / Writers Dr 80 p. 234
Clinton, George Wylie, 1859-1921
Preacher, editor
  Bio Dict S Suth p. 88 / Culp. Twen
  p. 114-15 il / Dict Am Biog 30, 3:
  228-29 / Dict Am Biog 58, 2-1: 228-29 /
  Haley. Ency p. 118-24 por / Penn. Press
  p. 309-312 / Who Col Race p. 69

Cobb, Bessie A.
Poet
Murphy. N Voices p. 35
Cobb, Charlie, 1944-
Poet, essayist
Jones. Fire p. 659
Cobb, Janice, 1952-
Poet
Blk Am Wr 1: 160-61
Cobb, W(illiam) Montague, 1904-
Professor of anatomy, author, essayist
Dreer. Am Lit p. 126 / Ebony Success
1: 73 por / Historical N Bio 174-75 /
Who Blk Am 77 p. 174
Cobbs, Price M(ashaw), 1928-
Psychiatrist
Con Auth 21-24R: 181 / Ebony Success
1: 73 por / Who Am 80, 1: 628 / Who
Blk Am 77 p. 174
Coffin, Frank Barbour, 1871-
Druggist, poet
White. Verse p. 217 / Who Col Race
p. 71
Cole, Johnetta B.
Professor of anthropology
Chapman. New p. 491
Cole, Robert, 1868-1911
Playwright, composer
Blk Am Wr 1: 162
Coleman, Anita Scott
Teacher, poet, short story writer
Murphy. Ebony p. 48 / Murphy. N
Voices p. 36
Coleman, Ethel
Poet
Murphy. N Voices p. 38
Coleman, Horace Wendell, Jr., 1943-
Poet, short story writer
Blk Am Wr 1: 163-64 / Broadside
Auth p. 107-108
Coleman, Jayme H.
Poet
Murphy. Ebony p. 52
Coleman, Larry G., 1946-
Teacher, editor, film critic, actor
Blk Am Wr 1: 164
Coleman, Lucretia Newman
Journalist, novelist, poet
Majors. Wom p. 197 / Penn. Press
p. 384-86 / Scruggs. Wom p. 210-11
Coleman, Merton H., 1889-
Living BAA p. 32
Coleman, Wanda
Television script writer, poet, playwright,
short story writer
Blk Am Wr 1: 165

Collier, Eugenia, 1928-
Educator, poet, essayist, short story writer
Blk Am Wr 1: 165 / Con Auth 49-52:
122 / Living BAA p. 32 / Selected
BAA p. 49-50 por / Who Blk Am 77
p. 181 / Writers Dr 76 p. 207 / Writers
Dr 80 p. 245
Collins, Durward, Jr., 1937-
Educator, poet
Blk Am Wr 1: 166
Collins, Helen Armstead Johnson, 1918-
Professor of English, poet, writer on
black theatre
Blk Am Wr 1: 166 / Bontemps. American
74 p. 221-22 / Hughes. Poet p. 597 /
Murphy. N Voices p. 87
Collins, Leslie M(organ), 1914-
Educator, poet, librarian
Blk Am Wr 1: 166 / Bontemps. American
63 p. 188 / Bontemps. American 74
p. 217 / Dr Am Schol 74, 2: 121-22 /
Handbk Librns p. 163 / Hughes. Poet p.
597-98
Colter, Cyrus J., 1910-
Public official, novelist, short story writer,
poet
Afro-Am Novel p. 42 / Blk Am Wr 1:
167-68 / Blk Plots p. 211 / Chapman.
New p. 69 / Con Auth 65-68: 133 /
Con Novel 76 p. 296-97 / Ebony Success
1: 76 por / Hughes. Best p. 499 / Living
BAA p. 32-33 / Selected BAA p. 50-51
por / Who Am 80, 1: 682 / Who Blk Am
77 p. 184 / Writers Dr 80 p. 259
Comer, James P(ierpont), 1934-
Educator, author
Con Auth 61-64: 134 / Ebony Success
1: 77 por / Who Blk Am 77 p. 185
Cone, James H., 1938-
Educator, theologian, author, lecturer
Bio Dr Min 75 p. 103-104 / Con Auth
33-36R: 203 / Ebony Success 1: 77 por /
Living BAA p. 33 / Who Blk Am 77
p. 185-86 / Young. Since 1940 p. 132-33,
141-42
Conley, Allen. See Elam, Dorothy
Conley, Everett Nathaniel. 1949-
Poet
Innis. Profiles p. 196-97 por / Living
BAA p. 33
Conner, Charles H., 1864-
Poet
Blk Am Wr 1: 168 / Kerlin. Poets 23
p. 209-210 il, p. 270 / Kerlin. Poets
35 p. 335

Conyus, 1942-
Poet
    Adoff. Poet p. 520 / Blk Am Wr 1: 168
Cook, Mary V. (Grace Ermine), 1883-
Teacher, editor, journalist
    Majors. Wom p. 195-96 / Penn. Press
    p. 367-74 / Scruggs. Wom p. 120-21
Cook, Mercer, 1903-
Educator, editor, poet, diplomat
    Ency Blk Am p. 287 / Historical N Bio
    p. 175 por / Living BAA p. 34 / Negro
    Alm 71 p. 287 / Negro Alm 76 p.
    347 / Scally. Catholic p. 38-40
Cook, Mike, 1939-
Poet
    Broadside Auth p. 39
Coombs, Orde
Compiler of literary anthologies, short story
writer, essayist
    Blk Am Wr 1: 171-72 por / Con Auth
    73-76: 131 / Who Blk Am 77 p. 189
Cooper, Ada A., 1861-
Lecturer, teacher, poet
    Majors. Wom p. 298-304
Cooper, Anna Julia, 1858-1964
Educator, essayist, lecturer
    Afro-Am Ency 3: 666 / Blk Am Wr 1:
    172 / Lerner. Wom p. 572 / Loewenberg.
    Wom p. 317-18 / Majors. Wom p.
    284-87 / Notable Am Wom 4: 163-65 /
    Scruggs. Wom p. 207-209 / Who Col Am
    40 p. 132-33 / Who Col Am 42 p. 133 /
    Who Col Race p. 76
Cooper, Charles B., 1948-
Poet
    Adoff. Blk out p. 77 / Adoff. Poet p.
    520 / Shuman. Nine p. 24
Cooper, Clarence, Jr.
Novelist, short story writer
    King. Spirits p. 209
Cooper, Edward E.
Journalist, editor
    Culp. Twen p. 464-65 por / Penn. Press
    p. 334-39
Cooper, William Arthur, 1895-
Minister, artist, author
    Who Col Am 40 p. 134-35, por p. 131 /
    Who Col Am 42 p. 134
Copeland, Emily America
Educator, librarian
    Bio Dr Librns 70 p. 219 / Josey. Blk
    Librn p. 77-91 / Who Blk Am 77 p. 191
Coppin, Fannie M(uriel) Jackson, 1835-1912
Educator, lecturer, missionary
    Afro-Am Ency 3: 668-69 / Brawley.
    Builders p. 273-77 / Brown. Homespun

Coppin, Fannie M(uriel) Jackson (cont'd) ...
    p. 119-26, por opp. p. 96 / Daniel.
    Wom 70 p. 219-39 il / Dannett. Profiles
    1: 246-47 il / Ency Blk Am p. 288 /
    Historical N Bio p. 67 il / Lerner. Wom
    p. 88 / Loewenberg. Wom p. 302-303 /
    Majors. Wom p. 170-75 / Notable Am
    Wom 1: 383-85 / Scruggs. Wom p. 75-77 /
    Williams. Wom p. 177
Corbett, Maurice Nathaniel, 1859-
Government employee, poet
    Kerlin. Poets 23 p. 270 / Kerlin. Poets
    35 p. 335
Corbin, Lloyd M., Jr. (Djangatolum), 1949-
Educational media specialist, poet
    Adoff. Poet p. 522 / Blk Am Wr 1:
    174-75 / Cele p. 255
Cornish, Sam(uel James), 1935?-
Poet, writer of fiction for children
    Adoff. Poet p. 520 / Con Auth 41-44R:
    154 / Con Poets 70 p. 234-35 / Con
    Poets 75 p. 306-307 / Con Poets 80
    p. 302-304 / Jones. Fire p. 660 / Living
    BAA p. 34-35 / Major. Poet p. 146 /
    Selected BAA p. 54 / Something ATA
    23: 51-52 / Writers Dr 76 p. 221 /
    Writers Dr 80 p. 263 / Writers Dr 82
    p. 201
Cornish, Samuel E., 1790-1859
Journalist, editor, minister
    Afro-Am Ency 3: 671 il / Bennett.
    Pioneers p. 58-66 por / Historical N Bio
    p. 68 / Sterling. Speak p. 373
Corrothers, James David, 1869-1917
Minister, poet, playwright, autobiographer
    Barton. Witness p. 18-23 / Blk Am Wr 1:
    175-76 / Davis. Cav p. 189 / Hughes.
    Poet p. 598 / Johnson. Book p. 72 /
    Kendricks. Voices p. 198 / Kerlin. Poets
    23 p. 86 il, p. 270 / Kerlin. Poets 35
    p. 335 / Robinson. Poets p. 263 / White.
    Verse p. 163-68 / Who Col Race p. 77
Cortez, Lynne, 1937-
Educator, publisher, poet
    Adoff. Poet p. 520 / Blk Am Wr 1: 177 /
    Chapman. New p. 233 / Exum. Keep p.
    283 / Living BAA p. 35
Cosby, Bill, 1937?-
Actor, comedian, author
    Con Auth 81-84: 100-101 / Cur Biog Yrbk
    67 p. 82-84 por / Dr Perf Arts 78
    p. 80-81 / Who Am 80, 1: 722 / Who Blk
    Am 77 p. 193

Coston, Julia Ringwood, ca. 1860-
Journalist
Majors. Wom p. 251 / Scruggs. Wom
p. 140-43
Cotter, Joseph (Seamon), 1861-1949
Poet
Afro-Am Ency 3: 674 / Am Auth & Bks
72 p. 139 / Blk Am Wr 1: 178-79 / Blk
Plots p. 212 / Brown. Caravan p. 343 /
Cullen. Carol p. 10-11 / Hughes. Poet
p. 598 / Kerlin. Poets 23 p. 70, 271 /
Kerlin. Poets 35 p. 335 / Lincoln Lib
Arts 2: 509 / Negro Alm 71 p. 671 /
Robinson. Poets p. 195 / Sherman.
Invisible p. 164-66 / White. Verse p.
146 / Who Col Am 33 p. 108 / Who
Col Am 37 p. 136 / Who Col Am 40
p. 135-36 / Who Col Am 42 p. 136
Cotter, Joseph Seamon, Jr., 1895-1919
Poet
Adoff. Poet p. 520 / Blk Am Wr 1: 178 /
Blk Plots p. 212 / Brown, Caravan p.
346 / Cullen. Carol p. 99-100 / Ham-
mond. Van p. 162-70 por / Johnson.
Book p. 185 / Kerlin. Poets 23 p.
270-71, por p. 81 / Negro Alm 71 p.
671 / Negro Alm 76 p. 720 / White.
Verse p. 180
Council(l), William Hooper, 1848-1909
Educator, attorney, minister, editor,
historian
Afro-Am Ency 3: 678-79 / Culp. Twen p.
324-25 / Historical N Bio p. 68 / Paths
p. 147 por
Cousins, William
Poet
Murphy. Ebony p. 53
Cox, James Monroe, 1860-1948
Educator, essayist
Culp. Twen p. 294-95 por / Who Was 2:
132 / Who Col Race 1: 78
Cox, Ollie H.
Educator, poet
Shuman. Galaxy p. 283
Craft, Ellen, 1826-1897
Narrator of personal experiences
Afro-Am Ency 3: 682-83 il / Bontemps.
Great p. 269-331 / Chittenden. Profiles
p. 68-87 / Dannett. Profiles 1: 126-31
il / Historical N Bio p. 69-70 il /
Lerner. Wom p. 65-66 / Notable Am
Wom 1: 396-97 / Robinson. Prose p.
141-56 / Simmons. Men p. 83-86 / Sterl-
ing. Fore p. 2-59

Craft, William
Narrator of personal experiences
Afro-Am Ency 3: 682-83 il / Bontemps.
Great p. 269-331 / Chittenden. Profiles
p. 68-87 / Historical N Bio p. 69-70 il /
Lerner. Wom p. 65-66 / Robinson. Prose
p. 141-56 / Simmons. Men p. 83-86 /
Sterling. Speak p. 156-60
Cravat, John A., 1831-1897
Soldier, narrator of experiences
Barksdale. Writers p. 263-65
Crawley, Hazel L., 1921-
Poet, playwright
Nat Play Dr p. 54 por
Crayton, James E(dward), 1943-
Librarian, essayist
Josey. What p. 303 / Who Blk Am
77 p. 200
Crayton, Pearl
Writer of short stories, editor
Adoff. Brothers p. 232 / Hughes.
Best p. 499
Crews, Donald
Illustrator
Illus Bks YP 75 p. 45-46 / Illus Ch Bks
67 p. 110
Crews, Stella Louise, 1950-
Poet
Blk Am Wr 1: 183 / Broadside Auth p. 40
Crichlow, Ernest T., 1914-
Illustrator
Afro-Am Art p. 64-65 / Blk Am Ency
p. 292 / Fourth Bk p. 107-108 / Illus
Bks YP 70 p. 27 / Illus Bks YP 75
p. 46 / Illus Ch Bks 57 p. 96
Crogman, William H(enry), 1841-1931
Educator, historian, lecturer
Afro-Am Ency 3: 687-88 il / Culp.
Twen p. 6-7 / Ency Blk Am p. 295 /
Simmons. Men p. 480-82 / Thorpe.
Hist p. 151 / Who Col Am 29 p. 93 /
Who Col Race p. 81 / Who Was 1:
278
Cromwell, John Wesley, 1846-
Lawyer, editor, journalist, historian
Culp. Twen p. 290-91 por / Dreer. Am
Lit p. 106 / Penn. Press p. 154-58 /
Simmons. Men p. 637-43 il / Thorpe.
Hist p. 146-47 / Who Col Race p. 81
Crouch, Stanley, 1945-
Musician, music critic, poet, columnist,
playwright
Adoff. Poet p. 520 / Cele p. 255 /
Coombs. Speak p. 240 / King. Spirits
p. 244 / Major. Poets p. 146

Crummel(l), Alexander, 1819-1898
  Clergyman, scholar, essayist
    Afro-Am Ency 3: 694 / Alli Sup 1: 426 /
    Am Auth & Bks 72 p. 147 / Barksdale.
    Writers p. 101-103 / Blk Plots p. 213-14 /
    Brawley. Builders p. 207-208 / Brawley.
    Early p. 299-301 / Cromwell. Read p.
    364-65 / Dict Am Auth p. 81 / Ency
    Blk Am p. 296 por / Great Negroes 69
    p. 39 / Haley, Ency p. 561 / Long.
    Writing 1: 117-18 / Northrop. College
    p. 44 por / Simmons. Men p. 357-61 por /
    Sterling. Speak p. 373 / Young. 1755 p.
    110-13, 125-26
Cruse, Harold W.
  Film editor, drama critic, free lance writer
    Blk Am Wr 1: 183-84 / Davis. Cav p.
    853 / Ebony Success 1: 83 por / Jones.
    Fire p. 660 / Living BAA p. 35-36 /
    Selected BAA p. 56-57 por / Who Blk Am
    77 p. 204
Cruz, Victor Hernandez, 1949-
  Poet, writer, teacher
    Adoff. Blk out p. 77 / Adoff. Poet p.
    521 / Afro-Am Ency 3: 695 / Chapman.
    New p. 237 / Con Poets 70 p. 251 /
    Con Poets 75 p. 331-32 / Con Poets
    80 p. 326-27 / Jones. Fire p. 660 /
    Miller. Dices p. 139 / Writers Dr 80
    p. 282 / Writers Dr 82 p. 215-16
Cuffe, Paul, 1759-1817
  Colonizer, autobiographer
    Afro-Am Ency 3: 696-99 / Brawley.
    Builders p. 35-39 / Dict Am Biog 30,
    4: 585 / Dict Am Biog 58, 2-2: 585 /
    Great Negroes 69 p. 27 / Mott. Bio
    p. 26-31 / Who Was H: 129 / Who Was
    HR: 198
Cullen, Countee (Porter), 1903-1946
  Novelist, poet, playwright
    Adams. Auth p. 20 / Adoff. Poet
    p. 521 / Afro-Am Ency 3: 699-700 /
    Am Auth & Bks 72 p. 147 / Anth Mag
    Verse 26, Pt. 4 p. 11 / Barksdale.
    Writers p. 529-30 / Blk Am Wr 1: 184 /
    Bone. Novel p. 78 / Bontemps. American
    63 p. 188 / Bontemps. American 74 p.
    217 / Broadside Auth p. 40-41 / Brown.
    Caravan p. 357 / Chamber p. 338 /
    Chapman. Blk V p. 381-82 / Cromwell.
    Read p. 365 / Cullen. Carol p. 179 /
    Davis. Cav p. 323-24 / Davis. Dark
    p. 74-75 / Dict Lit Biog 4: 103-104 /
    Dr Perf Arts 78 p. 83 / Dreer. Am Lit

Cullen, Countee (Porter) (cont'd) ...
    p. 67 / Emanuel. Dark p. 172-75 / Ency
    Blk Am p. 297, il p. 522 / Ford. Insights
    p. 78-79 / Great Negroes 69 p. 154 il /
    Historical N Bio p. 176 / Hughes. Poet
    p. 599 / Johnson. Book p. 219-21 /
    Kendricks. Voices p. 235 / Kerlin 35
    p. 336 / Locke. Four p. 31 / Long.
    Writing 2: 417 / Margolies. Read p.
    354-55 / Negro Alm 71 p. 671-72 por /
    Negro Alm 76 p. 720 por / Oxford Am
    65 p. 198-99 / Penguin Am Lit p. 67 /
    Reader's Adviser 74, 1: 293 / Reader's
    Ency 62 p. 228 / Rollins. Famous p.
    75-79 por / Sign Am Auth p. 38 /
    Something ATA 18: 64-68 por / Turner.
    Voices p. 261 / Twen CA 42 p. 336-
    37 por / Twen CA Sup 55 p. 250 /
    Wagner. Poets p. 284-91 / White. Verse
    p. 210 / Whitlow. Lit p. 83-86 / Who
    Col Am 37 p. 138 / Who Col Am 40
    p. 140 / Who Col Am 42 p. 140 /
    Who Was 2: 138
Culp, Daniel Wallace, 1854-
    Culp. Twen p. 15-16 il
Culver, Eloise Crosby, 1915-1972
  Poet, teacher
    Blk Am Wr 1: 190
Cumberbatch, Lawrence S., 1946-
  Poet
    Coombs. Speak p. 240
Cumbo, Kattie M., 1938-
  Poet, teacher, journalist
    Adoff. Blk out p. 77 / Blk Am Wr 1:
    190-91 / Living BAA p. 36 / Shuman.
    Galaxy p. 72 / Shuman. Nine p. 43
Cuney, (William) Waring. 1906-
  Musician, poet
    Afro-Am Ency 3: 701 / Blk Am Wr 1:
    191 / Bontemps. American 63 p. 189 /
    Bontemps. American 74 p. 217 / Brown.
    Caravan p. 374 / Cromwell. Read p. 365 /
    Cullen. Carol p. 207-208 / Cuney. Linc
    p. 68 / Davis. Cav p. 374 / Ency Blk
    Am p. 297 / Johnson. Book p. 283 /
    Kerlin. Poets 35 p. 336
Cuney-Hare, Maud, 1874-1936
  Concert pianist, lecturer, writer, biographer
    Blk Am Wr 1: 193 / Ency Blk Am p.
    416 / Who Col Race 1: 129-30
Cunningham, James (Olumbo), 1936-
    Broadside Auth p. 91 / Cele p. 263 /
    Chapman. New p. 483
Cunningham, Margaret Essie. *See* Danner,
    Margaret Essie

Cunningham, William D., 1937-
Educator, librarian, essayist
Bio Dr Librn 70 p. 239 / Josey. Blk
Librn p. 284-89 / Josey. What p. 304 /
Who Blk Am 77 p. 206
Curry, George E(dward), 1947-
Reporter, author
Con Auth 69-72: 162 / Who Blk Am 77
p. 207
Curtis, Thomas A., 1862-
Essayist
Haley. Ency p. 76-77 por
Curtwright, Wesley, 1910-
Poet
Blk Am Wr 1: 194 / Cullen. Carol p. 224

Dabney, Wendell Phillips, 1865-1952
Editor, musician
Brown, Caravan p. 1000 / Dabney. Cin
p. 360 / Ohio Auth p. 152 / Who Col
Am 33 p. 115 / Who Col Am 42 p. 142 /
Who Col Race p. 85
Dalcour, Pierre, 1805-
Poet
Afro-Am Ency 3: 707 / Hughes. Poet
p. 599-600
Damas, Leon, 1912-
Poet, public official
Afro-Am Ency 3: 707
Dancy, John C., 1857-
Educator, editor, political activist
Afro-Am Ency 3: 708 / Penn. Press
p. 197-250
Dancy, Walter, 1946-
Poet
Blk Am Wr 1: 195 / Coombs. Speak
p. 240 / Henderson. Under p. 383
Dandridge, Raymond Garfield, 1882-1930
Poet, literary editor
Adoff. Poet p. 521 / Blk Am Wr 1:
196 / Johnson. Book p. 190 / Kerlin.
Poets 23 p. 271 / Kerlin. Poets 35
p. 336 / Ohio Auth p. 153 / White. Verse
p. 191
Daniel, Portia Bird
Poet
Murphy. N Voices p. 43
Danner, Margaret (Margaret Essie Cun-
ningham), 1915-
Poet, editor
Adoff. Poet p. 521 / Afro-Am Ency 3:
711 / Bontemps. American 63 p. 189 /
Bontemps. American 74 p. 217-18 /

Danner, Margaret (Margaret Essie Cun-
ningham) (cont'd) ...
Broadside Auth p. 41-42 / Cele p. 255 /
Con Auth 29-32R: 153 / Con Poets 70
p. 265 / Hayden. Kal p. 124 / Hughes.
New p. 119 / Living BAA p. 36-37 /
Long. Writing 2: 633 / Who Blk Am 77
p. 212
Danridge, Dorothy, 1923-1965
Actress, autobiographer
Dr Perf Arts 78 p. 85-86
Darben, Althea Gibson. *See* Gibson (Darben),
Althea
Dario, Ruben, 1867-1916
Poet
Afro-Am Ency 3: 712
Darity, William A., Jr., 1953-
Orator, author
Living BAA p. 37
Davis, A. I.
Playwright, writer of short stories
Blk Am Wr 1: 197-98
Davis, Allison, 1902-
Anthropologist, psychologist, author
Brown. Caravan p. 1024 / Living BAA
p. 37 / Selected BAA p. 59
Davis, Angela (Yvonne), 1944-
Activist, autobiographer
Afro-Am Ency 3: 715-16 por / Con Auth
57-60: 159 / Negro Alm 76 p. 1003-1004 /
Pol Profiles: Nixon p. 162-63 / Selected
BAA p. 60 por / Wom Am p. 12-13
Davis, Arthur P(aul), 1904-
Professor of English, essayist, editor, auto-
biographer, short story writer
Afro-Am Ency 3: 716 / Blk Am Wr 1:
198 / Chapman. Blk V p. 605-606 /
Con Auth 61-64: 146-47 / Davis. Cav
p. 428 / Dr Am Schol 78, 2: 155 /
Emanuel. Dark p. 517-18 / Ency Blk Am
p. 303 / Living BAA p. 38 / Negro
Alm 71 p. 672 / Negro Alm 76 p.
720-21 / Selected BAA p. 60-61 / Who
Blk Am 77 p. 216-17 / Who Col Am
50 p. 138 por
Davis, Barbara (Thulani Nkabinde), 1949-
Poet
Blk Am Wr 1: 200
Davis, Benjamin J(efferson), Jr., 1903-1964
Lawyer, public official, autobiographer,
political organizer
David. Defiance p. 102-103 / Who Col
Am 50 p. 138-39

Davis, Daniel Webster, 1862-1913
  Clergyman, educator, poet
    Blk Am Wr 1: 201 / Culp. Twen p.
    38-39 il / Johnson. Book p. 81 / Penn.
    Press p. 326-30 / Robinson. Poets p.
    262-63 / Sherman. Invisible p. 172-78 /
    Wagner. Poets p. 138 / White. Verse p. 98
Davis, Elizabeth Lindsay, 1855-
  Teacher, writer
    Afro-Am Ency 3: 720
Davis, Frank Marshall, 1905-
  Journalist, poet
    Adoff. Poet p. 521 / Afro-Am Ency 3:
    721 / Blk Am Wr 1: 202-203 / Blk Plots
    p. 215 / Bontemps. American 63 p. 189 /
    Bontemps. American 74 p. 218 / Brown.
    Caravan p. 391-92 / Davis. Dark p. 121 /
    Ford. Insights p. 157 / Hayden. Kal
    p. 104 / Hughes. Poet p. 600 / Kerlin.
    Poets 35 p. 346 / Murphy. Ebony p. 54 /
    Murphy. N Voices p. 45 / Selected BAA
    p. 61 por / Wagner. Poets p. 187
Davis, George B., 1939-
  Novelist, short story writer
    King. Story p. 339
Davis, Harry E., 1882-1955
  Public official, attorney, writer on
  freemasonry
    Davis. Memorable p. 48-49 por
Davis, I. D.
  Minister, educator
    Culp Twen p. 124 il
Davis, James A.
  Pulpit orator, theologian
    Haley. Ency p. 584-87 por
Davis, Katie Chapman
  Poet, short story writer
    Northrop. College p. 102 il
Davis, Lenwood G., 1939-
  Educator, bibliographer
    Con Auth 25-28R: 179 / Living BAA
    p. 38-39
Davis, Nolan, 1942-
  Novelist, journalist, TV scriptwriter
    Blk Am Wr 1: 205 / Con Auth 49-52:
    142-43
Davis, Ossie, 1917-
  Playwright, actor, film director, editor
    Adoff. Blk on p. 228 / Afro-Am Ency 3:
    725 il / Am Auth & Bks 72 p. 157 /
    Blk Am Wr 1: 206-207 por / Blk Plots
    p. 215 / Broadside Auth p. 42-43 /
    Childress. Scenes p. 149 / Con Drama
    73 p. 191-93 / Cur Biog Yrbk 69 p.

Davis, Ossie (cont'd) ...
    114-17 por / Davis. Cav p. 627 / Dict
    Lit Biog 7-1: 144-47 / Dr Perf Arts
    78 p. 89-90 / Ebony Success 1: 90 por /
    Ency Blk Am p. 304 / Hill. Anger p.
    215 / Lincoln Lib Arts 2: 519 / Living
    BAA p. 39 / Negro Alm 71 p. 765 /
    Negro Alm 76 p. 824-25 por / Negro
    Handbk 66 p. 399 / Notable Names p.
    667-68 / Oliver. Drama p. 123-24 /
    Selected BAA p. 62 por / Southern Wr
    p. 117-18 / Whitlow. Lit p. 148 / Who
    Blk Am 77 p. 223 / Wor Auth 70-75,
    p. 189-92 por / Writers Dr 80 p. 301
Davis, Ronda Marie
  Poet, teacher
    Broadside Auth p. 43 / King. Spirits
    p. 244
Davis, Sammy, Jr., 1925-
  Entertainer, autobiographer
    Afro-Am Ency 3: 725-26 il / Bio Hist
    p. 276-77 / David. Soldier p. 131-46 /
    Dr Perf Arts 78 p. 90-91 / Ebony
    Success 2: 56-59 il / Historical N Bio
    p. 180 por / Lincoln Lib Arts 2: 519 /
    Negro Alm 71 p. 765 / Negro Alm 76
    p. 825 por / Negro Handbk 66 p. 399 /
    Rollins. Enter p. 57-62, por p. 10 /
    Who Blk Am 77 p. 224
Dawley, Jack H., 1924-
  Poet
    Cuney. Linc p. 68
Day, Caroline Bond
  Short story writer, essayist, teacher
    Cromwell. Read p. 365
Day, William Howard, 1825-1900
  Minister, editor, public official
    Davis. Mem p. 18-19 / Sterling. Speak
    p. 374
Deadwood, Dick. See Love, Nat
Dean, Philip Hayes
  Playwright, dramatist
    Dr Perf Arts 78 p. 92-93 / King. Drama
    p. 301
DeAnda, Peter
  Actor, playwright
    King. Drama p. 475
DeBaptiste, Georgia Mable, 1867-
  Journalist
    Majors. Wom p. 297-98 / Penn. Press
    p. 386-88
DeCoy, Robert H(arold), Jr., 1920-
  Radio program and news director, writer,
  publisher
    Blk Am Wr 1: 211 / Con Auth 25-28R:
    181-82 / Robinson. Nommo p. 477

Dedeaux, Richard Anthony, 1940-
Poet
Blk Am Wr 1: 212 / Who Blk Am 77
p. 230
Dee, Ruby (Ruby Ann Wallace; Mrs. Ossie
Davis), 1924-
Actress, editor of poetry anthology for
children
Blk Am Wr 1: 213 / Cur Biog Yrbk 70 p.
107-110 por / Dannett. Profiles 2: 188-94
por / Ebony Success 1: 92 por / Fax.
Leaders p. 220-36 / Lincoln Lib Arts 2:
519 / Negro Alm 71 p. 765 / Negro
Alm 76 p. 824-25 / Notable Names
p. 670 / Who Blk Am 77 p. 230 /
Who Theatre 77 p. 540-41
Delany, Clarissa Scott, 1901-1927
Poet, educator, essayist
Adoff. Poet p. 521-22 / Afro-Am Ency 3:
743 / Blk Am Wr 1: 214 / Bontemps.
American 63 p. 189 / Bontemps. American
74 p. 218 / Cromwell. Read p. 365 /
Cullen. Carol p. 140 / Ency Blk Am p.
306 / Hughes. Poet p. 601 / Kerlin.
Poets 35 p. 336
Delany, Martin R., 1812-1885
Orator, editor, explorer, journalist
Afro-Am Ency 3: 742-43 por / Barksdale.
Writers p. 192-94 / Blk Am Wr 1:
214-15 / Brawley. Builders p. 88-94 /
Brawley. Early p. 216-19 / Brown. Cara-
van p. 151, 633-34 / Bruce. Sketches
p. 38-50 / Davis. Cav p. 65-66 / Dict
Am Biog 30, 5: 219-20 / Dict Am Biog
59, 3-1: 219-20 / Ency Am Biog p.
270-71 / Ency Blk Am p. 306-307 / Great
Negroes 69 p. 66 il / Greene, Defenders
p. 63-64 por / Historical N Bio p. 72
il / Negro Alm 71 p. 672, por p.
673 / Negro Alm 76 p. 721 il / Sterling.
Speak p. 374, il p. 293 / Webster Am
Biog p. 267-68 / Whitlow. Lit p. 48-49 /
Who Was H: 144 / Who Was HR: 213
Delany, Samuel R(ay), 1942-
Professor of English, novelist, writer of
science fiction
Blk Am Wr 1: 217-18 / Con Auth 81-84:
120-21 / Con Novel 76 p. 351-52 / Dict
Lit Biog 8: 119-28 por, il / Writers Dr
76 p. 260-61 / Writers Dr 80 p. 308
DeLarge, Robert C., 1842-1874
Congressman, orator
Bio Dr Am Cong 61 p. 786 / Chris-
topher. Congress p. 97 / Who Was H:

DeLarge, Robert C. (cont'd) ...
144 / Who Was HR: 213 / Woodson.
Orators p. 295
De Legall, Walter, 1936-
Poet
Blk Am Wr 1: 218 / Henderson. Under
p. 383 / Jones. Fire p. 660
DeLerma, Dominique-Rene, 1928-
Professor of musicology, librarian, writer
Bio Dr Librns 70 p. 258 / Con Auth
45-48: 122
Delphy, A. C., 1857-
Journalist
Penn. Press p. 566-67
Dember, Jean Wilkins, 1930-
Poet
Living BAA p. 39-40 / Who Blk Am 77
p. 233
Demby, Edward Thomas, 1869-
Bishop
Who Col Am 40 p. 152, 155
Demby, William, 1922-
Novelist, filmscript writer
Afro-Am Novel p. 55 / Barksdale.
Writers p. 768 / Blk Am Wr 1: 218-19 /
Blk Lit HS p. 58-59 / Blk Plots p. 216 /
Bone. Novel p. 191-92 / Davis. Cav p.
489 / Lincoln Lib Arts 2: 522 / Living
BAA p. 40 / Margolies. Read p. 355 /
Penguin Am Lit p. 71 / Whitlow. Lit
p. 122-25
Dendy, J. Brooks, III
Painter, graphic artist, educator
Afro-Am Art p. 76
Denmark, James, 1936-
Painter, sculptor, graphic artist
Afro-Am Art p. 76
Dent, Thomas C. (Kush)
Poet, playwright
Blk Am Wr 1: 219-20 / Hughes. New
p. 119
DePriest, Oscar Stanton, 1871-
Congressman, realtor, orator
Boulware. Oratory p. 149 / Christopher.
Congress p. 168-75 / Great Negroes 69
p. 116 / Historical N Bio p. 181-82 por /
Negro Alm 76 p. 322-23 por / Who Col
Am 40 p. 155 por
Deshong, J. M. W., 1853-
Clergyman, editor, publisher of church
publication
Haley. Ency p. 593-94

Dett, R. Nathaniel, 1882-1943
Composer, poet, essayist
AmSCAP 80 p. 123 / Blk Am Wr 1:
221 / Great Negroes 69 p. 177 il /
Johnson. Book p. 196 / Kerlin. Poets
23 p. 271 / Who Col Am 40 p. 155-56 /
Who Col Am 42 p. 156
De Veaux, Alexis, 1948-
Singer, novelist, children's author, short
story writer
Nat Play Dr p. 64 por
Dharr, Abu
Poet
Afro Am Ency 3: 770
Dickinson, Blanche Taylor, 1896-
Teacher, poet
Blk Am Wr 1: 222 / Cullen. Carol
p. 105
Diggs, Margaret Agneta, 1909-
Historian
Scally. Catholic p. 43-44
Dillon, Leo (Lionel J.), 1933-
Illustrator
ALA Yrbk (77) 2: 55 / Auth Bk YP Sup
79 p. 68-69 / Illus Ch Bks 67 p.
113-14, il p. 8 / Something ATA 15:
98-99 por, il
Dinkins, Charles R.
Minister, poet
White. Verse p. 105
Dismond, Henry Binga, 1891-1956
Physician, poet
Blk Am Wr 1: 223 / Hughes. Poet p.
601 / Kerlin. Poets 35 p. 347 / Murphy.
Ebony p. 58 / Who Col Am 37 p.
158 / Who Col Am 40 p. 160, por p. 161
Djangatolum. *See* Corbin, Lloyd M., Jr.
Dodson, Owen (Vincent), 1914-
Playwright, poet, novelist
Adoff. Poet p. 522 / Afro-Am Ency
3: 782 / Blk Am Wr 1: 224 / Blk
Plots p. 217-18 / Bontemps. American 63
p. 189 / Bontemps. American 74 p. 218 /
Broadside Auth p. 43-44 / Brown. Cara-
van p. 543 / Cele p. 255 / Chapman.
Blk V p. 450 / Con Auth 65-68: 174 /
Davis. Cav p. 394 / Dr Perf Arts 78
p. 100-101 / Ency Blk Am p. 318 /
Hayden. Kal p. 118 / Hughes. Best p.
500 / Hughes. Poet p. 601-602 / Lin-
coln Lib Arts 2: 528 / Living BAA p.
41 / Negro Alm 71 p. 673 / Negro Alm
76 p. 722 / Notable Names p. 683-84 /
Selected BAA p. 65-66 por / Who Am
80, 1: 890

Dolan, Harry, 1927-
Playwright, TV scriptwriter, editor, writer
of short fiction
David. Defiance p. 200-209 / Ford.
Insights p. 296 / Watts Wr p. 25
Donaldson, Ulysses S.
Minister, essayist
Dreer. Am Lit p. 197
Dooley, Thomas (Ebon), 1942-
Poet
Adoff. Poet p. 523 / Broadside Auth
p. 45 / Henderson. Under p. 384
Douglas, Aaron, 1899-
Painter, illustrator
Afro-Am Art p. 80-81 / Ency Blk Am
p. 319 / Negro Alm 76 p. 763
Douglas, Elroy
Poet
Murphy. Ebony p. 59
Douglas, Glenn. *See* Duckett, Alfred A.
Douglass, Frederick (Frederick Augustus Wash-
ington Bailey), 1817-1895
Abolitionist, journalist, publisher, orator,
autobiographer
Adams. Auth p. 7 / Adoff. Blk on p.
228 / Afro-Am Ency 3: 788-842 il /
Alexander. Young p. 4-16 por / Alli Sup
1: 506-507 / Barksdale. Writers p. 66-69 /
Barton. Witness p. 172-74 / Bennett.
Pioneers p. 196-217 / Bio Dict S. Auth
p. 125 / Bio Hist p. 282-83 / Blk Am
Wr 1: 228 / Blk Lit HS p. 134 / Blk
Pioneer 1 / Blk Plots p. 219-20 /
Bormann. Fore p. 154-57 / Brawley.
Builders p. 61-66 por / Brawley. Early
p. 175-79 / Brawley. Lit p. 55-58 /
Brown. Caravan p. 606-608 / Bruce.
Sketches p. 30-35 / Chapman. Blk V
p. 231-32 / Cromwell. Read p. 365 /
David. Living p. 216-27 / Davis. Cav
p. 82-83 / Davis. South p. 350 / Dict
Am Biog 20, 5: 406-407 / Dict Am Biog
59, 3-1: 406-407 / Dict Lit Biog 1:
46-47 por / Dreer. Am Lit p. 187-88 /
Emanuel. Dark p. 12-13 / Ency Am Biog
p. 291-93 / Fauset. Freedom p. 62-76 il /
Ford. Insights p. 5-6 / Gayle. Bond p.
148 / Great Negroes 69 p. 34-36 il /
Haley. Ency p. 395 / Historical N Bio
p. 74 il / Kendricks. Voices p. 62 /
King. Famous p. 79-86 / Long. Writing
1: 59-60 / Lyons. Leader p. 23-51 /
Margolies. Read p. 355-56 / Miller. Ten
p. 34-40 / Negro Alm 71 p. 287-88 por /

DuBois, W(illiam) E(dward) B(urghardt)
(cont'd) ...
    40 p. 166, por p. 167 / Who Col Am
    42 p. 166 / Who Col Race p. 95-96 /
    Young. Since 1940 p. 17-19, 24-25 /
    Young, M. Lead p. 18-20 por
Dubonee, Ylessa
  Poet
    Murphy. Ebony p. 60
Du Cille, Ann, 1949-
  Teacher, poet
    Blk Am Wr 1: 241-42 / Exum. Keep
    p. 283-84
Duckett, Alfred A. (Glenn Douglas), 1917-
  Journalist, poet
    Adoff. Poet p. 522 / Blk Am Wr 1:
    242 / Bontemps. American 63 p. 189 /
    Con Auth 45-48: 137-38 / Hughes. Poet
    p. 602
Dumas, Henry L., 1934-1968
  Poet, writer of short stories
    Adoff. Blk out p. 77-78 / Adoff.
    Brothers p. 232 / Adoff. Poet p. 522 / Blk
    Am Wr 1: 243 / Cele p. 256 / Con
    Auth 85-88: 155 / Jones. Fire p. 660-61 /
    Selected BAA p. 71 por / Shuman.
    Galaxy p. 292
Dunbar, Paul Laurence, 1872-1906
  Novelist, poet, short story writer, librettist,
  essayist
    Adams. Auth p. 14 / Adoff. Poet p.
    522-23 / Afro-Am Ency 3: 856 il / Am
    Auth & Bks 72 p. 182 / Barksdale.
    Writers p. 349-50 / Bio Hist p. 286-87 /
    Blk Am Wr 1: 244 / Blk Plots p. 221 /
    Bone. Novel p. 38-39 / Bontemps. Amer-
    can 63 p. 189 / Bontemps. American
    74 p. 218 / Brawley. Builders p. 158-66 /
    Brawley. Lit p. 64-68 / Brown. Caravan
    p. 303-304 / Chamber p. 409 / Chapman.
    Blk V p. 354 / Cromwell. Read p. 366 /
    Cullen. Carol p. 1-2 / David. Living
    p. 62-63 / Davis. Cav p. 205-206 /
    Dict Am Biog 30, 5: 505-506 / Dict Am
    Biog 59, 3-1: 505-506 / Dreer. Am Lit
    p. 26-27 / Emanuel. Dark p. 36-37 /
    Fauset. Freedom p. 151-61 il / Ford.
    Insights p. 44-45 / Great Negroes 69 p.
    152 il / Haslam. Forgot p. 272 / Hayden.
    Kal p. 14 / Nistorical N Bio p. 77 /
    Hughes. Best p. 500 / Hughes. Poet p.
    602-603 / Johnson. Book p. 49-52 / Ken-
    dricks. Voices p. 184 / Long. Writing 1:
    213 / Nat Cyclo 9: 276 por / Negro Alm

Dunbar, Paul Laurence (cont'd) ...
    71 p. 675 / Negro Alm 76 p. 722 por /
    Ohio Auth p. 181-83 / Oxford Am 65 p.
    239 / Penguin Am Lit p. 79 / Poets
    p. 335-37 / Reader's Adviser 74, 1:
    260-61 / Reader's Ency 62 p. 288-89
    por / Robinson. Prose p. 172 / Rogers.
    World p. 364-71 / Rollins. Famous p.
    38-52 por / Rollins. They p. 59-62 /
    Selected BAA p. 72-73 por / Sign Am
    Auth p. 18 / Turner. Voices p. 263 /
    Wagner. Poets p. 73-80 / Webster Am
    Biog p. 296-97 / White. Verse p. 184 /
    Whitlow. Lit p. 54-55
Dunbar-Nelson, Alice Ruth Moore (Alice Ruth
  Moore), 1875-1935
  Journalist, poet, short story writer
    Adoff. Poet p. 532 / Am Women Wr 3:
    247-49 / Blk Am Wr 1: 253 / Cromwell.
    Read p. 369 / Cullen. Carol p. 71 /
    Culp. Twen p. 138-39 il / Ency Blk Am
    p. 636 / Hughes. Poet p. 618 / John-
    son. Book p. 164 / Kerlin. Poets 23
    p. 271-72 / Kerlin. Poets 35 p. 337 /
    Notable Am Wom 2: 614-15 / Selected
    BAA p. 207 / Who Col Am 33 p. 316 /
    Who Col Am 37 p. 388 / Who Col
    Lo p. 76-77, 122-23 / Who Col Race
    p. 96
Dunham, Katherine (Kaye Dunn), 1910-
  Dancer, choreographer, poet, autobiog-
  rapher, essayist
    Afro-Am Ency 3: 859 / AmSCAP 66 p.
    190-91 / Bio Hist p. 289-90 / Blk Am
    Wr 1: 255-56 / Brown. Caravan p.
    990-91 / Con Auth 65-68: 183-84 /
    Dannett. Profiles 2: 172-78 por / Dr
    Perf Arts 78 p. 105 / Ebony Success 1:
    101 por / Great Negroes 69 p. 169 il /
    Historical N Bio p. 188 il / Hughes.
    Best p. 500 / Lincoln Lib Arts 2:
    533 / Living BAA p. 42 / Negro Alm
    71 p. 767 / Negro Alm 76 p. 826 /
    Notable Names p. 695 / Reader's Ency
    62 p. 289 / Richardson. Great 56 p.
    68-78 il / Richardson. Great 76 p. 72-81
    por / Selected BAA p. 73 por / Shuman.
    Galaxy p. 297 / Sign Am Wom p. 61 il /
    Webster Am Biog p. 297 / Who Theatre
    77 p. 565-66
Dunjee, Roscoe, 1883-
  Publisher, editor, poet
    Blk Am Wr 1: 257 / Who Col Am 50
    p. 169

Endicott, Stephen. *See* Roberts, Walter
Adolphe
England, Jay Raymond
    Poet
        Murphy. N Voices p. 57
English, Jeanne
    Librarian
        Josey. What p. 304
Equiano, Olaudah. *See* Vassa, Gustavus
Ermine, Grace. *See* Cook, Mary V.
Evans, Don, 1938-
    Educator, essayist, playwright
        Blk Am Wr 1: 279-80 por / Nat Play
        Dr 77 p. 79 por / Who Blk Am 77 p. 276
Evans, Emmery, Jr., 1943-
    Poet
        Watts Wr p. 195
Evans, Mari, 1923-
    Poet, musician, writer of fiction for young
    people
        Adoff. Blk out p. 78 / Adoff. Poet p.
        523 / Afro-Am Ency 3: 908 / Auth Bk
        YP Sup 79 p. 80 / Bontemps. American
        63 p. 189 / Bontemps. American 74 p.
        219 / Broadside Auth p. 49 / Cele p.
        256 / Chapman. Blk V p. 478 / Chap-
        man. New p. 244-45 / Con Auth 49-52:
        174 / Con Poets 75 p. 454 / Con
        Poets 80 p. 455 / Coombs. Speak
        p. 241 / Crowell CAP p. 119 / Ebony
        Success 1: 108 por / Emanuel. Dark p.
        507-508 / Exum. Keep p. 284 / Hayden.
        Kal p. 172 / Hughes. New p. 120 /
        Hughes. Poet p. 604 / King. Spirits
        p. 244 / Lincoln Lib Arts 2: 545 /
        Living BAA p. 47 / Long. Writing 2:
        681 / Negro Alm 71 p. 675-76 / Negro
        Alm 76 p. 723 / Margolies. Read p. 356 /
        Something ATA 10: 39 / Who Am 80,
        1: 1026 / Who Blk Am 77 p. 278 /
        Writers Dr 76 p. 318 / Writers Dr 80
        p. 373-74 / Writers Dr 82 p. 286
Evans-Charles, Marti
    Playwright
        Dr Perf Arts 78 p. 114
Everett (Karenga), Ron(ald), 1941-
    Playwright
        Haskins. Profiles p. 217-38 / Who Blk
        Am 77 p. 280
Exum, Pat Crutchfield
    Poet
        Exum. Keep p. 284

Fabio, Sarah Webster, 1928-
    Poet, teacher
        Adoff. Poet p. 523 / Afro-Am Ency 3:
        915 / Blk Plots p. 224 / Broadside
        Auth p. 50 / Cele p. 256 / Hughes.
        Poet p. 604 / Living BAA p. 48 /
        Miller. Dices p. 138 / Selected BAA p. 81
Fagan, Eleanora Gough. *See* Holiday, Billie
Fair, Ronald L., 1932-
    Novelist, poet, short story writer
        Afro-Am Novel p. 59 / Blk Plots p.
        224-25 / Chapman. New p. 106-107 /
        Hughes. Best p. 501 / Jones. Fire p.
        661 / Living BAA p. 48 / Negro Alm
        76 p. 723 / Who Blk Am 77 p. 281
Farmer, James L., 1920-
    Orator, author
        Boulware. Oratory p. 220-22 / Negro Alm
        76 p. 222-23 / Negro Handbk 66 p. 401 /
        Sterne. Dream p. 143-66
Farrison, William Edward, 1902-
    Professor of English, critic, author
        Blk Am Wr 1: 284 / Con Auth 29-32R:
        199 / Dr Am Schol 69, 2: 163 / Dr Am
        Schol 74, 2: 190 / Dr Am Schol 78,
        2: 204 / Ency Blk Am p. 383 / Who Blk
        Am 77 p. 283
Farrow, William McKnight, 1885-
    Artist, editor, author
        Afro-Am Art p. 92 / Who Col Am 40
        p. 181, por p. 183
Fauset, Arthur Huff, 1899-
    Anthropologist, critic, short story writer,
    essayist, novelist, biographer
        Blk Plots p. 225 / Con Auth 25-28R:
        231 / Ency Blk Am p. 384 / Living
        BAA p. 48 / Selected BAA p. 82 /
        Who Col Am 50 p. 182-83
Fauset, Jessie Redmond, 1884?-1961
    Poet, novelist, short story writer
        Adoff. Poet p. 523 / Afro-Am Ency 3:
        921-22 / Am Auth & Bks 72 p. 205 /
        Am Women Wr 2: 18-20 / Blk Plots
        p. 225 / Brown. Caravan p. 189 /
        Cromwell. Read. p. 366 / Cullen. Carol
        p. 64-65 / Dannett. Profiles 2: 226-31
        por / Davis. Cav p. 354 / Davis. Dark
        p. 90-91 / Dreer. Am Lit p. 255 / Ency
        Blk Am p. 384 por / Hughes. Poet p.
        604-605 / Johnson. Book p. 205 / Ken-
        dricks. Voices p. 216 / Kerlin. Poets 23
        p. 216 / Kerlin. Poets 35 p. 337 / Negro
        Alm 71 p. 676 / Negro Alm 76 p.
        723-24 / Noble. Beautiful p. 159-62 /

Fauset, Jessie Redmond (cont'd) ...
Notable Am Wom Mod p. 225-27 / Selected BAA p. 83 por / Sign Am Wom p. 41 / Southern Wr p. 152-54 / Twen CA p. 441 / Twen CA Sup p. 318 / White. verse p. 193 / Who Col Am 37 p. 181 / Who Col Am 40 p. 181

Faust, Naomi F(lowe)
Teacher, poet, writer on education
Con Auth 61-64: 190

Fax, Elton Clay, 1909-
Illustrator, author, educator
Afro-Am Art p. 92-93 / Con Auth 13-14: 149 / Living BAA p. 49 / Negro Alm 76 p. 771-72 por / Something ATA 25: 106-107 por, il / Who Blk Am 77 p. 284

Feelings, Muriel, 1938-
Author of books for young people
Con Auth 93-96: 148 / Fourth Bk p. 129-31 / Living BAA p. 49 / Profiles Lit / Selected BAA p. 84 / Something ATA 16: 104-105 por

Feelings, Tom, 1933-
Illustrator, writer for young people
Afro-Am Art p. 93 / Blk Plots p. 225-26 / Books Are p. 69-73 / Con Auth 49-52: 180 / Illus BYP 70 p. 37 / Illus BYP 75 p. 57 / Illus Ch Bks 67 p. 117, il p. 62 / Living BAA p. 49-50 / Profiles Lit / Selected BAA p. 84 por / Something ATA 8: 55 / Third Bk p. 81-82 por / Who Blk Am 77 p. 284

Felton, (Elmer) B(uford), 1934-
Writer of poetry and fiction
Blk Plots p. 226 / Broadside Auth p. 50-51

Felton, Haleemon Shaik, 1913-
Playwright, actor
Scally. Catholic p. 48-50

Fenderson, Harold, 1910-
Short story writer
Blk Am Wr 1: 290

Fentress, John W.
Poet
Murphy. Ebony p. 62

Ferdinand, Val (Kalamu ya Salaam), 1947-
Short story writer, drama critic, playwright, poet
Coombs. What p. 205-206

Ferguson, Cecil L. (Duke), 1931-
Illustrator
Ebony Success 1: 110 por / Who Blk Am 77 p. 285

Ferguson, Clarence Clyde, Jr., 1924-
Educator, lawyer, writer
Con Auth 7-8: 160 / Who Blk Am 77 p. 285-86

Fernandis, Sarah Collins, 1863-
Poet
White. Verse p. 212

Ferris, William H., 1874-1941
Author, lecturer, literary editor
Ency Blk Am p. 385 / Who Col Am 27 p. 65 / Who Col Am 33 p. 494 / Who Col Am 40 p. 182

Fields, Julia, 1938-
Poet, playwright, short story writer
Adoff. Blk out p. 78 / Adoff. Poet p. 523 / Afro-Am Ency 4: 950 / Blk Am Wr 1: 293-94 / Bontemps. American 63 p. 190 / Bontemps. American 74 p. 219 / Broadside Auth p. 51 / Cele p. 257 / Hayden. Kal p. 220 / Hughes. New p. 120 / Hughes. Poet p. 605 / Jones. Fire p. 661 / King. Story p. 167 / Living BAA p. 50-51 / Major. Poet p. 147 / Owen. Poet p. 148 / Shuman. Galaxy p. 301 / Shuman. Nine p. 67 / Southern Wr p. 155-56

Fields, Maurice C., 1915-
Poet
Scally. Catholic p. 50-52

Finley, Catherine L.
Poet
Murphy. Ebony p. 63

Fisher, Leland Milton, 1875-1904
Poet
Blk Am Wr 1: 296 / Kerlin. Poets 23 p. 272 / Kerlin. Poets 35 p. 338

Fisher, Miles Mark, 1899-1970
Clergyman, educator, historian, writer on Negro songs
Con Auth 15-16: 148 / Con Auth P-1: 213 / Ency Blk Am p. 386 / Paths p. 150 por / Nat Cyclo 56: 143-44 por / Selected BAA p. 86 por / Who Col Am 37 p. 185 / Who Col Am 40 p. 185

Fisher, Rudolph, 1897-1934
Physician, novelist, playwright, short story writer
Afro-Am Ency 4: 954 por / Barksdale. Writers p. 590-91 / Blk Am Wr 1: 296-98 / Brown. Caravan p. 54 / Chapman. Blk V p. 73 / Cromwell. Read p. 366 / Davis. Cav p. 337 / Davis. Dark p. 98-99 / Emanuel. Dark p. 110-11 / Ency Blk Am p. 386 / Historical N Bio

Fisher, Rudolph (cont'd) ...
    p. 191 por / Hughes. Best p. 501 /
    Long. Writing 2: 403 / Negro Alm 71
    p. 676 / Negro Alm 76 p. 724 / Selected
    BAA p. 87 por / Sign Am Auth p. 41 /
    Who Col Am 33 p. 153 / Who Col Am
    37 p. 602
Fitzbutler, Henry
    Journalist
    Penn. Press p. 314-20
Fitzgerald, Ella, 1918-
    Singer, autobiographer
    Ebony Success 1: 112 por / Who Am
    80, 1: 1098
Fitzhugh, George, 1806-1881
    Lawyer, journalist
    Afro-Am Ency 4: 956-57
Fleming, George James, 1904-
    Educator, journalist, writer on politics
    Living BAA p. 51 / Who Blk Am 77
    p. 292-93 / Who Col Am 40 p. 185-86 /
    Who Col Am 50 p. 187
Fleming, Ray(mond R.), 1945-
    Educator, poet
    Broadside Auth p. 52 / Who Blk Am
    77 p. 293
Fleming, Sarah Lee Brown
    Poet, novelist, teacher
    Brown. Homespun p. 17, 151 / Kerlin.
    Poets 23 p. 338
Fletcher, Robert E. (Bob Fletcher), 1938-
    Photographer, film maker, writer, poet
    Blk Am Wr 1: 299 / Major. Poet p. 147 /
    Who Blk Am 77 p. 293-94
Flipper, Henry O., 1877-1940
    Autobiographer
    Greene. Defenders p. 113-14 por / Negro
    Alm 71 p. 609 / Negro Alm 76 p.
    659-60
Flipper, Joseph Simeon, 1859-1944
    Educator, minister, author
    Culp. Twen p. 256-57 il / Who Col
    Race p. 104
Forber, Calvin L., 1945-
    Educator, poet
    Adoff. Poet p. 523 / Blk Am Wr 1:
    301-302 / Chapman. New p. 247-48 /
    Con Auth 49-52: 188 / Who Blk Am
    77 p. 296
Ford, Annie L., 1938-
    Poet
    Selected BAA p. 87-88
Ford, George (Jr.)
    Painter, illustrator
    Afro-Am Art p. 95 / Illus Ch Bks 67
    p. 118-19

Ford, Gregory J.
    Poet
    Afro-Am Ency 4: 972
Ford, Nick Aaron, 1904-
    Poet, short story writer, essayist
    Blk Am Wr 1: 301-303 / Con Auth
    25-28R: 242 / Ency Blk Am p. 390 /
    Ford. Insights p. 122-23 / Murphy. N
    Voices p. 58 / Selected BAA p. 88-89
    por
Ford, R. Edgar, 1869-
    Poet
    Bruce. Sketches p. 75-76
Ford, Robert B., Jr.
    Librarian
    Josey. What p. 304
Forten, Charlotte L. (Mrs. Francis Grimké),
    1838-1914
    Poet, autobiographer
    Afro-Am Ency 4: 1098-99 por / Am
    Women Wr 2: 69-71 / Barksdale. Writers
    p. 275-76 / Blk Am Wr 1: 304-305 /
    Blk Pioneers 1 / Blk Plots p. 228 / Chitten-
    den. Profiles p. 107-124 / Dannett.
    Profiles 1: 86-91 il / Davis. Cav p.
    108-109 / Dict Am Biog 31, 6: 536-37 /
    Dict Am Biog 59, 3-2: 536-37 / Historical
    N Bio p. 86 / Kerlin. Poets 23 p. 273 /
    Lerner. Wom p. 94-95, 365 / Loewen-
    berg. Wom p. 283-85 / Majors. Wom p.
    213-15 / Negro Alm 71 p. 676 / Negro
    Alm 76 p. 724 / Notable Am Wom 2:
    95-97 / Scruggs. Wom p. 193-96 /
    Selected BAA p. 89 / Sherman. Invisible
    p. 88-93
Forten, James, 1766-1842
    Businessman, abolitionist, orator
    Afro-Am Ency 4: 974-79 / Bio Hist p.
    297-99 / Ency Am Biog p. 374-76 /
    Great Negroes p. 28 il / Historical N
    Bio p. 19-20 / O'Neill. Speeches p. 13-14 /
    Sterling. Speak p. 375 / Woodson. Orators
    p. 41-42
Forten, Sarah Louise
    Essayist
    Dannett. Profiles 1: 82-84 / Sterling.
    Speak p. 375
Fortune, Timothy Thomas, 1856-1928
    Journalist, publisher, author, poet
    Afro-Am Ency 4: 981-82 por / Alli Sup
    1: 615 / Am Auth & Bks 72 p. 222 /
    Blk Am Wr 1: 306 / Brown. Caravan
    p. 880 / Culp. Twen p. 226-27 / Ency
    Am Biog p. 376-77 / Historical N Bio

Fortune, Timothy Thomas (cont'd) ...
p. 81 il / Penn. Press p. 133-38 / Robin-
son. Poets p. 247-48 / Selected BAA
p. 89-90 / Sherman. Invisible p. 141-50 /
Simmons. Men p. 549-54 il / White. Verse
p. 114 / Who Col Race p. 106
Foster, Craig Curtis, 1947-
Writer on black studies
Living BAA p. 51
Foster, Francis M.
Poet
Murphy. Ebony p. 64
Fox, Mamie Eloise, 1871-
Poet
Blk Am Wr 1: 307 / Majors. Wom p.
125-28
Francis, John R., 1856-
Physician, essayist
Culp. Twen p. 204-205 il
Franklin, Clarence
Poet
Jones. Fire p. 661
Franklin, J(ennie) E(lizabeth), 1937-
Playwright, short story writer
Blk Am Wr 1: 307-308 / Con Auth
61-64: 198-99 / Dr Perf Arts 78 p. 124 /
King. Story p. 349 / Nat Play Dr p. 93
por
Franklin, Jimmie L., 1939-
Educator, historian
Ency Blk Am p. 393
Franklin, John Hope, 1915-
Historian
ALA Yrbk 76 p. 104 por / Afro-Am
Ency 4: 992 por / Am Auth & Bks 72
p. 226 / Bio Hist p. 299-300 / Con
Auth 1: 90 / Con Auth 1R: 203 /
Con Auth NR-3: 208-209 / Ebony Success
1: 117 por / Ency Blk Am p. 393-94 /
Great Negroes p. 146 il / Historical N
Bio p. 192 por / Jordan. Soul p. [ii] /
Living BAA p. 52 / Negro Alm 71 p.
676-77 por / Negro Alm 76 p. 724-25
por / Negro Handbk 66 p. 401 / Selected
BAA p. 90-92 por / Thorpe. Hist p.
180-81 / Webster Am Biog p. 365 /
Who Am 62 p. 1059 / Who Am 80, 1:
1146 / Who Blk Am 77 p. 306 / Who
Col Am 50 p. 195 / Writers Dr 80 p.
417-18 / Writers Dr 82 p. 319
Franklin, W. H., 1852-
Minister, journalist
Penn. Press p. 347-52 / Who Col Race
p. 108

Fraser, Al
Poet
Jones. Fire p. 661
Fraser, Walter
Librarian
Josey. What p. 304
Frazier, Edward Franklin, 1894-1962
Sociologist, author
Afro-Am Ency 4: 994 por / Am Auth &
Bks 72 p. 226 / Bio Hist p. 300-301 /
Brown. Caravan p. 904 / Cur Biog 40
p. 314-15 por / Ency Am Biog p.
381-82 / Historical N Bio p. 192-93 /
Negro Alm 71 p. 677 / Negro Alm 76 p.
725 por / Selected BAA p. 92-93 / Web-
ster Am Biog p. 366 / Who Col Am
37 p. 195 / Who Col Am 50 p. 195-96 /
Who Was 4: 329
Frazier, Victoria Q.
Publisher, author
Who Col Am 40 p. 192
Freeman, Carol S., 1941-
Poet, playwright
Adoff. Poet p. 524 / Afro-Am Ency 4:
1005 / Blk Am Wr 1: 308-309 / Cele
p. 257 / Jones. Fire p. 661
French, James Edgar
Poet
Kerlin. Poets 35 p. 338
Friedman, Bruce Jay, 1930-
Playwright, editor
Nat Play Dr p. 96 por
Frierson, Augustus Ulysses
Essayist
Culp. Twen p. 240-41 il
Fuller, Charles H., Jr., 1939-
Novelist, playwright, short story writer
Alhamisi. Arts p. 75 / Blk Am Wr 1:
309-311 por / Dr Perf Arts 78 p. 128 /
Jones. Fire p. 661-62 / King. Story p.
141 / Nat Play Dr p. 99 por
Fuller, Hoyt (Williams), 1927-1981
Editor, poet, short story writer
Adoff. Poet p. 524 / Afro-Am Ency 4:
1020, 1022 / Blk Am Wr 1: 311 por /
Con Auth 53-56: 208 / Con Auth 103:
152 / Ebony Success 1: 119 por / Ency
Blk Am p. 400 / Innis. Profiles p. 86-87
por / Living BAA p. 52-53 / Long.
Writing 2: 667 / Selected BAA p. 93-94
por / Who Blk Am 77 p. 314
Fuller, Meta Vaux Warrick, 1877-1967
Sculptor, illustrator, writer
Afro-Am Art p. 98-99 / Ency Blk Am
p. 400 / Notable Am Wom Mod p. 255-56

Gault, Charlayne Hunter, 1942-
Journalist, short story writer, teacher
Ebony Success 1: 122 por / Negro Alm
76 p. 1005 / Who Blk Am 77 p. 323
Gavins, Raymond, 1942-
Historian, educator
Ency Blk Am p. 403
Gayle, Addison, Jr., 1932-
Critic, biographer, short story writer, essayist
Afro-Am Ency 1: 294 / Blk Am Wr 1:
320-22 por / Broadside Auth p. 54 /
Chapman. New p. 524 / Con Auth 25-
28R: 260 / Con Novel 76 p. 1622 / Ency
Blk Am p. 403 / Gayle. Bond p. 149 /
Living BAA p. 54-55 / Selected BAA p.
96-97 / Who Blk Am 77 p. 324
Gayles, G(eorge) W(ashington), 1844-
Minister, legislator, editor
Penn. Press p. 142-44 / Simmons. Men
p. 404-406 il / Who Col Race 1:
113-14
Geary, Bruce (K. Sayif M. Shabazz), 1942-
Poet
Broadside Auth p. 54-55
Geary, Efton F., 1940-
Poet
Blk Am Wr 1: 322
Gelbert, Jack, 1932-
Playwright
Who Am 78, 1: 1176 / Writers Dr 82
p. 341
Gerald, Carolyn Fowler, 1937-
Educator, critic, essayist, poet
Blk Am Wr 1: 323
Gex, Quo Vadis. *See* Gamble, Quo Vadis Gex
Gibbs, Mifflin W(ister), 1823-1903
Jurist, autobiographer, newspaper publisher,
lecturer
Afro-Am Ency 4: 1058-59 por / Historical
N Bio p. 82-83 il / Katz. West p. 139-42
por / Simmons. Men p. 407-411 il /
Sterling. Speak p. 376-77 / Who Col
Race p. 114
Gibson (Darben), Althea, 1927-
Tennis player, autobiographer
Afro-Am Ency 4: 1059-60 por / Bio
Hist p. 305-307 / Cur Biog Yrbk 57
p. 203-204 por / Ebony Success 1: 123
por / Historical N Bio p. 194-95 por /
Living BAA p. 37 / Negro Alm 71 p.
651 / Negro Alm 76 p. 698 / Richardson.
Great 76 p. 300-308 por / Who Blk Am
77 p. 327
Gibson, Charline, 1937-
Writer on baseball
Living BAA p. 55

Gibson, D(aniel) Parke, 1930-1979
Economist, author
Con Auth 93-96 p. 171 / Ebony Success
1: 124 por / Negro Alm 76 p. 102-127 /
Who Blk Am 77 p. 327
Gibson, Edna, 1946-
Watts Wr p. 187
Giddings, Paula
Poet, journalist, biographer
Coombs. Speak p. 242
Gilbert, John Wesley, 1864-
Archeologist, essayist
Afro-Am Ency 4: 1063 / Culp. Twen
p. 190-91 il
Gilbert, Matthew William, 1862-
Minister
Culp. Twen p. 286-87 por / Who Col
Race 1: 115
Gilbert, Mercedes, ?-1952
Poet, playwright, novelist
Blk Am Wr 1: 325
Gilbert, (Lerman) Zack, 1925-
Preacher, poet
Adoff. Poet p. 524 / Blk Am Wr 1:
325-26 / Broadside Auth p. 55 por /
Cele p. 257 / Hughes. Poet p. 605 /
Murphy. Ebony p. 65
Giles, Louise, 1930-
Librarian, bibliographer
Bio Dr Librns 70 p. 390 / Josey.
What p. 304
Gillespie, Marcia Ann, 1944-
Editor, writer
Auth News 2: 119 por / Living BAA p.
55-56 / Selected BAA p. 97-98 / Who Blk
Am 77 p. 331
Gillison, Lenora
Poet
Murphy. Ebony p. 66
Gilmore, Al-Tony, 1946-
Professor of history, author
Con Auth 57-60: 228 / Ency Blk Am p.
405 / Selected BAA p. 98
Giovanni, Nikki (Yolande Cornelis Giovanni,
Jr.), 1943-
Poet, autobiographer
Adoff. Blk out p. 78 / Adoff. Poet p.
524 / Afro-Am Ency 4: 1068 / Auth Bk
YP Sup 79 p. 100 / Blk Am Wr 1:
326-28 / Broadside Auth p. 55-57 / Cele
p. 257 / Chester. Rising p. 358 / Con
Auth 29-32R: 237-38 / Con Poets 80 p.
557-58 / Cur Biog Yrbk 73 p. 148-51 por /
Dict Lit Biog 5-1: 286-90 por / Ebony

Giovanni, Nikki (Yolande Cornelis Giovanni,
Jr.) (cont'd) ...
    Success 1: 125 por / Ency Blk Am p.
    405 / King. Story p. 19 / Living BAA
    p. 56 / Major. Poet p. 147-48 / Negro
    Alm 76 p. 726 por / Reader's Adviser
    74, 1: 340-41 / Selected BAA p. 98-99
    por / Southern Wr p. 179-80 / Turner.
    Voices p. 264 / Twen CCW p. 511-12 /
    Whitlow. Lit p. 177 / Who Blk Am 77
    p. 333 / Wor Auth 70-75 p. 308-311 por /
    Writers Dr 76 p. 391 / Writers Dr 80
    p. 458 / Writers Dr 82 p. 350
Glanville, Maxwell
    Screenplay writer, novelist
    Nat Play Dr p. 107 por
Gloster, Hugh Morris, 1911-
    Critic, educator, essayist
    Blk Am Wr 1: 328 / Ency Blk Am p.
    406 / Living BAA p. 56-57 / Selected
    BAA p. 99-100 / Who Blk Am 77 p. 336
Glover, Archibald F., 1902-
    Engineer, writer on race relations
    Scally. Catholic p. 52-53
Goddard, Nettye George, 1923-
    Teacher, writer on black literature
    Living BAA p. 57
Golden, Bernette
    Afro-Am Ency 4: 1070
Gonclaves, Joe (Dingane), 1937-
    Poet, essayist
    Alhamisi. Art p. 19 / Blk Am Wr 1:
    329 / Broadside Auth p. 57 / Jones.
    Fire p. 662
Goode, Kenneth G., 1932-
    Educational administrator, educator
    Con Auth 49-52: 217 / Living BAA p.
    57 / Who Blk Am 77 p. 339 / Writers
    Dr 80 p. 470-71
Goodwin, George Augustus, 1861-
    Minister, educator
    Culp. Twen p. 132-33 il
Goodwin, Leroy
    Poet
    Jones. Fire p. 662
Goodwin, Ruby Berkley, 1903-
    Poet, short story writer, autobiographer
    Blk Am Wr 1: 329-30 / David. Roots
    p. 175-85 / Murphy. Ebony p. 67 /
    Murphy. N Voices p. 61
Gordon, Charles B. W., 1861-
    Clergyman, editor
    Penn. Press p. 194-96
Gordon, Charles Franklin (Oyamo), 1921-
    Playwright, drama critic
    Nat Play Dr p. 235

Gordon, Edmund Wyatt, 1921-
    Psychologist, writer on education
    Living BAA p. 58
Gordon, Edythe Mae
    Short story writer, poet
    Murphy. N Voices p. 65
Gordon, N. Antonia
    Poet
    Scruggs. Wom p. 217-21
Gordon, Roland, 1944-
    Writer, actor
    Selected BAA p. 100
Gordon, Taylor, 1893-
    Autobiographer, singer
    Barton. Witness p. 115-22 / Blk Am
    Wr 1: 330-31
Gordon, William Henry Barefield, 1906-
    Poet
    Cuney. Linc p. 68
Gordone, Charles, 1925?-
    Playwright, poet
    Afro-Am Ency 4: 1075 / Con Auth 93-96:
    184-87 / Con Drama 73 p. 299-300 /
    Con Drama 77 p. 307-308 / Dict Lit
    Biog 7: 227-31 por / Dr Perf Arts 78
    p. 136-37 / Ency Blk Am p. 406 / Ford.
    Insights p. 326 / Oliver. Drama p.
    383-84 / Selected BAA p. 100 / Who
    Blk Am 77 p. 344 / Who Theatre 77 p.
    663 / Writers Dr 76 p. 406 / Writers
    Dr 80 p. 475 / Writers Dr 82 p. 363
Gorham, Myrtle Campbell
    Poet
    Murphy. Ebony p. 71
Goss, Clay(ton) (Bill Pickett Clay), 1946-
    Playwright, poet, writer for children and
    young people
    Blk Am Wr 1: 333 / Con Auth 57-60:
    236-37 / Coombs. Speak p. 242 / Dr Perf
    Arts 78 p. 139 / Who Blk Am 77 p. 345
Goss, Linda McNear (Mrs. Clayton Goss),
    1947-
    Poet
    Coombs. Speak p. 242
Goss, William Thompson
    Poet
    Murphy. Ebony p. 72
Govan, Oswald
    Poet
    Henderson. Under p. 385
Graham, Donald L., 1944-1970
    Poet
    Adoff. Poet p. 524 / Blk Am Wr 1:
    334 / Hayden. Kal p. 230-31 / Jones.
    Fire p. 662

Graham, Linda B., 1958-
Poet
Shuman. Galaxy p. 313
Graham, Lorenz B(ell), 1902-
Social worker, writer for children and
young people, poet, short story writer
Auth Bk YP Sup p. 104 / Blk Am Wr 1:
335-36 por / Con Auth 9: 180-81 /
Living BAA p. 58-59 / More Books p.
193-99 por / Selected BAA p. 101 por /
Something ATA 2: 122-23 por / Third
Bk p. 108-109 por / Twen CCW p.
524-26 / Who Blk Am 77 p. 347
Graham, Rudy Bee, 1947-
Poet
Jones. Fire p. 662
Graham, Shirley Lola. *See* DuBois, Shirley
Graham
Grainger, Porter
Playwright, composer
Dr Perk Arts 78 p. 138
Grant, John Wesley, 1850-
Novelist
Blk Am Wr 1: 338
Grant, Micki (Mrs. Roy McCutcheon), 1943-
Composer, singer, poet
Abdul. Enter p. 66-72 por / Blk Am Wr
1: 338-39 por / Dr Perf Arts 78 p. 139 /
Who Blk Am 77 p. 349
Grant, Richard E., 1949-
Poet
Adoff. Poet p. 524 / Blk Am Wr 1: 338
Gray, Darrell M., 1950-
Poet, writer of short stories
Shuman. Galaxy p. 100
Grayson, Bessie R.
Librarian, educator
Josey. What p. 305
Greaves, Donald, 1943-
Screenplay writer, poet
Blk Am Wr 1: 340 por / King. Drama
p. 253
Green, Carl H., 1945-
Poet
Shuman. Galaxy p. 315
Green, Donald
Poet, actor
Coombs. Speak p. 243
Green, John Paterson, 1845-
Public official, orator, autobiographer,
writer on race relations
Culp. Twen p. 88-89 il / Davis. Mem
p. 26-27 por / Who Col Race 1: 120-21

Green, Robert L., 1933-
Psychologist, writer on education
Living BAA p. 60 / Who Blk Am 77
p. 355
Greene, Carl H., 1945-
Artist, poet
Broadside Auth p. 57-58
Greene, Charles Clarence Edward
Playwright
Who Blk Am 77 p. 356
Greene, Emily Jane
Poet
Murphy. Ebony p. 73
Greene, Lorenzo Johnston, 1899-
Educator, historian, essayist
Afro-Am Ency 4: 1090 / Dreer. Am Lit
p. 154 / Ency Blk Am p. 408-409 /
Living BAA p. 60-61 / Who Blk Am 77
p. 357
Greener, Richard Theodore, 1844-1922
Lawyer, editor, educator, librarian, political
leader
Afro-Am Ency 4: 1090-91 por / Dict Am
Biog 31, 7: 578-79 / Dict Am Biog 60,
4-1: 578-79 / Gayle. Bond p. 148 /
Historical N Bio p. 83-84 il / Woodson.
Orators p. 473-74
Greenfield, Eloise, 1929-
Writer of children's books, biographer
Con Auth 49-52: 225 / Int Auth & Wr 77
p. 391 / Living BAA p. 61 / Selected
BAA p. 104 / Somthing ATA 19: 141 /
Who Am 80, 1: 1344 / Who Blk Am 77
p. 358 / Writers Dr 80 p. 492 / Writers
Dr 82 p. 376
Greenlee, Sam, 1930-
Novelist, playwright, short story writer
Afro-Am Novel p. 71 / Blk Am Wr 1:
341 / Con Auth 69-72: 289-90 / King.
Story p. 91 / Living BAA p. 62 / Selected
BAA p. 104 por / Who Blk Am 77 p.
358
Greenridge, Edwin, 1929-
Living BAA p. 61
Greenwood, Theresa (Winfrey), 1936-
Teacher, poet
Blk Am Wr 1: 342-43 / Con Auth 29-32R:
255
Gregory, Carole E. *See* Clemmons, Carole
Gregory
Gregory, Dick (Richard Claxton), 1932-
Social satirist, autobiographer, lecturer
Adoff. Blk on p. 230 / Afro-Am Ency 4:
1093 il / Con Auth 45-48: 201 / Cur

Gregory, Dick (Richard Claxton) (cont'd) ...
Biog Yrbk 62 p. 168-70 por / David.
Growing p. 241-54 / David. Roots p.
211 / Ebony Success 1: 134 por / Living
BAA p. 62 / Negro Handbk 66 p. 402 /
Pol Profiles: Johnson p. 235 / Richard-
son. Great 76 p. 82-93 / Selected BAA
p. 104 por / Who Blk Am 77 p. 359 /
Writers Dr 76 p. 420 / Writers Dr 80
p. 494

Gregory, James Monroe, 1848-1915
Linguist, educator, essayist
Simmons. Men p. 433-43 il

Gregory, Yvonne, 1919-
Poet
Bontemps. American 63 p. 190 / Bon-
temps. American 74 p. 219

Grier, William H., 1926-
Psychiatrist, educator, author
Selected BAA p. 105 / Who Blk Am
77 p. 360

Griffin, Amos J.
Poet
Murphy. Ebony p. 74

Griffin, Judith Berry
Author of books for young people, teacher
Auth Bk YP Sup 79 p. 110

Griggs, Sutton Elbert, 1872-1930
Minister, short story writer, novelist
Blk Am Wr 1: 343 / Bone. Novel p.
32-35 / Davis. Cav p. 163 / Robinson.
Prose p. 200 / Selected BAA p. 106 /
Who Col Race p. 125

Grigsby, J(efferson) Eugene, Jr., 1918-
Artist, educator, author
Afro-Am Art p. 111 / Who Blk Am 77
p. 363

Grimké, Angelina Weld, 1880-1958
Poet, playwright, writer of short stories,
teacher
Adoff. Poet p. 524 / Am Auth & Bks
72 p. 262 / Blk Am Wr 1: 345-47 /
Bontemps. American 63 p. 190 / Bon-
temps. American 74 p. 219 / Brown.
Caravan p. 341 / Cromwell. Read p. 366 /
Cullen. Carol p. 35 / Hughes.
Poet p. 605-606 / Kerlin. Poets
23 p. 272 / Kerlin. Poets 35 p. 338 /
Selected BAA p. 106 / Who Col Am 33
p. 182 / Who Col Am 37 p. 221 /
Who Col Am 40 p. 221 / Who Col Am
42 p. 219

Grimké, Archibald H., 1849-1930
Attorney, educator, editor, biographer
Afro-Am Ency 4: 1098 por / Am Auth &

Grimké, Archibald H. (cont'd) ...
Bks 72 p. 262-63 / Brown. Caravan p.
804-808 / Dict Am Auth p. 158 / Ency
Am Biog p. 410 / Historical N Bio p.
85 / Nat Cyclo 26: 341-42 por / Rollins.
They p. 72-74 / Selected BAA p. 106
por / Who Was 1: 489 / Who Col Race
p. 125

Grimké, Charlotte Forten. *See* Forten,
Charlotte L.

Grimké, Francis James, 1850-1937
Minister, civic leader, essayist
Afro-Am Ency 4: 1099 / Brawley. Builders
p. 209 / Culp. Twen p. 426-27 il / Ency
Blk Am p. 410 / Historical N Bio p.
86-87 il / Simmons. Men p. 416-19 /
Who Col Race p. 125 / Woodson. Orators
p. 690

Grit. *See* Bruce, John E(dward)

Grosvenor, Verta Mae, 1938-
Short story writer, poet, autobiographer
Blk Am Wr 1: 347 / Con Auth 69-72:
293 / Living BAA p. 62-63 / Selected
BAA p. 107

Grovenor, Kali (Kali)
Poet, short story writer
King. Spirits p. 246

Guffy, Ossie, 1931-
Activist, autobiographer
Wom Am p. 13-14

Guillén, Nicholas, 1904-
Poet
Afro-Am Ency 4: 1101

Gunn, William Harrison (Bill), 1934-
Playwright, actor, director, novelist
Auth News 1: 206 / Con Auth 13-14:
187 / Dr Perf Arts 78 p. 145

Guy, Rosa Cuthbert Glanze (Mrs. Warner
Guy), 1926-
Playwright, novelist, short story writer,
editor, writer for young people
Blk Am Wr 1: 348 / Con Auth 17:
304 / Con Auth 17-18R: 194 / Selected
BAA p. 107 / Something ATA 14: 77
por / Twen CCW p. 554-55

Gwaltney, John Langston, 1928-
Anthropologist, ethnographer, educator
Con Auth 33-36R: 361 / Living BAA p.
63 / Selected BAA p. 108 / Who Blk
Am 77 p. 367 / Writers Dr 76 p. 431 /
Writers Dr 82 p. 387

Hackley, Emma Azalia Smith, 1867-1922
Singer, music educator, writer
Afro-Am Ency 4: 1107 / Brown.

Hackley, Emma Azalia Smith (cont'd) ...
Homespun p. 231-36 por / Dannett. Pro-
files 1: 262-63 il / Notable Am Wom 2:
106-108
Hadhbuti, Mwalimu Haki R. *See* Lee, Don L.
(Mwalimu Haki R. Madhubuti)
Hagan, Roosevelt (Sonebeyatta Amungo),
1956-
Broadside Auth p. 20
Hairston, Loyle, 1926-
Essayist, short story writer
Afro-Am Ency 4: 1109 / Blk Am Wr 1:
348-49 / Ency Blk Am p. 411 / Living
BAA p. 63
Hairston, William, 1927-
Playwright
Dr Perf Arts 78 p. 147 / Who Blk Am
77 p. 368
Hale, Frank Wilbur, Jr., 1927-
Educator, writer on speech
Ency Blk Am p. 411 / Living BAA
p. 64 / Who Blk Am 77 p. 369
Haley, Alex(ander Palmer), 1921-
Journalist, author, lecturer, historian
Au Speaks p. 448-51 / Con Auth 77-80:
205-207 / Cur Biog Yrbk 77 p. 184-87
por / Ebony Success 1: 136 por / Ency
Blk Am p. 411-12 / Greene. Defenders
p. 196 por / Living BAA p. 64 / Selected
BAA p. 109 / Southern Wr p. 195-97 /
Who Am 76, 1: 1291 / Who Blk Am 77
p. 368 / Writers Dr 80 p. 511 / Writers
Dr 82 p. 391
Hall, Agnes Maxwell, 1894-
Poet
Afro-Am Ency 4: 1111
Hall, James C., Jr., 1932-
Living BAA p. 64-65
Hall, Kirk, 1944
Poet
Chapman, New p. 254 / Jones. Fire p.
662
Hall, Nathaniel B., 1916-
Teacher, writer on sociology
Living BAA p. 65 / Writers Dr 80 p. 514
Hall, Prince, 1748?-1807
Orator, petitionist
Bennett. Pioneers p. 28-39 il / Brawley.
Early p. 96 / Historical N Bio p.
20-21 / Negro Alm 76 p. 601 / Robinson.
Prose p. 47
Halliburton, Warren J., 1924-
Teacher
Con Auth 33-36R: 368 / Living BAA p.
65-66 / Selected BAA p. 109-110

Hamer, Martin J., 1931-
Poet, short story writer
Adoff. Brothers p. 234 / Afro-Am Ency 4:
1116-17 / Living BAA p. 66
Hamilton, Charles V(ernon), 1929-
Educator, political scientist
Adoff. Blk out p. 230-31 / Afro-Am Ency
4: 1117 / Ebony Success 1: 138 por /
Living BAA p. 66 / Selected BAA p. 110 /
Who Blk Am 77 p. 372
Hamilton, Robert (Bobb), 1928-
Poet, short story writer, sculptor
Adoff. Blk out p. 78 / Afro-Am Ency 4:
1117 / Alhamisi. Arts p. 123 / Broad-
side Auth p. 58 / Living BAA p. 66-67
Hamilton, Virginia (Esther), 1936-
Children's author, biographer, short story
writer
ALA Yrbk 76 p. 104 por / Afro-Am
Novel p. 73 / Am Women Wr 2: 232-34 /
Auth & Ill 72 p. 186-92 / Auth Bk YP
71 p. 223 / Auth News 1: 3-5 por / Blk
Am Wr 1: 351-53 / Con Auth 25-28R:
299 / More Books p. 199-207 por /
Selected BAA p. 110-111 por / Some-
thing ATA 4: 97-99 por, il / Twen CCW
p. 569-70 / Writers Dr 80 p. 518
Hammon, Briton
Slave narrator
Blk Am Wr 1: 352 / Robinson. Prose
p. 108-114
Hammon, Jupiter, 1720-1800
Poet, essayist
Afro-Am Ency 4: 1119-20 / Am Auth &
Bks 72 p. 273 / Barksdale. Writers
p. 45-46 / Blk Am Wr 1: 352 / Brawley.
Early p. 21-22 / Brawley. Lit p. 12-14 /
Dict Am Biog 32, 8: 201-202 / Dict Am
Biog 60, 4-2: 201-202 / Historical N Bio
p. 21 / Hughes. Poet p. 606 / Kendricks.
Voices p. 30 / Kerlin. Poets 23 p. 273 /
Negro Alm 71 p. 678 / Negro Alm 76 p.
726-27 / Oxford Am 65 p. 346 / Rollins.
Famous p. 15-17 / Selected BAA p.
111-12 / Who Was H: 231 / Who Was
HR: 300
Hammond, Edward W. S., 1842-
Clergyman, editor, writer
Northrop. College p. 55
Hammond, Francis M., 1911-
Educator, writer, reviewer
Scally. Catholic p. 54-55
Hand, Q. R., Jr., 1937-
Poet
Jones. Fire p. 663

Handy, D. Antoinette
  Musician, lecturer, author
    Williams. Wom p. 178
Handy, W(illiam) C(hristopher), 1873-1958
  Composer, song publisher, editor,
  autobiographer
    Afro-Am Ency 4: 1128-29 por / Am Auth
    & Bks 72 p. 274 / AmSCAP 66 p. 307 /
    Barton. Witness p. 57-67 / Bontemps.
    Golden p. 209 / Cur Biog Yrbk 41 p.
    361-62 por / Dr Perf Arts 78 p. 153 /
    Ency Am biog p. 480-81 / Ency Blk Am
    p. 415 il / Great Negroes 69 p. 178-79
    il / King. Famous p. 35-39 / Lincoln
    Lib Arts 2: 591 / Negro Alm 71 p.
    806 / Negro Alm 76 p. 879 / Oxford
    Am 65 p. 346 / Rollins. They p. 75-79 /
    Turner. Voices p. 264 / Webster Am
    Biog p. 451 / Who Col Am 33 p. 189,
    por p. 191
Hankins, Paula
  Short Story writer
    King. Spirits p. 97
Hannibal, Gregor
  Poet
    Henderson. Under p. 386
Hansberry, Lorraine, 1930-1965
  Playwright
    Afro-Am Ency 4: 1131-32 por / Am Auth
    & Bks 72 p. 274 / Am Women Wr 2:
    236-39 / Auth News 2: 211 / Bio Hist
    p. 312-13 / Blk Am Wr 1: 355 / Blk
    Auth / Blk Lead / Childress, Scenes
    p. 149-50 / Crowell CD p. 223-24 /
    Davis. Dark p. 204 / Dict Lit Biog 7-1:
    247-54 por / Dr Perf Arts 78 p. 153-54 /
    Dramatists 79 p. 96-98 / Ford. Insights
    p. 278-79 / Kendricks. Voices p. 339 /
    Lincoln Lib Arts 2: 591 / McGraw Ency
    WD 2: 286 / Nat Cyclo 60: 273 / Negro
    Alm 71 p. 678 por / Negro Alm 76 p.
    727 por / Noble. Beautiful p. 182-84 /
    Notable Am Wom Mod p. 310-12 /
    Oliver. Drama p. 29 / Reader's Ency
    62 p. 425 / Selected BAA p. 112 por /
    Whitlow. Lit p. 141 / Who Was 4: 403 /
    Wor Auth 50-70 p. 614-15
Hansberry, William Leo, 1894-1965
  Educator, historian, anthropologist
    Afro-Am Ency 4: 1132 / Ency Blk Am
    p. 415-16 / Selected BAA p. 112-13
Harding, Vincent, 1931-
  Historian, educator, essayist
    Blk Am Wr 1: 358 / Ebony Success 1:

Harding, Vincent (cont'd) ...
    141 por / Ency Blk Am p. 416 / Living
    BAA p. 67 / Selected BAA p. 113-14
    por / Who Blk Am 77 p. 378 / Who
    Am 74, 1: 1316
Hardnett, Linda G., 1950-
    Shuman, Galaxy p. 107
Hare, Nathan, 1933-
  Publishing executive, essayist, professor of
  education, poet, journalist
    Barksdale. Writers p. 836 / Blk Am Wr
    1: 359, por p. 360 / Chapman. New
    p. 425 / Con Auth 41-44R: 290-91 /
    Ebony Success 1: 141 por / Jones.
    Fire p. 663 / Living BAA p. 67-68 /
    Negro Alm 76 p. 1028 / Selected BAA
    p. 114-15 / Who Blk Am 77 p. 379
Harllee, M. W., 1852-
  Public official, educator, essayist
    Culp. Twen p. 298-99 il
Harmon, Florence M.
  Short story writer
    Cromwell. Read p. 366
Harper, Frances E(llen) W(atkins) (Effie
Afton), 1825-1911
  Poet, novelist, lecturer
    Afro-Am Ency 4: 1141 il / Am Auth &
    Bks 72 p. 675 / Am Wom Wr 2:
    244-46 / Barksdale. Writers p. 224-25 /
    Blk Am Wr 1: 361 / Brawley. Early p.
    290-92 / Brown. Homespun p. 97-103
    por / Dannett. Profiles 1: 102-109 il /
    Davis. Cav p. 101 / Ency Blk Am p.
    419 / Haley. Ency p. 592-93 / Hayden.
    Kal p. 12 / Historical N Bio p. 88 il /
    Hughes. Poet p. 606-607 / Kendricks.
    Voices p. 80 / Kerlin. Poets 23 p. 27
    il, p. 273 / Kerlin. Poets 35 p. 339 /
    Lerner. Wom p. 243-46 / Loewenberg.
    Wom p. 243-44 / Majors. Wom p. 23-27 /
    Negro Alm 71 p. 678-79 / Negro Alm
    76 p. 727 / Notable Am Wom 2: 137-39 /
    Penn. Press p. 420-22 por / Robinson.
    Poets p. 26-27 / Rollins. Famous p.
    22-27 / Rollins. They p. 80-82 / Scruggs.
    Wom p. 6-13 / Selected BAA p. 115 il /
    Sherman. Invisible p. 62-66 / Sign Am
    Auth p. 19 / Sterling. Speak p. 37 /
    White. Verse p. 39-40
Harper, Michael S(teven), 1938-
  Professor of English, poet
    Adoff. Poet p. 524-25 / Blk Am Wr 1:
    364 / Cele p. 257 / Chapman. New
    p. 255-56 / Con Auth 33-36: 410-11

Harper, Michael S(teven) (cont'd) ...
Con Auth 33-36R: 378-79 / Con Poets
75 p. 636-37 / Con Poets 80 p. 643-44 /
Ebony Success 1: 141 por / Living BAA
p. 68 / Negro Alm 76 p. 728 / Selected
BAA p. 116 / Who Blk Am 77 p. 382 /
Writers Dr 76 p. 450 / Writers Dr 80
p. 528-29 / Writers Dr 82 p. 404

Harrell, Dennis, 1949-
Sports writer, poet
Shuman. Galaxy p. 322

Harrington, Oliver Wendell, 1913-
Cartoonist, illustrator, biographer
Afro-Am Art p. 118-19

Harrington, W. R.
Essayist
Haley. Ency p. 596-97 por

Harris, Abrams L(incoln), Jr., 1899-1963
Economist, author
Afro-Am Ency 4: 1142-43 / Bio Hist
p. 313 / Brown. Caravan p. 910 /
Selected BAA p. 116-17 / Who Col Am
37 p. 233 / Who Col Am 40 p. 230

Harris, H(erman) K., II, 1940-
Poet
Blk Am Wr 1: 365

Harris, Helen C.
Poet
Murphy. Ebony p. 78

Harris, James Leon, 1934-
Novelist
Blk Am Wr 1: 366, por p. 367

Harris, Janette Hoston, 1939-
Poet
Living BAA p. 68-69

Harris, Jessie Redmond. *See* Fauset, Jessie
Redmond

Harris, Leon R., 1881-1960
Poet, novelist
Blk Am Wr 1: 366 / Kerlin. Poets 23
p. 273-74 / Kerlin. Poets 35 p. 339 /
Ohio Auth p. 276

Harris, Middleton A., 1908-
Historian
Living BAA p. 69 / Negro Alm 76 p.
728-29 phot / Selected BAA p. 117

Harris, Neil, 1936-
Playwright, poet
Blk Am Wr 1: 366-67, por p. 368 /
Nat Play Dr p. 132 por

Harris, William J(oseph), 1942-
Poet
Adoff. Blk out p. 79 / Adoff. Poet
p. 525 / Blk Am Wr 1: 368 / Cele
p. 258 / Chapman. New p. 260 / Con
Auth 53-56: 271 / Shuman. Galaxy p.
109 / Shuman. Nine p. 90

Harrison, DeLeon, 1914-
Teacher of art, poet
Adoff. Poet p. 525 / Blk Am Wr 1:
369 / Miller. Dices p. 138

Harrison, Deloris, 1938-
Teacher of English
Con Auth 61-64: 240 / Something ATA
9: 97-98 por

Harrison, Hubert Henry, 1883-1927
Essayist
Afro-Am Ency 4: 1148 / Rogers. World
p. 432-42

Harrison, James Minnis, 1873-
Poet
Blk Am Wr 1: 369

Harrison, Juanita
Traveler, autobiographer
Barton. Witness p. 89-92

Harrison, Paul Carter, 1936-
Playwright
Blk Am Wr 1: 369-70 / Dr Perf Arts
78 p. 156

Harrison, Zechariah, 1886-
Essayist
Haley. Ency p. 597-99 por

Haskett, Edythe R(ance), 1915-
Teacher, writer for young people,
autobiographer
Con Auth 21-24R: 385-86 / Living BAA
p. 69-70 / Selected BAA p. 117-18

Haskins, James, 1941-
Professor of English, biographer, writer on
black culture, author of books for young
people
Auth Bk YP Sup 79 p. 119 / Con Auth
33-36: 382 / Negro Alm 76 p. 729, 731 /
Selected BAA p. 118-19 / Something ATA
9: 100-101 por / Writers Dr 82 p. 412

Hassan, Umar Abdul-Rahim. *See* Rutherford,
Tony

Hawkins, Darnell Felix, 1946-
Poet
Blk Am Wr 1: 370 / Broadside Auth
p. 59

Hawkins, Odie, 1937-
Screenplay writer, novelist
Blk Am Wr 1: 370 / Con Auth 57-60:
264 / Selected BAA p. 120

Hawkins, Walter Everette, 1886-
Blk Am Wr 1: 370-71 / Kerlin. Poets 23
p. 119-22 por / Kerlin. Poets 35 p. 339

Hayden, Robert C., 1937-
Writer of non-fiction for children and
young people, teacher of science, editor
Con Auth 69-72: 307-308 / Selected BAA
p. 120 / Writers Dr 80 p. 544

Hayden, Robert Earl, 1913-1980
Professor of English, poet
Bontemps. American 63 p. 190 / Bon-
temps. American 74 p. 219 / Cele p.
258 / Con Poets 70 p. 485 / Con Poets
75 p. 656-58 / Con Poets 80 p. 664 /
Long. Writing 2: 561-62 / Margolies.
Read p. 357 / Robinson. Nommo p. 478 /
Who Am 80, 1: 1484 / Writers Dr 80
p. 666
Hayes, Donald Jeffrey, 1904-
Musician, poet
Adoff. Poet p. 525 / Afro-Am Ency 4:
1159 / Blk Am Wr 1: 372 / Bontemps.
American 63 p. 190 / Bontemps. Ameri-
can 74 p. 220 / Cullen. Carol p. 188 /
Hughes. Poet p. 607
Hayes, Elizabeth Ross, 1883-1953
Lerner. Wom p. 255-56 / Notable Am
Wom Mod p. 324-25
Hayes, George Edmund, 1880-
Sociologist, author
Afro-Am Ency 4: 1163-64 il / Who Col
Am 37 p. 224, por 241 / Who Col
Am 40 p. 244 / Who Col Am 42 p.
244-45 / Who Col Am 50 p. 252-53
Haynes, Albert E., Jr.
Artist, poet
Jones. Fire p. 663
Haynes, George Edmund, 1880-1960
Sociologist, educator, author
Afro-Am Ency 4: 1163-64 il / Cur Biog
Yrbk 46, p. 251-52 por / Cur Biog Yrbk
60 obit p. 184 / Who Col Am 37 p. 244,
por p. 241 / Who Col Am 42 p. 244-45 /
Who Col Am 50 p. 252-53
Haynes, Lemuel B., 1753-1833
Theologian
Barksdale. Writers p. 226-27 / Historical
N Bio p. 22-23 il / Nat Cyclo 12: 256-57 /
Robinson. Prose p. 19-20 / Simmons.
Men p. 467-68
Haynes, Samuel A.
Poet
Murphy. Ebony p. 80
Heard, Josephine Henderson (Josie), 1861-
Poet
Blk Am Wr 1: 372 / Majors. Wom p.
261-68 / Robinson. Poets p. 261-63
Heard, Nathan C(liff), 1936-
Teacher of English, novelist
Afro-Am Novel p. 76 / Blk Am Wr 1:
372 / Living BAA p. 70-71 / Robinson.
Nommo p. 478 / Selected BAA p. 121-22

Heard, William Henry, 1850-1937
Minister, missionary, essayist
Afro-Am Ency 4: 1168-69 / Culp. Twen
p. 442-43 il / Who Col Race 1: 134
Hedgeman, Anna Arnold, 1899-
Teacher, public official, editor, columnist,
autobiographer
Afro-Am Ency 4: 1171 / Con Auth 15-16:
204 / Con Auth P-1: 279-80 / Lerner.
Wom p. 489 / Negro Alm 71 p. 876 /
Negro Alm 76 p. 1006-1007 por / Negro
Handbk 66 p. 403 / Selected BAA p.
122-23 por
Height, Dorothy Irene, 1910-
Association executive, writer on civil rights
Cur Biog Yrbk 72 p. 216-18 por / Ebony
Success 1: 149 por / Ency Blk Am p.
434 / Negro Alm 76 p. 1007 por / Negro
Handbk 66 p. 403 / Who Blk Am 77
p. 403
Henderson, David, 1942-
Poet, editor
Adoff. Blk out p. 79 / Adoff. Poet
p. 525-26 / Afro-Am Ency 4: 1172 /
Broadside Auth p. 60-61 / Cele p. 258 /
con Auth 25-28R: 316 / Con Poets 70 p.
492 / Hayden. Kal p. 222 / Hughes.
New p. 120-21 / Hughes. Poet p. 608 /
Jones. Fire p. 663 / Jordan. Soul p. 139 /
King. Spirits p. 245 / Major. Poet p.
148-49 / Selected BAA p. 123-24
Henderson, George Wylie, 1904-
Novelist, short story writer
Am Auth & Bks 72 p. 290 / Bone.
Novel p. 123 / Brown. Caravan p. 231 /
Selected BAA p. 124
Henderson, Mattie Allison, 1868-
Teacher, editor
Majors. Wom p. 121-23
Henderson, Stephen E., 1925-
Professor of English, anthologist,
essayist, critic, short story writer
Con Auth 29-32R: 291-92
Henry, Carol, 1928-
Poet
Blk Am Wr 1: 374 por
Henson, Josiah, 1789-1883
Minister, narrator of experiences
Afro-Am Ency 4: 1177-85 il / Blk Pio-
neers 2 / Brawley. Early p. 160-61 /
Dict Am Biog 32, 8: 564-65 / Dict Am
Biog 62, 4-2: 564-65 / Historical N Bio
p. 89-90 il / Miller. Ten p. 67-71 / Oxford
Am 65 p. 367 / Reader's Ency 62
p. 459-60 / Robinson. Prose p. 135-40 /
Who Was H: 247 / Who Was HR: 317

Henson, Matthew Alexander, 1866-1955
Explorer, autobiographer
Barton, Witness p. 52-56 / Bio Hist
p. 320-22 / Brawley. Builders p.
173-76 / Ency Blk Am p. 436 por /
Great Negroes p. 69 p. 67 il / Historical
N Bio p. 203 por / King. Famous p. 105 /
Rollins. They p. 83-87 / Who Col Am 42
p. 249, por p. 251
Hercules, Frank (E. M.), 1917-
Novelist
Blk Am Wr 1: 374 / Con Auth 2:
76 / Con Auth NR-2: 316 / Selected
BAA p. 124
Herndon, Angelo, 1913-
Labor leader, autobiographer
Barton. Witness p. 193-205 / Brown.
Caravan p. 777 / David. Growing p. 57-59
Hernton, Calvin C., 1933-
Poet, playwright, novelist, short story writer
Adoff. Blk out p. 79 / Adoff. Poet p.
526 / Afro-Am Ency 4: 1188 / Blk Am
Wr 1: 375-76 / Cele p. 258 / Con Auth
11-12: 174 / Con Auth NR-3: 271 / Con
Poets 75 p. 677-78 / Con Poets 80 p.
687-88 / Ency Blk Am p. 436 / Hayden.
Kal p. 194 / Hughes. New p. 121 /
Hughes. Poet p. 608 / Jones. Fire
p. 663-64 / Jordan. Soul p. 139-40 /
Living BAA p. 71 / Major. Poet p. 149 /
Miller. Dices p. 138 / Selected BAA p.
124-25 / Who Blk Am 77 p. 411 /
Writers Dr 76 p. 476 / Writers Dr 80
p. 559 / Writers Dr 82 p. 428
Hewett, Mary Jane
Author, lecturer, educator
Williams. Wom p. 178
Hewett, Vivian Davidson
Librarian, lecturer, writer on librarianship
ALA Yrbk 79 p. 52 por / Bio Dr Librns
70 p. 480 / Josey. Blk Librn p. 253-72 /
Josey. What p. 305 / Who Blk Am 77 p.
412
Hill, Abram (Barrington), 1911-
Playwright
Blk Am Wr 1: 376-77 / Dr Perf Arts
78 p. 168-69
Hill, Elton (Abu Ishak), 1950-
Poet
Blk Am Wr 1: 377 / Major. Poet p. 149
Hill, Errol (Gaston), 1921-
Educator, playwright, essayist, editor
Blk Am Wr 1: 377-78 / Con Auth 45-48:
234-35 / Dr Perf Arts 78 p. 169 / King.
Drama p. 553 / Who Blk Am 77 p. 418 /
Writers Dr 80 p. 568

Hill, John H., 1852-1936
Educator, author
Ency Blk Am p. 437-38
Hill, Leslie Pinckney, 1880-1960
Educator, poet
Adoff. Poet p. 526 / Afro-Am Ency 4:
1199 / Blk Am Wr 1: 378-79 / Brown.
Caravan p. 338 / Cromwell. Read p.
367 / Dreer. Am Lit p. 48 / Johnson.
Book p. 152 / Kerlin. Poets 23 p. 131
il / Kerlin. Poets 35 p. 339 / Selected
BAA p. 125 por / Southern Wr p.
225-26 / White. Verse p. 194 / Who Col
Am 40 p. 255 / Who Col Race p. 137-38 /
Who Was 3: 401
Hill, Mars, 1927-
Playwright
Blk Am Wr 1: 380
Hill, Roy L., 1925-
Educator, poet, lecturer, writer of short
stories
Blk Am Wr 1: 380
Hill, William Allyn, 1908-
Poet
Cuney. Linc p. 69
Hilyer, Andrew Franklin, 1858-
Accountant, essayist
Culp. Twen p. 374-75 il / Who Col
Race 1: 139
Himes, Chester (Bomar), 1909-
Novelist, autobiographer, short story writer
Afro-Am Ency 4: 1204 / Afro-Am Novel
p. 78 / Barksdale. Writers p. 618-20 /
Blk Am Wr 1: 380 / Chapman. New p.
393-94 / Con Auth 25-28: 324-25 / Con
Novel 72 p. 611-12 / Con Novel 76 p.
651-52 / Davis. Cav p. 481 / Davis.
Dark p. 162 / Dict Lit Biog 2: 240-44
por / Ency Blk Am p. 439 / Hughes.
Best p. 501 / Int Auth & Wr 77 p.
466-67 / Living BAA p. 72 / Margolies.
Read p. 357 / Selected BAA p. 125-26 /
Southern Wr p. 226-27 / Who Am 80, 1:
1558 / Who Blk Am 77 p. 422 / Wor
Auth p. 643-45 / Writers Dr 80 p. 572
Hines, Carl Wendell, Jr., 1940-
Poet
Blk Am Wr 1: 383 / Bontemps. American
63 p. 190 / Bontemps. American 74 p.
220 / Hayden. Kal p. 226 / Southern Wr
p. 227-28
Hoagland, Everett, III, 1942-
Poet, teacher
Blk Am Wr 1: 383-84 / Broadside Auth
p. 62 / Cele p. 259 / Chapman. New

Hoagland, Everett, III (cont'd) ...
p. 262 / Con Auth 33-36R: 408 / Major.
Poet p. 149 / Selected BAA p. 127 /
Who Blk Am 77 p. 423
Hobson, Julius W(ilson), 1922-1977
Auth Blk YP Sup 79 p. 130
Hodges, Frenchy Jolene, 1940-
Teacher, poet, actress
Blk Am Wr 1: 384, por p. 385 / Broad-
side Auth p. 62-63 por
Hodges, Norman Edward, 1939-
Educator, writer on black history
Living BAA p. 72 / Who Blk Am 77,
p. 425
Holden, Matthew, Jr., 1931-
Professor of political science, writer on
race relations
Con Auth 57-60: 280-81 / Living BAA
p. 73 / Who Blk Am 77 p. 426 /
Writers Dr 76 p. 489 / Writers Dr 80
p. 585 / Writers Dr 82 p. 448
Holiday, Billie (Eleanora Gough Fagan),
1915-1959
Singer, autobiographer
Afro-Am Ency 4: 1211 por / David.
Living p. 153-64 / Dr Perf Arts 78 p.
173 / Negro Alm 76 p. 880 por / Noble.
Beautiful p. 246-49 / Notable Am Wom
Mod p. 346-48 / Sign Am Wom p. 42
il / Webster Am Biog p. 497
Holland, Jerome Heartwell, 1916-
Educator, diplomat
Afro-Am Ency 4: 1212-13 / Ebony
Success 1: 154 por / Ebony Success 2:
104-107 il / Selected BAA p. 128 /
Who Blk Am 77 p. 426
Holland, Justin Miner, 1819-1887
Musician, composer, linguist, author
Davis. Mem p. 15
Hollingsworth, Alvin C., 1930 or 1931-
Painter, illustrator, educator
Afro-Am Art p. 129-30 / Illus Bks YP
75 p. 77
Holloway, John Wesley, 1865-1935
Teacher, minister, poet
Blk Am Wr 1: 387 / Hughes. Poet p.
608 / Johnson. Book p. 134 / White.
Verse p. 183 / Who Col Am 40 p. 258,
por p. 253
Holloway, Lucy Ariel Williams, 1905-
Teacher of music, poet
Afro-Am Ency 4: 1217 / Blk Am Wr 1:
387 / Bontemps. Golden p. 215 / Brown.
Caravan p. 377 / Cullen. Carol p. 201 /
Johnson. Book p. 288

Holly, James Theodore, 1829-1911
Clergyman, educator, historian
Brawley. Builders p. 207 / Dict Am
Biog 32, 9: 156-57 / Dict Am Biog 61,
5-1: 156-57 / Who Am 10, p. 931-32 /
Who Was 1: 580
Holman, M(oses) Carl, 1919-
Poet, playwright
Adoff. Poet p. 526 / Blk Am Wr 1:
387-88 por / Bontemps. American 63
p. 190 / Bontemps. American 74 p.
220 / Hayden. Kal p. 162 / Hill.
Anger p. 215 / Hughes. Poet p. 609 /
Jordan. Soul p. 140 / Who Am 80, 1:
1537 / Who Blk Am 77 p. 429
Holmes, Gene
Poet
Murphy. Ebony p. 83
Holmes, R(obert) Ernest, 1943-
Attorney, poet, short story writer, lecturer
Blk Am Wr 1: 389 / Coombs. Speak
p. 243 / Coombs. What p. 206 / Who Blk
Am 77 p. 430
Holsey, Lucius, 1842-1920
Clergyman, educator, autobiographer
Brawley. Builders p. 206-207 / Culp.
Twen p. 46-47 por / Dict Am Biog 32,
9: 176-77 / Dict Am Biog 61, 5-1:
176-77 / Haley. Ency p. 599-601 por /
Who Col Race p. 142 / Who Was 4:
456
Holt, Leonard W.
Lawyer, writer on civil rights
Afro-Am Ency 4: 1220
Holtzclaw, William H.
Autobiographer
David. Growing p. 127-46
Hood, James Walker, 1831-1918
Clergyman, church historian
Dict Am Biog 32, 9: 192-93 / Dict Am
Biog 61, 5-1: 192-93 / Who Was 1: 584
Hooks, Julia A.
Essayist
Haley. Ency p. 563
Hoover, Dorothy Estheryne McFadden, 1918-
Con Auth 49-52: 263 / Living BAA
p. 73-74 / Who Blk Am 77 p. 432-33 /
Writers Dr 80 p. 593
Hope, Lezli
Poet
Exum. Keep p. 285
Hopkins, Pauline Elizabeth
Literary editor, dramatist, novelist
Blk Am Wr 1: 389-90

Horne, Frank S., 1899-1974
Physician, poet, short story writer,
autobiographer
Adoff. Poet p. 526 / Afro-Am Ency 4:
1229-30 / Blk Am Wr 1: 390-91 / Bon-
temps. American 63 p. 190-91 / Bontemps.
American 74 p. 220 / Bontemps. Golden
p. 208-209 / Con Auth 53-56: 298 (obit) /
Cullen. Carol p. 111-12 / Ency Blk Am
p. 444 / Hayden. Kal p. 64 / Hughes.
Poet p. 609-610 / Johnson. Book p. 268 /
Selected BAA p. 128
Horne, Lena (Mary Calhoun), 1917-
Singer, actress, autobiographer
Afro-Am Ency 4: 1230 por / Bio Hist
p. 324-26 / David. Roots p. [62] / Dr
Perf Arts 78 p. 176-77 / Ebony Success
1: 159 por / Negro Handbk 66 p. 404 /
Noble. Beautiful p. 249-50
Horne, Theodore R., 1937-
Broadside Auth p. 63
Hornsby, Alton, Jr., 1940-
Educator, historian
Con Auth 37-40R: 260-61 / Ency Blk Am
p. 444 / Who Blk Am 77 p. 434 /
Writers Dr 80 p. 597
Horton, George Moses, 1797-1883
Poet
Barksdale. Writers p. 219-20 / Blk Am
Wr 1: 391-92 / Brawley. Early p.
110-112 / Brawley. Lit p. 42-44 / Brown.
Caravan p. 287-88 / Davis. Cav p. 33-35 /
Davis. South p. 363 / Hayden. Kal p. 8 /
Kerlin. Poets 35 p. 340 / Long. Writing
1: 41 / Nat Cyclo 7: 93 / North Car
Auth p. 64-65 / Paths p. 160 por /
Richmond. Bid p. 81-177 / Robinson.
Poets p. 18-19 / Selected BAA p. 129 /
Sherman. Invisible p. 5-11 / Walser.
Young p. 5 por / White. Verse p. 33-34
House, Eddie, Jr., "Son," 1902-
Preacher, poet, teacher, blues singer
Henderson. Under p. 387
House, Gloria Larry
Poet, teacher of English
Alhamisi. Arts p. 112
Houston, Drusilla Dunjee
Writer on Africa
Williams. Wom p. 178
Houston, Gordon David, 1880-
Professor of English, essayist
Who Col Am 33 p. 219 / Who Col Am
37 p. 263 / Who Col Am 40 p. 262
Houston, Virginia
Poet
Murphy. N Voices p. 76

Howard, Clarence J., 1907-
Clergyman, journalist, editor
Scally. Catholic p. 56-57
Howard, Floretta
Poet
Dreer. Am Lit p. 52
Howard, Vanessa, 1955-
Poet, short story writer
Jordan. Soul p. 140
Howard, Vilma
Poet
Hughes. New p. 121
Hubert, James A., 1906-
Librarian, writer on library science
Living BAA p. 75
Huggins, Nathan Irvin, 1927-
Historian, editor
Con Au 29-32R: 318-19 / Ency Blk Am
p. 456 / Living BAA p. 74-75 / Who
Blk Am 77 p. 443
Huggins, Willis N., 1886-1940
Historian, educator
Ency Blk Am p. 456
Hughes, Langston, 1902-1967
Poet, novelist, playwright, autobiographer,
writer for children and young people
Adams. Auth p. 28 / Adoff. Blk on
p. 231 / Adoff. Blk out p. 79 / Afro-Am
Ency 4: 1245 por / AmSCAP 66 p. 351 /
AmSCAP 80 p. 239 / Am Auth & Bks 72
p. 315 / Auth Bk YP Sup 67 p. 151 /
Barksdale. Writers p. 514-17 / Barton.
Witness p. 206-220 / Bio Hist p. 326-28 /
Blk Am Wr 1: 395-96 / Blk Auth
Blk Lead / Bontemps. American 63
p. 191 / Bontemps. American 74 p.
220-21 / Broadside Auth p. 63-65 / Cele
p. 259 / Chapman. Blk V p. 96-97 /
Con Poets 75 p. 1760-61 / Cromwell.
Read p. 367 / Crowell CD p. 239 /
Cullen. Carol p. 144-45 / Cuney. Linc
p. 69 / David. Living p. 165-71 /
David. Roots p. 167 / Davis. Dark p.
61-63 / Dict Lit Biog 4: 213-14 por /
Dict Lit Biog 7: 314-24 por / Dr Perf
Arts 78 p. 179-80 / Emanuel. Dark
p. 191-203 / Ency Am Biog p. 552-53 /
Ford. Insights p. 140 / Fourth Bk p.
185-87 por / Gayle. Bond p. 149 / Great
Negroes 69 p. 157 il / Guide Am Lit
p. 95 / Haslam. Forgot p. 282 / Hayden.
Kal p. 84-85 / Historical N Bio p.
207-208 por / Johnson. Book p. 232-34 /
Kendricks. Voices p. 202 / Kerlin. Poets

Imani. *See* Rodgers, Carolyn M(arie)
Imes, William Lloyd, 1889-
Clergyman, author
Jenness. Twelve p. 35-52 / Who Col Am
37 p. 275 / Who Col Am 42 p. 270-73
Iola. *See* Wells (Barnett), Ida B(ell)
Ishak, Abu. *See* Hill, Elton
Islew, Bert. *See* Lewis, Lillian A.

Jackmon, Marvin (Marvin X; El Muhajir),
1944-
Poet, playwright, lecturer
Blk Am Wr 2: 558-59 / Con Auth 49-52:
278-79 / Jones. Fire p. 664 / Selected
BAA p. 201-202
Jackson, Angela, 1951-
Poet
Blk Am Wr 2: 411 / Cele p. 259
Jackson, Blyden, 1910-
Professor of English, novelist, critic
Afro-Am Ency 5: 1289 / Blk Am Wr 2:
411-12 / Chapman. Blk V p. 622-23 /
Con Auth 57-60: 296 / Dr Am Schol
78, 2: 336 / Ency Blk Am p. 465 /
Who Blk Am 77 p. 456
Jackson, Booker, 1929-
Poet, songwriter
Blk Am Wr 2: 413
Jackson, Clyde Owen, 1928-
Composer, writer on race relations, historian
Living BAA p. 76-77 / Selected BAA p.
133-34 por / Writers Dr 76 p. 536 /
Writers Dr 80 p. 629 / Writers Dr 82
p. 482
Jackson, Emma Lou
Blk Am Wr 2: 413
Jackson, Eugenia Lutcher
Writer, playwright, producer, composer
Blk Am Wr 2: 414
Jackson, Franklin Jefferson. *See* Watkins, Mel
Jackson, George Lester, 1941-1971
Revolutionary, writer
Selected BAA p. 134
Jackson, Jacquelyne Johnson, 1932-
Sociologist, educator, author
Con Auth 37-49R: 272-73 / Ebony Success
1: 167 por / Ency Blk Am p. 466 /
Who Am 80, 1: 1682 / Who Blk Am
77 p. 459
Jackson, James Thomas
Poet, short story writer
Watts Wr p. 147

Jackson, Jesse, 1908-
Writer of fiction for children, biography
and essays on race relations
Afro-Am Novel p. 91 / Auth Bk YP 67
p. 155 / Auth Bk YP 71 p. 260 /
Blk Am Wr 2: 414-15 por / Con Auth
25-28: 373 / Con Auth 25-28R: 355-56 /
Living BAA p. 77 / Ohio Auth p. 335 /
Selected BAA p. 135 por / Something
ATA 2: 150-52 por / Twen CCW p.
645-46 / Writers Dr 80 p. 630 / Writers
Dr 82 p. 482
Jackson, John Glover, 1907-
Author
Living BAA p. 77
Jackson, Joseph H(arrison), 1904-
Clergyman, orator
Afro-Am Ency 5: 1292 / Boulware.
Oratory p. 194-97 / Ebony Success 1:
168 por / Ency Blk Am p. 466 / Negro
Alm 76 p. 975 / Negro Handbk 66 p.
405 / Selected BAA p. 135-36 por / Who
Blk Am 77 p. 460
Jackson, Lena Terrell, 1865-
Teacher, essayist
Culp. Twen p. 304-305 il
Jackson, Luther Porter, 1892-1950
Educator, historian, journalist
Afro-Am Ency 5: 1293 / Ency Blk Am p.
467 / Historical N Bio p. 209
Jackson, Mae, 1946-
Teacher, writer of short stories and children's
plays, poet
Adoff. Blk out p. 79 / Adoff. Poet p.
526-27 / Blk Am Wr 2: 416 / Broadside
Auth p. 65 / Con Auth 81-84: 264 /
King. Spirits p. 245 / Selected BAA
p. 136-37
Jackson, Marsha Ann
Poet
Afro-Am Ency 5: 1294
Jackson, Miles M(errill), Jr., 1929-
Educator, librarian, writer on librarianship
Bio Dr Librns 70 p. 533 / Con Auth
41-44: 343-44 / Josey. Blk Librn p.
43-49 / Josey. What p. 305 / Living BAA
p. 77-78 / Who Blk Am 77 p. 462
James, Charles Lyman, 1934-
Editor, teacher
Con Auth 29-32R: 332 / Living BAA p.
78 / Selected BAA p. 137
James, Harold L.
Illustrator
Illus Bks YP 76 p. 80

Jamison, Roscoe Conkling, 1888-1918
Poet
Blk Am Wr 2: 417
Jarry, Hawke, 1938-
Playwright, short story writer
Blk Am Wr 2: 417
Jasper, John, 1812-1901
Minister, orator
Great Negroes 69 p. 104 il
Jeffers, Lance, 1919-
Poet, fiction writer, educator
Adoff. Poet p. 527 / Broadside Auth
p. 66 / Cele p. 259 / Chapman. Blk
V p. 473 / Chapman. New p. 264 / Con
Auth 65-68: 318 / Davis. Cav p. 768 /
Living BAA p. 79 / Major Poet p. 149 /
Owen. Poet p. 151-52 / Selected BAA
p. 137-38 / Shuman. Nine p. 116
Jefferson, Issac
Narrator of experiences
David. Growing p. 73-93
Jemand, Amanda Berry Smith. *See* Smith
(Jemand), Amanda Berry
Jemmott, Claudia E., 1949-
Actor, teacher, poet
Shuman. Galaxy p. 352
Jenkins, Clarke, 1917-
Writer on religion
Living BAA p. 79
Jenkins, Deaderick Franklin, 1910-
Novelist, essayist
Blk Am Wr 2: 418-19 por
Jenrette, Corinne McLemore, 1903-
Poet
Blk Am Wr 2: 419-20
Jessye, Eva Alberta, 1897-
Music director, poet, columnist
Afro-Am Ency 5: 1322-23 por / AmSCAP
66 p. 365 / Blk Am Wr 2: 420 / Ency
Blk Am p. 470-71 / Kerlin. Poets 23
p. 274-75 / Kerlin. Poets 35 p. 340 /
Who Col Am 33 p. 238 / Who Col Am
37 por p. 284
Jiggetts, Bess
Poet, author
Blk Am Wr 2: 420-21
Joans, Ted, 1928-
Artist, jazz musician, poet
Adoff. Blk out p. 79 / Adoff. Poet
p. 527 / Afro-Am Ency 5: 1327 / Blk Am
Wr 2: 421-22 / Bontemps. American 63
p. 191 / Bontemps. American 74 p. 221 /
Broadside Auth p. 66-67 / Cele p. 260 /
Con Auth 45-48: 262 / Hayden. Kal p.
190 / Hughes. New p. 121 / Hughes.
Poet p. 611 / Selected BAA p. 138

John, Errol
Actor, playwright
Dr Perf Arts 78 p. 190-91
Johns, Vernon S.
Minister, writer of published sermons
Dreer. Am Lit p. 210
Johnson, Alicia Loy, 1944-
Poet
Adoff. Blk out p. 79 / Blk Am Wr 2:
422 / Broadside Auth p. 67-68 / Living
BAA p. 79-80 / Shuman. Galaxy p.
338 / Shuman. Nine p. 145
Johnson, Amelia E., 1858-
Novelist, poet, publisher
Blk Am Wr 2: 422-23 / Majors. Wom
p. 210 / Penn. Press p. 424-27 / Scruggs.
Wom p. 116-19
Johnson, Charles Bertram, 1880-
Minister, poet
Blk Am Wr 2: 423 / Johnson. Book
p. 198 / Kerlin. Poets 23 p. 95-97 por;
p. 275 / Kerlin. Poets 35 p. 95-97 por;
p. 341 / White. Verse p. 189-90
Johnson, Charles S(purgeon), 1893-1956
Sociologist, educator, author
Afro-Am Ency 5: 1331-32 por / Brown.
Caravan p. 896 / Cur Biog Yrbk 46 p.
285-87 por / Ency Am Biog p. 586-87 /
Great Negroes 69 p. 115 / Historical N
Bio p. 329-31 / Hughes. Harlem p.
215-46 / Reader's Ency 62 p. 549 /
Selected BAA p. 139-40
Johnson, Don Allen, 1942-
Poet
Afro-Am Ency 5: 1335 / Blk Am Wr 2:
423 / Hughes. New p. 121-22 / Hughes.
Poet p. 611
Johnson, Dorothy Vena, ?-1970
Teacher, poet
Afro-Am Ency 5: 1335 / Blk Am Wr 2:
424 / Bontemps. Golden p. 210 / Hughes.
Poet p. 612 / Murphy. Ebony p. 91 /
Murphy. N Voices p. 83
Johnson, Edward Austin, 1860-1944
Novelist, historian, politician, lawyer,
educator
Ency Blk Am p. 473 / Robinson. Prose
p. 211 / Thorpe. Hist p. 149-50 / Who
Col Am 42 p. 285
Johnson, Eugene Harper
Illustrator
Illus Bks YP 75 p. 81-82 / Illus Ch Bks
57 p. 127

Johnson, Fenton, 1885-1958
Poet
Adoff. Poet p. 527 / Afro-Am Ency 5:
1336 / Barksdale. Writers p. 455 / Blk Am
Wr 2: 424-25 / Bontemps. Golden p.
210-11 / Brown. Caravan p. 347 / Chap-
man. Blk V p. 366-67 / Cullen. Carol
p. 61-62 / Ency Blk Am p. 473 / Hayden.
Kal p. 40 / Johnson. Book p. 140-41 /
Kerlin. Poets p. 275 / Long. Writing
1: 283 / Negro Alm 71 p. 683 / Negro
Alm 76 p. 731 / Robinson. Poets p.
145-46 / Wagner. Poets p. 179 / White.
Verse p. 160 / Who Col Race p. 156
Johnson, Frederick, Jr., 1940-
Educator, poet
Adoff. Poet p. 527 / Cele p. 260 / Who
Blk Am 77 p. 482
Johnson, George Perry, 1887-
Producer, screenplay writer
Dr Perf Arts 78 p. 191
Johnson, Georgia Douglas, 1886-1966
Poet, playwright
Adoff. Poet p. 527 / Afro-Am Ency 5:
1337-38 / Blk Am Wr 2: 426 / Bontemps.
American 63 p. 191 / Bontemps. American
74 p. 221 / Bontemps. Golden p. 211 /
Brown. Caravan p. 339 / Cromwell. Read
p. 367 / Cullen. Carol p. 74-75 / Dreer.
Am Lit p. 73 / Ency Blk Am p. 473 /
Hayden. Kal p. 38 / Johnson. Book p.
181 / Kerlin. Poets 23 p. 275 / Negro
Alm 71 p. 683 / Negro Alm 76 p. 731 /
Selected BAA p. 141-42 / Southern Wr
p. 246-47 / White. Verse p. 208
Johnson, (Francis) Hall, 1888-1970
Musician, playwright
Afro-Am Ency 5: 1338 / AmSCAP 66
p. 367 / AmSCAP 80 p. 251 / Blk Am
Wr 2: 427-28 / Dr Perf Arts 78 p.
191-92 / Historical N Bio p. 211
Johnson, Harry Alleyn, 1920-
Educator, writer on Afro-American materials
Afro-Am Ency 5: 1340 / Con Auth
45-48: 263 / Living BAA p. 81 / Who
Blk Am 77 p. 483
Johnson, Harvey, 1843-1923
Clergyman
Afro-Am Ency 5: 1340 il / Historical N
Bio p. 91-92 por / Simmons. Men
p. 506-511 il
Johnson, Helen Armstead. *See* Collins, Helen
Arnstead Johnson

Johnson, Helene (Hubbell), 1907-
Adoff. Poet p. 527 / Afro-Am Ency 5:
1341 / Anth Mag Verse 26, pt. 4 p. 22 /
Bontemps. American 63 p. 191 / Bon-
temps. American 74 p. 222 / Bontemps.
Golden p. 211 / Cromwell. Read p. 367 /
Cullen. Carol p. 215 / Hughes. Poet p.
612 / Johnson. Book p. 279
Johnson, Henry Theodore 1857-1910
Poet, essayist
Blk Am Wr 2: 428
Johnson, Herbert Clark, 1911-
Poet
Afro-Am Ency 5: 1341 / Blk Am Wr 2:
428 / Hughes. Poet p. 613
Johnson, Herschell Lee, 1948-
Editor
Coombs. Speak p. 244 / Who Blk Am
77 p. 484
Johnson, James Weldon, 1871-1938
Poet, lyricist, critic, translator, novelist,
editor, autobiographer
Adoff. Poet p. 527-28 / Am Auth & Bks
72 p. 333 / AmSCAP 80 p. 252 / Anth
Mag Verse 26 pt 4, p. 22 / Barksdale.
Writers p. 480-82 / Barton. Witness p.
221-37 / Bio Hist p. 336-38 / Blk Am Wr
2: 429-30 / Blk Auth / Bone. Novel
p. 45-49 / Bontemps. American 63
p. 191-92 / Bontemps. American 74
p. 222 / Bontemps. Golden p. 212 /
Boulware. Oratory p. 81-86 / Brawley.
Lit p. 97-104 / Brown. Caravan p.
324-25 / Chapman. Blk V p. 269-70 / Con
Am Anth 40 p. 409-411 / Cromwell. Read
p. 367 / Cullen. Carol p. 15-17 / David.
Living p. 29-36 / Davis. Dark p. 25-27 /
Davis. South p. 901 / Dreer. Am Lit
p. 173-78 / Dr Perf Arts 78 p. 192-93 /
Emanuel. Dark p. 69-70 / Ency Am Biog
p. 590-91 / Ford. Insights p. 61 / Fourth
Bk p. 199-201 por / Great Negroes 69
p. 155 il / Haslam. Forgot p. 278 /
Hayden. Kal p. 26 / Historical N Bio
p. 213-14 por / Hughes. Poet p. 613 /
Johnson. Book p. 114-17 / Jordan. Soul
p. 140 / Kendricks. Voices p. 112 /
Kerlin. Poets 23 p. 90-92 por; p. 275 /
Kerlin. Poets 35 p. 90-92 por; p. 341 /
Lincoln Lib Arts 2: 618 / Long. Writing
2: 310-11 / Margolies. Read p. 358 /
Negro Alm 71 p. 683 / Negro Alm 76 p.
242 / Ovington. Portraits p. 1-17 / Oxford
Am p. 429 / Penguin Am Lit p. 138 /

Johnson, James Weldon (cont'd) ...
Poets p. 530-31 / Reader's Advisor 74,
1: 260 / Reader's Ency 62 p. 549 /
Richardson. Great 56 p. 131-49 il /
Richardson. Great 76 p. 118-28 por /
Rollins. Famous p. 28-31 / Rollins. They
p. 88-90 / Selected BAA p. 142-43 por /
Southern Wr p. 249-51 / Sterling. Lift
p. 82-110 il / Turner. Voices p. 266 /
Twen CA p. 728 / Wagner. Poets p.
352-53 / Webster Am Biog p. 552 / White.
Verse p. 170 / Whitlow. Lit p. 65-67 /
Who Col Am 33 p. 243 / Who Col
Am 37 p. 289 / Who Col Am 40 p.
289-90 / Who Was 1: 639 / Woodson.
Orators p. 663
Johnson, Jesse J., 1914-
Editor, historical novelist, military official,
writer on blacks in military service
Blk Am Wr 2: 434 / David. Soldier p.
167-78 / Living BAA p. 81 / Who Blk Am
77 p. 485 / Writers Dr 80 p. 642
Johnson, Joe, 1940-
Poet, short story writer
Adoff. Poet p. 528 / Blk Am Wr 2:
434-35 / Cele p. 260 / Living BAA p. 82
Johnson, John Quincy, 1865-
Minister, writer
Culp. Twen p. 270-71 il / Who Col Race
1: 156-57
Johnson, Joseph A., Jr., 1914-1979
Clergyman, author
Con Auth 89-92: 274 (obit.) / Ebony
Success 1: 178 por
Johnson, Leanna F.
Poet
Murphy. Ebony p. 95
Johnson, Mae Smith, 1890-
Poet
Blk Am Wr 2: 434
Johnson, Marguerite. *See* Angelou, Maya
Johnson, Mordecai Wyatt, 1890-1976
Minister, educator, orator
Afro-Am Ency 5: 1351-52 por / Bio Dr
Min 65 p. 200 / Boulware. Oratory p.
70-77 / Brawley. Builders p. 221-25 /
Ency Blk Am p. 475 por / Historical
N Bio p. 215-16 por / Richardson.
Great 56 p. 167-76 il / Woodson.
Orators p. 658 / Young. Since 1940 p.
27-28, 31-33
Johnson, Percy, 1930-
Teacher, editor, playwright, poet
Blk Am Wr 2: 437

Johnson, Ray
Poet
Jones. Fire p. 664
Johnson, Ruth Brownlee
Poet
Murphy. Ebony p. 96
Johnson, William B., 1856-
Minister, editor, teacher
Penn. Press p. 235-37
Johnson, William Decker, 1842-
Clergyman, orator
Haley. Ency p. 591-92 por
Johnson, William Matthews, 1905-
Novelist, short story writer, essayist
Blk Am Wr 2: 436 / Living BAA p. 82
Johnson, Yvette
Social worker, poet
Afro-Am Ency 5: 1358
Johnston, Brenda A(rlivia), 1944-
Author of children's books
Con Auth 57-60: 305-306
Jones, Absalom, 1746-1818
Clergyman, pamphleteer
Brawley. Builders p. 30-34 / Brawley.
Early p. 87-89 / Historical N Bio p.
24 / Robinson. Nommo p. 24 por
Jones, Clara, 1915-
Library administrator, writer on librarianship
Afro-Am Ency 5: 1363 / ALA Yrbk 76,
1: 106 por / Ency Blk Am p. 476 /
Josey Blk Librn p. 19-42 / Who Blk Am
77 p. 469
Jones, Daniel, 1830-
Minister, orator
Simmons. Men p. 394-97
Jones, E. H., 1925-
Playwright, poet
Blk Am Wr 2: 438
Jones, Edward Smyth(e)
Poet
Blk Am Wr 2: 438-39 / Johnson. Book
p. 147 / White. Verse p. 154
Jones, Gayl Amanda, 1949-
Novelist, poet, playwright, short story writer
Afro-Am Novel p. 95 / Am Women Wr 2:
421-22 / Blk Am Wr 2: 439-40 por / Exum.
Keep p. 285 / Jordan. Soul p. 140 / Selected
BAA p. 145 por
Jones, Georgia Holloway
Librarian, poet
Murphy. Ebony p. 98
Jones, Hettie, 1934-
Editor, biographer, children's author
Auth Bk YP Sup 79 p. 144 / Con Auth
81-84: 274

Jones, Howard O., 1922-
  Minister, author
    Afro-Am Ency 5: 1368-69
Jones, J. McHenry, 1859-1909
  Minister, novelist, editor, orator, educator
    Afro-Am Ency 5: 1376 / Blk Am Wr 2:
    441 / Historical N Bio p. 92
Jones, James Arlington, 1936-
  Painter, sculptor, poet
    Blk Am Wr 2: 441 / Shuman, Galaxy p.
    347 / Shuman. Nine p. 163
Jones, John, 1816-1879
  Civil rights activits, pamphleteer
    Great Negroes 69 p. 81 il / Katz.
    West p. 66-70 por, il / Sterling. Speak
    p. 377-78 por
Jones, Joseph Endom, 1850-
  Minister, educator, writer
    Afro-Am Ency 5: 1372-74 / Simmons.
    Men p. 143-48 por
Jones, Joshua H., 1856-1912
  Minister, educator
    Culp. Twen p. 82-83 por / Who Col Race
    p. 161 / Who Was 1: 649
Jones, Joshua Henry, Jr., 1876-1953
  Poet, journalist
    Blk Am Wr 2: 441 / Johnson. Book
    p. 201 / Kerlin. Poets 23 p. 113-14 por,
    p. 276 / Kerlin. Poets 35 p. 113-14 por,
    p. 342
Jones, Jymi, 1940-
  Poet
    Kendricks. Voices p. 347
Jones, (Everette) Le Roi (Imamu Amiri
Baraka), 1934-
  Playwright, poet, essayist
    Adoff. Blk on p. 231-32 / Adoff. Blk
    out p. 77 / Adoff. Poet p. 518 / Afro-Am
    Ency 5: 1374-75 / Barksdale. Writers
    p. 745-47 / Bio Hist p. 340-41 / Blk Am
    Wr 1: 50 / Bontemps. American 63 p.
    192 / Bontemps. American 74 p. 222 /
    Broadside Auth p. 24-25 / Cele p. 251 /
    Chapman. Blk V p. 482-83 / Chapman.
    New p. 207-208 / Con Auth 21-24R:
    455-66 / Con Drama 77 p. 429-35 / Con
    Novel 76 p. 733-37 / Con Poets 70 p.
    574-76 / Con Poets 75 p. 799-82 /
    Crowell CD p. 268-69 / Cur Biog Yrbk
    70 p. 204-207 por / Davis. Cav p. 646 /
    Dict Lit Biog 5-1: 21-27 por / Dict Lit
    Biog 7-1: 49-56 / Dr Perf Arts 78 p.
    17-18 / Dramatists 79 p. 324-29 / Ebony
    Success 1: 19 por / Emanual. Dark p.

Jones, (Everette) Le Roi (Imamu Amiri
Baraka) (cont'd) ...
    513-14 / Ency Blk Am p. 166, por p.
    536 / Ford. Insights p. 322-23 / Guide
    Am Lit p. 111 / Haslam. Forgot p. 351 /
    Hayden. Kal p. 208-209 / Hill. Anger p.
    215-16 / Hughes. New p. 122 / Hughes.
    Poet p. 613-14 / Int Auth & Wr 77 p.
    527 / Jordan. Soul p. 140-41 / King.
    Drama p. 11 / King. Spirits p. 243 /
    King. Story p. 117 / Lincoln Lib Arts
    2: 620 / Living BAA p. 9 / Long.
    Writing 2: 693-94 / Margolies. Read p.
    358 / Notable Names p. 539 / Pol Pro-
    files: Nixon p. 332-34 / Robinson.
    Nommo p. 478-79 / Selected BAA p. 13 /
    Turner. Voices p. 266 / Webster Am
    Biog p. 63 / Whitlow. Lit p. 170 / Who
    Am 80, 1: 170 / Who Blk Am 77 p. 41 /
    Who Theatre 77 p. 384 / Wor Auth 50-70
    p. 734-37 por / Writers Dr 76 p. 544 /
    Writers Dr 80 p. 649 / Writers Dr 82
    p. 498
Jones, Marte
  Poet
    Exum. Keep p. 285
Jones, Ralph H., 1906-
  Poet, editor
    Blk Am Wr 2: 442-43 por
Jones, Reginald L., 1931-
  Educator, psychologist
    Con Auth 45-48: 265 / Living BAA
    p. 83 / Who Blk Am 77 p. 505
Jones, Richard A., 1847-
  Editor
    Penn. Press p. 292-95
Jones, Robert Elijah, 1872-
  Minister, editor
    Afro-Am Ency 5: 1379
Jones, Rossie Lee Logan. See Logan (Jones),
Rossie Lee
Jones, Sarah Gibson, 1845-
  Poet, teacher, writer, lecturer
    Brown. Homespun p. 247, por opp. p.
    248 / Majors. Wom p. 138-40
Jones, Silas, 1940-
  Short story writer, television documentary
  writer
    Blk Am Wr 1: 443-44 / Nat Play Dr
    p. 154
Jones, Virginia Lacy
  Library school dean, writer on librarianship
    ALA Yrbk (77) 2: 59-60 por / ALA Yrbk
    (81) 6: 75 por / Bio Dr Librns 70 p.

Kennedy, Adrienne, 1931-
Playwright
Blk Am Wr 2: 455 / Blk Plots p.
256 / Con Auth 103: 256 / Con Drama
73 p. 435-37 / Con Drama 77 p. 445-46 /
Crowell CD p. 271 / Dr Perf Arts 78
p. 204 / Living BAA p. 87 / Notable
Names p. 882-83 / Oliver. Drama p. 189 /
Selected BAA p. 152 por / Who Am 80, 1:
1809 / Who Blk Am 77 p. 517 / Wor
Auth 70-75 p. 447-49 por / Writers Dr
76 p. 573 / Writers Dr 80 p. 671 /
Writers Dr 82 p. 514
Kennedy, Florynce, R(ae), 1916-
Attorney, lecturer, author
Living BAA p. 88 / Who Blk Am 77
p. 517
Kennedy, Paul H., 1848-
Clergyman, editor, author of church
publications
Haley. Ency p. 613-14 por
Kennedy, Vallejo Ryan, 1947-
Poet
Watts Wr p. 137
Kent, George Edward, 1920-
Professor of English, critic, short story
writer
Blk Am Wr 2: 456-57 / Chapman. Blk V
p. 690-91 / Living BAA p. 88 / Selected
BAA p. 152 / Who Blk Am 77 p. 518
Kerr, S.
Minister, essayist
Culp. Twen p. 320-21 il
Kewus, Lillial Akbeeta. *See* Lewis, Lillian A.
Kgositsile, Keorpetse (William), 1938-
Poet
Adoff. Poet p. 528 / Alhamisi. Arts p.
118 / Broadside Auth p. 70 / Con Auth
77-80: 302 / Con Poets 80 p. 833-34 /
Jones. Fire p. 665 / Robinson. Nommo
p. 479 / Selected BAA p. 153 / Turner.
Voices p. 267 / Writers Dr 80 p. 678 /
Writers Dr 82 p. 519
Kilgore, James C(olumbus), 1928-
Professor of English, short story writer,
novelist, dramatist
Blk Am Wr 2: 459-60 / Con Auth
33-36R: 469 / Writers Dr 76 p. 579 /
Writers Dr 80 p. 679 / Writers Dr 82
p. 520
Killens, John Oliver, 1916-
Playwright, novelist, essayist
Adams. Auth p. 82 / Adoff. Blk on p.
232 / Afro-Am Ency 5: 1415 / Afro-Am

Killens, John Oliver (cont'd) ...
Novel p. 107 / Blk Am Wr 2: 461 / Blk
Plots p. 257 / Con Auth 77-80: 304-305 /
Con Novel 72 p. 715-16 / Con Novel
76 p. 756 / Dr Perf Arts 78 p. 205 /
Ency Blk Am p. 485 / Ford. Insights
p. 319 / Int Auth & Wr 77 p. 555 /
Living BAA p. 89 / Long. Writing 2:
607-608 / Robinson. Nommo p. 479 /
Selected BAA p. 153-54 / Southern Wr
p. 264-65 / Who Blk Am 77 p. 520 /
Wor Auth 70-75 p. 452-53 por / Writers
Dr 76 p. 579 / Writers Dr 80 p. 679
Kilonfe, Oba (rob penny), 1940-
Poet
Adoff. Poet p. 532 / Blk Am Wr 2:
463-64
Kilson, Martin Luther, Jr., 1931-
Professor of political science
Con Auth 37-40: 268-69 / Con Auth
37-40R: 293-94 / Con Auth 103: 262 /
Ebony Success 1: 191 por / Living BAA
p. 89-90 / Who Blk Am 77 p. 521
King, Coretta Scott (Mrs. Martin Luther
King, Jr.), 1927-
Concert singer, civil rights activist,
autobiographer
Afro-Am Ency 5: 1418-20 il / Con Auth
29-33R: 360-61 / Cur Biog Yrbk 69 p.
239-41 por / Diamonstein. Open p.
248-49 / Ebony Success 1: 192 por /
Fax. Leaders p. 48-64 / Int Auth & Wr
77 p. 556 / Living BAA p. 90 / Negro
Alm 71 p. 879-80 / Negro Alm 76 p.
227-28 il / Oxford Am p. 192 por /
Selected BAA p. 154-55 / Who Am 80, 1:
1837 / Who Blk Am 77 p. 523
King, Helen H(ayes), 1931-
Children's author, poet, publisher
Blk Am Wr 1: 464 / Con Auth 33-36:
506 / Con Auth 33-36R: 471 / Ebony
Success 1: 193 por / Living BAA p.
90-91 / Selected BAA p. 155-56 / Who
Am 80, 1: 1838 / Who Blk Am 77 p. 523
King, John O. Taylor, 1921-
Professor of mathematics, college
administrator
Con Auth 25-28R: 387 / Ebony Success
1: 193 por / Who Blk Am 77 p. 524
King, Martin Luther, Jr., 1929-1968
Clergyman, civil rights leader
Adoff. Blk on p. 232-33 / Afro-Am Ency
5: 1421-23 por / Am Auth & Bks 72 p.
350 / Blk Am Wr 2: 464-65 / Blk Lead /

King, Martin Luther, Jr. (cont'd) ...
Boulware. Orators p. 243-75 / Con
Auth P-2: 289-91 / Cur Biog Yrbk 57 p.
299-301 / Cur Biog Yrbk 65 p. 220-23 /
Davis. Cav p. 779 / Ency Am Biog p.
620-22 / Ency Blk Am p. 486-89 il / Ford.
Insights p. 227 / Gayle. Bond p. 149 / Great
Negroes 69 p. 128-29 il / Long. Writing 2:
639-40 / Metcalf. Profiles p. 3-54 / Nat Cyclo
54: 1-2 por / Negro Alm 76 p. 243-45
por / Negro Handbk 66 p. 406 / O'Neill.
Speeches p. 151-52, por p. 153 / Oxford
Am 65 p. 445 / Pol Profiles: Eisen-
hower p. 335-38 / Pol Profiles: Johnson
p. 334-39 / Pol Profiles: Kennedy p.
286-89 / Reader's Ency 62 p. 571 /
Something ATA 14: 108-111 por / Web-
ster Am Biog p. 586 / Who Was 4:
1059 / Young. Since 1940 p. 108-111
King, William E., 1865-
Teacher, editor
Penn. Press p. 200-201 / Who Col Am
29 p. 224
King, Woodie, Jr., 1937-
Editor, playwright, short story writer
Blk Am Wr 2: 466-67 / Con Auth 103:
263-64 / King. Spirits p. 253 / King.
Story p. 310 / Selected BAA p. 157-58
por / Who Am 80, 1: 1782 / Who Blk
Am 77 p. 526
Kirpatrick, Oliver
Librarian
Josey. What p. 305-306
Kitt, Eartha (Mae), 1928-
Actress, entertainer, autobiographer
Con Auth 77-80: 308-309 / David. Roots
p. 126-36 / Living BAA p. 91 / Notable
Names p. 890 / Rollins. Enter p. 75-80,
por p. 11 / Who Blk Am 77 p. 528
Knight, Etheridge, 1931-
Poet, short story writer
Adoff. Blk out p. 80 / Adoff. Poet
p. 528 / Broadside Auth p. 72 por /
Cele p. 260 / Chapman. New p. 276 / Con
Auth p. 21-24R: 493 / Con Poets 70
p. 611 / Con Poets 75 p. 842-44 /
Con Poets 80 p. 846-47 / Living BAA
p. 92 / Major. Poet p. 150 / Robinson.
Nommo p. 479 / Selected BAA p.
158-59 / Whitlow. Lit p. 167 / Who Am
80, 1: 1867 / Writers Dr 76 p. 589 /
Writers Dr 80 p. 689 / Writers Dr
82 p. 528

Knight, Franklin Willis, 1942-
Historian, educator
Ency Blk Am p. 489
Knox, Clinton Everett, 1908-
Educator, historian, foreign service officer
Ency Blk Am p. 490 / Negro Alm 71 p.
291-92 / Negro Alm 76 p. 352 / Thorpe.
Hist p. 183
Koiner, Richard B., 1929-
Novelist, free-lance writer, cartoonist
Con Auth 17-20R: 414 / Living BAA
p. 92 / Selected BAA p. 159
Kunjufu, Johari M. Amini. *See* Latimore,
Jewel C.
Kush. *See* Dent, Thomas C.
Kwartler, Stephen, 1950-
Jordan. Soul p. 141

Labrie, Peter, Jr., 1940-
Essayist, educator, city planner
Jones. Fire p. 665 / Who Blk Am 77
p. 531
Lacey, Archie L(ouis), 1923-
Educator
Con Auth 9-10: 268 / Innis. Profiles
16-17 por / Who Blk Am 77 p. 531
Lacy, Leslie Alexander, 1937-
Essayist, teacher, lecturer, autobiographer
Con Auth 33-36: 489 / Living BAA p.
92 / Selected BAA p. 159-60
Ladner, Joyce A., 1943-
Sociologist, author
Ebony Success 1: 196 por / Ebony
Success 3: 108 por / Living BAA p.
93 / Who Blk Am 77 p. 532
La Grone, (Clarence) Oliver, 1906-
Teacher, sculptor, poet
Broadside Auth p. 73 / Chapman. New
p. 280 / Hughes. New p. 122 / Hughes.
Poet p. 614 / Living BAA p. 93-94 /
Selected BAA p. 160
Laine, Henry Allen, 1869-
Poet
Blk Am Wr 2: 470
Lakin, Mattie T., 1917-
Educator, poet
Blk Am Wr 2: 470 / Shuman. Galaxy
p. 366
LaMarre, Hazel Washington, 1917-1973
Poet, journalist
Blk Am Wr 2: 471 / Hughes. Poet p. 614
Lamb, Arthur Clifton, 1909-
Playwright
Blk Am Wr 2: 471 / Dr Am Schol 78,
2: 388

Lamont, Barbara, 1939-
Newscaster, author, writer of documentaries
Dr Perf Arts 78 p. 214 / Negro Alm 76
p. 1030 / Who Blk Am 77 p. 533
Lancaster, Ella Madden
Writer of short stories
Scally. Catholic p. 63-64
Lane, Isaac, 1834-1937
Bishop, college founder, autobiographer
Ency Blk Am p. 496-97 / Haley. Ency
p. 352-53 por / Who Col Am 33 p.
260-61 / Who Col Am 40 p. 316 /
Who Was 1: 702
Lane, Lunsford, 1803-
Narrator of experiences
David. Defiance p. 16-28 / Mezu. Leaders
p. 29
Lane, Pinkie Gordon, 1923-
Educator, peot
Blk Am Wr 2: 472 / Con Auth 41-44R:
396-97 / Dr Am Schol 69, 2: 308 /
Dr Am Schol 74, 2: 360 / Dr Am
Schol 78, 2: 389 / Selected BAA p. 161
Laney, Lucy Craft, 1854-1933
Educator, lecturer
Brawley. Builders p. 279-82 / Daniel.
Wom 70 p. 1-27 por / Dannett. Wom 1:
280 / Haley. Ency p. 108-109 / Lerner.
Wom p. 122-23 / Loewenberg. Wom p.
296-97 / Negro Alm 71 p. 880-81 / Negro
Alm 76 p. 1010 / Notable Am Wom 2:
265-67 / Ovington. Portraits p. 53-63 /
Who Col Am 29 p. 226 / Who Col Am
33 p. 261
Lange, Ted, III, 1947-
Actor, playwright, screenplay writer
Blk Am Wr 2: 473-74 / Dr Perf Arts
78 p. 214-15 / Who Am 80, 2: 1943
Langston, John Mercer, 1829-1897
Public official, educator, lawyer, orator,
autobiographer, pamphleteer
Afro-Am Ency 5: 1441 il / Alli Sup 2:
973 / Bio Dr Am Cong 61 p. 1191 /
Bio Dict S Auth p. 246 / Brawley.
Builders p. 139-46 / Brown. Caravan
p. 666-67 / Christopher. Congress p.
137-48 / Dict Am Biog 33, 10: 597-98 /
Dict Am Biog 61, 5-2: 597-98 / Great
Negroes 69 p. 42 il / Haley. Ency p.
40-42 por / Historical N Bio p. 93-94 il /
Nat Cyclo 3: 328 por / Negro Alm 76
p. 323-24 por / Ohio Auth p. 372 /
Selected BAA p. 162 / Simmons. Men p.
344-52 il / Webster Am Biog p. 607 /
Who Was H: 302-303 / Who Was HR:
373 / Woodson. Orators p. 387

Lanusse, Armand, 1812-1867
Poet
Afro-Am Ency 5: 1443 / Blk Am Wr 2:
474 / Hughes. Poet p. 615 / Selected
BAA p. 162
Larsen, Nella, 1893-1963
Novelist
Am Women Wr 2: 507-509 / Blk Am Wr
2: 475 / Bontemps. Harlem p. 83 /
Davis. Dark p. 94-95 / Ency Blk Am p.
497 / Noble. Beautiful p. 162-64 / Selected
BAA p. 163
LaSalle, Edward, 1900-
Writer of short stories
Scally. Catholic p. 65-66
Latimer, Bette Darcie, 1927-
Poet
Adoff. Poet p. 528 / Hughes. Poet p. 615
Latimer, Lewis Howard, 1848-1928
Engineer, poet, author
Afro-Am Ency 5: 1444 / Blk Am Wr 2:
477 / Ency Blk Am p. 792 / Negro Alm
71 p. 720 / Negro Alm 76 p. 792 / Who
Col Race p. 172
Latimore, Jewel C. (Johari M. Amini;
Johari M. Amini Kunjufu), 1935-
Poet, reviewer, teacher
Adoff. Poet p. 517 / Alhamisi. Arts p.
104 / Blk Am Wr 1: 31 por / Broad-
side Auth p. 19-20 / Cele p. 261 /
Con Auth 41-44R: 392 / Coombs. Speak
p. 244 / King. Spirits p. 243 / Selected
BAA p. 3-4 por
Lawrence, Harold G. (Harun Kofi Wangara),
1928-
Teacher, editor, poet, writer for children
Alhamisi. Arts p. 23 / Blk Am Wr 2:
736 / Broadside Auth p. 120-21
Lawrence, Jacob, 1917-
Painter, illustrator, author
Afro-Am Art p. 170-73 / Cur Biog
Yrbk 65 p. 252-54 / Ency Blk Am p.
498, il p. 514 / Fourth Bk p. 218-20
por / Historical N Bio p. 222 / Illus
Bks YP 70 p. 66-67 / Illus Bks YP 75
p. 93 / Who Blk Am 77 p. 539 /
Who Col Am 50 p. 332
Lawrence, Joyce Whitsitt (Maliaka Ayo
Wangara), 1938-
Poet
Broadside Auth p. 121 / Major. Poet
p. 156
Lawton, Maria Coles Perkins, 1864-
Lecturer, teacher, journalist
Who Col Am 29 p. 230, 233; por p.
235 / Who Col Am 33 p. 265 / Who

Lewis, James, Jr., 1930-
Educator
Con Auth 29-32R: 396 / Living BAA
p. 97 / Who Blk Am 77 p. 553
Lewis, Lillian A. (Lillial Akbeeta Kewus;
Bert Islew)
Journalist, lecturer
Penn. Press p. 381-84 por
Lewis, Ora Mae, 1918-
Poet, short story writer
Scally. Catholic p. 68-70
Lewis, Robert Benjamin, 1802-
Historian
Thorpe. Hist p. 33-34
Lewis, Samella Sanders, 1924-
Educator, writer on art
Afro-Am Art p. 180-81 / Selected BAA
p. 167-68 por / Who Blk Am 77 p. 555
Lewis, Theophilus, 1891-
Columnist, reviewer, literary critic
Blk Am Wr 2: 486 / Bontemps. Harlem
p. 171-89 / Scally. Catholic p. 75-77
Lewis, Walter I
Culp. Twen p. 272-73 il
Lewis, William H., 1868-1948
Lawyer, public official, orator
Woodson. Orators p. 562
Lightfoot, Claude M., 1910-
Historian, political activist
Living BAA p. 97-98 / Selected BAA
p. 168-69 / Who Blk Am 77 p. 556
Lilly, Charles
Illustrator
Illus Bks YP 75 p. 96
Lilly, Octave, Jr., 1908-1975
Poet
Blk Am Wr 2: 486-87 por / Murphy.
N Voices p. 97
Lincoln, Abbey (Gaby Lee; Anna Marie Wool-
ridge), 1930-
Singer, playwright
Childress. Scenes p. 152 / Dr Perf Arts
78 p. 224 / Negro Alm 76 p. 884
Lincoln, C(harles) Eric, 1924-
Professor of religion, social historian
Con Auth 2: 101 / Dr Am Schol 78,
4: 280 / Ebony Success 1: 203 por / Living
BAA p. 98-99 / Selected BAA p. 169-70
por / Something ATA 5: 111 / Who Am
78, 1: 1965 / Who Am 80, 1: 2031 /
Who Blk Am 77 p. 557 / Writers Dr
76 p. 640 / Writers Dr 80 p. 749 /
Writers Dr 82 p. 573 / Young. Since
1940 p. 88, 89, 95-96

Linde, Shirley Motter, 1929-
Writer on medicine, publisher
Con Auth 45-48: 327-28 / Living BAA
p. 99 / Who Am 80, 2: 2032 / Writers
Dr 76 p. 640-41 / Writers Dr 80 p.
750 / Writers Dr 82 p. 574
Linden, Charlotte E., 1859-1919
Poet, autobiographer
Ohio Auth p. 386
Lindsay, Powell
Playwright, poet
Blk Am Wr 2: 488-89 por
LinYatta. *See* Turner, Doris
Lipcombe, E. H., 1858-
Penn. Press p. 210-23
Little, Malcolm (Malcolm X), 1925-1965
Black nationalist, autobiographer
Adoff. Blk on p. 233 / Afro-Am Ency
6: 1563-67 / Alexander. Young p. 58-68
por / Alhamisi. Arts p. 138 / Am Auth
& Bks 72 p. 383 / Barksdale. Writers p.
873-74 / Bio Hist p. 358-68 / Blk Am Wr
2: 524-26 / Blk Lead / Blk Lit HS
p. 158 / Blk Plots p. 315 / Boul-
ware. Oratory p. 234-38 / Chapman.
Blk V p. 332-33 / David. Growing p.
195-202 / David. Living p. 300-309 /
David. Roots p. 195-210 / Ency Am
Biog p. 544 por / Ency Blk Am p.
723-24 / Fax. Leaders p. 1-17 / Ford.
Insights p. 332 / Gayle. Bond p. 151 /
Great Negroes 69 p. 131 / Haskins.
Profiles p. 103-110 / Haslam. Forgot p.
342 / Kendricks. Voices p. 312 / Long.
Writing 2: 653-54 / Margolies. Read p.
359-60 / Metcalf. Up p. 335-68 / Mezu.
Leaders p. 282-91 / Negro Alm 71 p. 235 /
Negro Alm 76 p. 245-46 por / O'Neill.
Speeches p. 247-48 / Pol Profiles: John-
son p. 403 / Pol Profiles: Kennedy p.
341 / Richardson. Great 76 p. 218-29
por / Selected BAA p. 170-71 por /
Turner. Voices p. 269 / Webster Am Biog
p. 683-84 / Young. Since 1940 p. 73-76,
80-81
Littleton, Arthur C., 1940-
Research psychologist, author, editor
Ebony Success 1: 204 por / Who Blk Am
77 p. 560
Llorens, David, 1939-1973
Editor, poet, essayist
Afro-Am Ency 5: 1496 / Blk Am Wr 2:
491 / Broadside Auth p. 78 / Jones.
Fire p. 665

Locke, Alain LeRoy, 1886-1954
Educator, historian, literary critic
Afro-Am Ency 5: 1496-97 / Am Auth &
Bks 72 p. 385 / Barksdale. Writers p.
573-75 / Bio Hist p. 352-54 / Blk Am Wr
2: 491-92 / Blk Plots p. 260 / Brown.
Caravan p. 948 / Chapman. Blk V p.
512 / Cromwell. Read p. 367-68 / Davis.
Dark p. 51-52 / Dreer. Am Lit p. 168 /
Emanuel. Dark p. 73-74 / Ency Am Biog
p. 677-78 / Ency Blk Am p. 539 /
Fauset. Freedom p. 171-77 il / Great
Negroes 69 p. 141 il / Historical N Bio
p. 222-23 por / Long. Writing 2: 333-34 /
Negro Alm 71 p. 686 / Negro Alm 76
p. 732 / Reader's Ency 62 p. 646 /
Selected BAA p. 171-72 / Twen CA p.
837 / Twen CA Sup·p. 588 / Webster
Am Biog p. 639-40 / Whitlow. Lit p.
73-74 / Who Col Am 37 p. 333, por
p. 335 / Who Col Am 40 p. 334 /
Who Col Race p. 178 / Who Was 3: 535
Lockett, Reginald, 1947-
Poet
Cele p. 261 / Jones. Fire p. 665
Lockett, Tena, 1945-
Teacher of linguistics, poet
Coombs. Speak p. 245
Loftin, Elouise, 1950-
Poet, editor
Adoff. Poet p. 529 / Blk Am Wr 2:
496 / Cele p. 261 / Selected BAA p. 172
Logan, Adella Hunt (Mrs. Warren Logan),
1863-1915
Culp. Twen p. 198-99 il / Dannett. Pro-
files 1: 283
Logan, Rayford W(hittingham), 1895-
Professor of history, historian
Afro-Am Ency 5: 1499-1500 / Brown.
Caravan p. 1042 / Con Auth 1-R: 388 /
Con Auth 2: 105 / Ency Blk Am p. 539 /
Historical N Bio p. 223 / Negro Alm 71
p. 686-87 / Negro Alm 76 p. 732-33 /
Selected BAA p. 172-73 / Thorpe. Hist
p. 173-75 / Who Am 78, 1: 418 / Who
Am 80, 2: 2057
Logan (Jones), Rossie Lee, 1924-
Teacher, poet, playwright
Blk Am Wr 2: 496 / Living BAA p. 84
Loguen, Jermain W(esley), 1814-1872
Preacher, narrator of experiences
Afro-Am Ency 5: 1500-1501 il / Dict Am
Bio 33, 9: 368-69 / Dict Am Bio 61,
6-1: 368-69 / Historical N Bio p. 97-98
il / Miller. Ten p. 27-33 / Who Was H:
319 / Who Was HR: 390

Lomax, Louis E(manuel), 1922-1970
Journalist, historian
Afro-Am Ency 5: 1501 por / Con Auth
25-28: 454 / Con Auth P-2: 321 / Ency
Blk Am p. 539-40 / Negro Handbk 66
p. 407 / Selected BAA p. 174 por
Lomax, Pearl Michelle Cleage (Pearl Michelle
Cleage), 1948-
Playwright, poet
Adoff. Poet p. 529 / Blk Am Wr 2:
497-98 / Broadside Auth p. 78-79 / Cele
p. 261 / Coombs. Speak p. 240 / Selected
BAA p. 174-75 / Who Blk Am 77 p. 563
Long, Charles Houston, 1926-
Professor of religion
Living BAA p. 100 / Selected BAA p.
175-76
Long, Doughtry, Jr. (Doc Long), 1942-
Poet
Adoff. Poet p. 529 / Afro-Am Ency 5:
1501-1502 / Blk Am Wr 2: 498 / Broad-
side Auth p. 79 / Cele p. 262 / Murphy.
Today p. 62
Long, Herman H., 1912-1976
Educator, author
Ebony Success 1: 205 por / Who Am 74,
1: 1912
Long, Jefferson F(ranklin), 1836-1900
U.S. congressman, orator
Christopher. Congress p. 25-37 / Dr Am
Cong 61 p. 1232 / Negro Alm 76 p. 324 /
Woodson. Orators p. 285
Long, Naomi Cornelia. See Madgett, Naomi
Long
Long, R. Charles, 1918-
Educator
Living BAA p. 100
Long, Richard A(lexander), 1927-
Educator, lecturer, editor
Bontemps. American 74 p. 223 / Chap-
man. New p. 419-20 / Con Auth 39-40R:
337-38 / Living BAA p. 101 / Selected
BAA p. 176 / Who Blk Am 77 p. 564
Long, Worth, 1936-
Poet
Major. Poet p. 151
Lorde, Audre (Mrs. Edwin Ashley Rollins),
1934-
Poet librarian, educator
Adoff. Poet p. 529-30 / Blk Am Wr 2:
500 / Bontemps. American 74 p. 223 /
Broadside Auth p. 80 / Cele p. 262 /
Chapman. New p. 288 / Con Poets 75 p.
935-36 / Henderson. Under p. 390 /

Lorde, Audre (Mrs. Edwin Ashley Rollins) (cont'd) ...
  Hughes. New p. 122 / Jordan. Soul p. 142 / Living BAA p. 101 / Major. Poet p. 151 / Margolies. Read p. 359 / Selected BAA p. 177 / Who Blk Am 77 p. 564 / Writers Dr 76 p. 654 / Writers Dr 82 p. 586
Love, George
  Poet
  Hughes. New p. 122-23
Love, Nat (Deadwood Dick), 1854-1921
  Cowboy, autobiographer
  Afro-Am Ency 3: 732 / Blk Pioneers 1 / David. Living p. 118-29 / Ency Blk Am p. 541 por / Negro Alm 76 p. 185 il
Lovinggood, Lillie England
  Essayist
  Haley. Ency p. 270
Lovinggood, R. S., 1864-
  Essayist
  Culp. Twen p. 48-49 il
Low, W. Augustus
  Educator, author, historian
  Ency Blk Am p. xi-xii
Lowe, E. K., 1850-
  Minister, editor
  Simmons. Men p. 321-22
Lowery, Samuel R., 1830-
  Minister, lawyer, editor
  Afro-Am Ency 5: 1514-15 il / Simmons. Men p. 77-80
Lucas, James Rowser, 1931-
  Poet
  Blk Am Wr 2: 501 / Broadside Auth p. 80-81 / Coombs. Speak p. 245
Lucas, Lawrence E(dward), 1933-
  Columnist, author
  Con Auth 65-68: 372-73 / Living BAA p. 102
Lucas, W(ilmer) F(rancis, Jr.), 1927-
  Short story writer, playwright
  Con Auth 77-80: 347-48 / Selected BAA p. 177-78 por / Who Blk Am 77 p. 568
Luper, Luther George, Jr.
  Pianist, poet
  Murphy. Ebony p. 102
Lyle, K. Curtis, 1944-
  Poet, playwright
  Chapman. New p. 292
Lyn. *See* Levy, Lyn A.
Lynch, Charles Henry, 1943-
  Poet, educator
  Adoff. Poet p. 530 / Blk Am Wr 2: 502 / Cele p. 262

Lynch, John Roy, 1847-1939
  Historian, military officer, orator
  Bio Dr Am Cong 61, p. 1245 / Ency Blk Am p. 541 / Greene. Defenders p. 143-44 por / Historical N Bio p. 98 por / Negro Alm 76 p. 324-25 por / Thorpe. Hist p. 147-48 / Who Col Am 33 p. 277 / Who Col Am 37 p. 338, 341 / Who Col Am 40 p. 342 / Who Was 1: 756 / Woodson. Orators p. 273
Lynch, Lorenzo, 1932-
  Author of children's books, illustrator
  Con Auth 29-32R: 414-15 / Something ATA 7: 161
Lyons, Maritcha Remond, 1848-1929
  Educator, autobiographer
  Sterling. Speak p. 378
Lyons, Martha E.
  Poet
  Murphy. Ebony p. 103

McBain, Barbara Mahone, 1944-
  Poet
  Adoff. Poet p. 530 / Broadside Auth p. 81 / Cele p. 263
McBrown, Gertrude Parthenia
  Dramatic artist, poet, historian
  Blk Am Wr 2: 504-505 / Cromwell. Read p. 368 / Innis. Profiles p. 28-29 por / Murphy. Ebony p. 104 / Who Blk Am 77 p. 596
McCabe, Edwin P., 1890-
  Public official, civic leader, journalist
  Katz. West p. 255-61 il, por / Simmons. Men p. 760-62 il
McCall, James Edward, 1880-
  Journalist, poet
  Blk Am Wr 2: 505 / Cullen. Carol p. 33-34 / Kerlin. Poets 23 p. 342
McCannon, Dindga
  Illustrator, painter
  Afro-Am Art p. 186
McClaurin, Irma Pearl, 1952-
  Poet
  Con Auth 57-60: 384
McClellan, George, 1860-1934
  Teacher, clergyman, writer, poet
  Blk Am Wr 2: 505-506 / Kerlin. Poets 23 p. 343 / Long. Writing 1: 237 / Robinson. Poets p. 121-22 / Robinson. Prose p. 165 / Who Col Race p. 187

McCluskey, John A., 1944-
Novelist, short story writer, educator
Blk Am Wr 2: 506 / Blk Plots p. 261-62 /
Con Auth 57-60: 385 / Coombs. What p.
207 / Selected BAA p. 178
McConnell, Roland C., 1910-
Historian, educator
Ency Blk Am p. 549-50 / Who Blk Am
77 p. 599
McCord, William Maxwell, 1930-
Professor of sociology, author
Am Auth & Bks 72 p. 417 / Con Auth
NR-1: 423-24 / Who BLk Am 77 p. 599
McCoy, Fleetwood M., Jr.
Poet
Murphy. Ebony p. 105
McElroy, Colleen J(ohnson), 1935-
Poet, short story writer
Con Auth 49-52: 363 / Con Auth NR-2:
451-52
McElwee, Samuel Allen
Lawyer, legislator, orator
Simmons. Men p. 335-41 il
McEwen, A. N.
Clergyman, editor
Penn. Press p. 300
McEwen, Alice E., 1870-
Journalist
Majors. Wom p. 250 / Penn. Press p.
369-400 / Scruggs. Wom p. 249-51
McFeely, William S(hield), 1830-
Professor of history, author
Con Auth 33-36R: 555 / Who Blk Am 77
p. 605
McGaugh, Lawrence Walter, Jr., 1940-
Art teacher, poet
Adoff. Black out p. 80 / Adoff. Poet p.
531 / Selected BAA p. 178-79
McGirt, James Ephraim, 1874-1930
Poet, magazine editor/publisher
Bio Dict S Auth p. 277 / North Car
Auth p. 79-80 / Sherman. Invisible p.
193-96
Mack, L. V., 1947-
Adoff. Poet p. 530 / Blk Am Wr 2: 509
MacKay, Charles, 1814-1899
Editor, composer
Afro-Am Ency 5: 1539
McKay, Claude, 1889-1948
Poet, novelist, short story writer,
autobiographer
Adams. Auth p. 24 / Adoff. Poet p. 531 /
Afro-Am Ency 5: 1543-44 por / Am Auth
& Bks 72 p. 420 / Barksdale. Writers

McKay, Claude (cont'd) ...
p. 489 / Bio Hist p. 367-69 / Blk Plots
p. 262 / Bontemps. American 63 p. 192 /
Bontemps. American 74 p. 223 / Bontemps. Golden p. 212-13 / Broadside Auth
p. 82-83 / Brown. Caravan p. 348-49 /
Chapman. Blk V p. 371-72 / Con Am
Auth p. 462-63 / Cromwell. Read p. 368 /
Cullen. Carol p. 81-83 / Davis. Dark
p. 33-34 / Dict Lit Biog 4: 281-82 por /
Dreer. Am Lit p. 44-45 / Emanuel. Dark
p. 85-88 / Ency Blk Am p. 551 / Ford.
Insights p. 154-55 / Great Negroes 69
p. 153 il / Hayden. Kal p. 44-45 / Hughes.
Poet p. 616 / Johnson. Book p. 165-68 /
Jordan. Soul p. 142 / Kendrick. Voices
p. 237 / Kerlin. Poets 23 p. 126-27 por /
Kerlin. Poets 35 p. 126-27 por; p. 343 /
Locke. Four p. 31 / Long. Writing 2:
375-76 / Margolies. Read p. 359 / Negro
Alm 71 p. 687 / Negro Alm 76 p. 733-34 /
Poets p. 676-79 / Reader's Ency 62 p.
678 / Scally. Catholic p. 79-80 / Selected
BAA p. 178-80 / Turner. Voices p. 270 /
Wagner. Poets p. 198-204 / White. Verse
p. 203-204 / Whitlow. Lit p. 76-77 / Who
Col Am 33 p. 288 / Who Col Am 37 p.
354 / Who Col Am 40 p. 363 / Who
Was 2: 361
McKeller, Ionora.
Actress, writer
Watts Wr p. 211
Mackey, William Wellington.
Playwright, author
Dr Perf Arts 78 p. 236-37 / King. Drama
p. 325
McKissick, Floyd B., 1922-
Organization official, lawyer, author
Cur Biog Yrbk 68 p. 238-41 por / Ebony
Success 1: 212 por / Haskins. Profiles p.
75-91 / Living BAA p. 103 / O'Neill.
Speeches p. 215-16, por p. 217
McLean, Eldon George
Poet
Murphy. Ebony p. 106
McLean, William Alfred, Jr.
Poet
Adoff. Blk out p. 80
McLemore, William P., 1931-
Educator, poet
Living BAA p. 103
McMillan, Herman L.
Poet
Afro-Am Ency 5: 1549 por

Mays, Benjamin Elijah, 1895-
  Theologian, educator, scholar
    Afro-Am Ency 6: 1618-19 por / Boul-
    ware. Oratory p. 184 / Con Auth 45-48:
    359 / Ebony Success 1: 218 por / Ency
    Blk Am p. 548 / Great Negroes 69 p.
    145 il / Living BAA p. 108-109 /
    Negro Handbk 66 p. 408 / Selected BAA
    p. 191-92 por / Thorpe. Hist p. 163-64 /
    Who Blk Am 77 p. 593 / Who Col Am 40
    p. 367, por p. [369] / Young. Since
    1940 p. 34-36, 43-45
Mays, James A(rthur)
  Cardiologist, novelist, song writer
    Con Auth 57-60R: 382 / Selected BAA
    p. 192 / Who Blk Am 77 p. 593
Mays, William Howard, Jr. (Willie Mays),
1931-
  Professional baseball player, autobiographer
    Historical N Bio p. 227 / King. Famous
    p. 107-113 / Richardson. Great 56 p. 302-
    316 il / Richardson. Great 76 p. 309-317
    por / Webster Am Biog p. 705
Mbende. *See* Smith, Milton
Meaddough, R. J., III, 1935-
  Short story writer
    Adoff. Brothers p. 235 / Hughes. Best
    p. 504
Mebane, Mary Elizabeth, 1933-
  Playwright, autobiographer
    Blk Am Wr 2: 539 / Con Auth 73-76:
    424 / Dr Am Schol 74, 2: 539 / Shuman.
    Galaxy p. 151
Menard, John Willis, 1838-1893
  Newspaper editor, politician, poet
    Afro-Am Ency 6: 1627-28 il / Blk Am
    Wr 2: 541 / Nistorical N Bio p. 99-100 /
    Sherman. Invisible p. 97-100 / Woodson.
    Orators p. 263-64
Menchan, W. McKinley, 1898-
  Educator
    Living BAA p. 109
Menken, Adah, 1835?-1868
  Poet
    Robinson. Poet p. 236-37
Meredith, James Howard, 1933-
  Civil rights advocate, autobiographer,
  lecturer
    Afro-Am Ency 6: 1630-31 il / David.
    Defiance p. 170-83 / Ency Blk Am p.
    553 / Flynn. Archive p. 159-67 / Met-
    calf. Profiles p. 219-54 / Webster Am
    Biog p. 715

Meriwether, Louise M.
  Short story writer, children's author,
  novelist
    Afro-Am Novel p. 125 / Blk Am Wr 2:
    542 / Blk Plots p. 268 / Con Auth 77-80:
    373 / Ebony Success 1: 220 por / King.
    Story p. 173 / Living BAA p. 110 /
    Who Blk Am 77 p. 623
Merriweather, Angela, 1951-
  Writer of short stories
    Shuman. Galaxy p. 158
Metcalfe, Ralph H., 1910-
  Athlete, writer of autobiographical account
    Scally. Catholic p. 82-84
Meyer, June. *See* Jordan, June
Micheaux, Oscar, 1884-1951
  Producer, director, novelist, publisher
    Am Auth & Bks 72 p. 428 / Blk Am Wr
    2: 543-44 / Dr Perf Arts 78 p. 251 /
    Selected BAA p. 193 / Who Col Am 29 p.
    262 / Who Col Am 33 p. 302 / Who Col
    Am 37 p. 372 / Who Col Am 40
    p. 371 / Who Col Am 42 p. 365
Millender, Dharathula H., 1920-
  Librarian, children's writer, educator
    Con Auth 19-20: 277-78 / Con Auth 21-
    24R: 510 / Selected BAA p. 193-94 /
    Who Blk Am 77 p. 626
Miller, Adam David, 1922-
  Poet, educator, critic, editor, anthologist
    Adoff. Poet p. 531 / Blk Am Wr 2:
    544-45 / Chapman. New p. 300-301 /
    Living BAA p. 110 / Miller. Dices p.
    141 / Selected BAA p. 194
Miller, Clifford L.
  Minister, columnist, poet
    Murphy. Ebony p. 108
Miller, Don, 1923-
  Painter, illustrator
    Afro-Am Art p. 198 / Something ATA
    15: 194-96 por, il
Miller, Flournoy E., 1887-1971
  Actor, composer, writer
    Dr Perf Arts 78 p. 252
Miller, Kelly, 1863-1939
  Historian, poet, short story writer
    Blk Am Wr 2: 545-46 / Brown. Caravan
    p. 884 / Cromwell. Read p. 368-69 /
    Davis. Cav p. 192 / Dreer. Am Lit
    p. 158 / Ency Am Biog p. 761-62 / Ford.
    Insights p. 17-18 / Gayle. Bond p. 150 /
    Kerlin. Poets 23 p. 277 / Kerlin. Poets
    35 p. 343 / Long. Writing 1: 243 /
    Selected BAA p. 194 por / Sterling.
    Speak p. 152 / Who Col Race p. 192-93

Miller, Larry A. (Sultani Katibu), 1949-
Poet, editor
Alhamisi. Arts p. 116 / Blk Am Wr 2:
451, por p. 452
Miller, Loren, 1903-
Jurist, author
Selected BAA p. 195
Miller, May (Mrs. John Sullivan)
Poet, playwright, teacher
Blk Am Wr 2: 546-47 / Blk Plots p.
268 / Davis. Dav p. 359 / Selected BAA
p. 195-96
Miller, Randolph
Newspaper publisher
Afro-Am Ency 6: 1647-48
Millican, Arthenia Bates (Arthenia Jackson
Bates), 1920-
Educator, short story writer, novelist
Blk Am Wr 1: 62 / Con Auth 57-60:
46-47 / Living BAA p. 110 / Who Blk
Am 77 p. 631
Milner, Ronald, 1938-
Playwright
Alhamisi. Arts p. 52 / Auth News 1:
348-50 por / Blk Plots p. 268 / Con
Auth 73-76: 438 / Con Drama 73 p. 546 /
Con Drama 77 p. 558 / Dr Perf Arts
78 p. 253-54 / Hughes. Best p. 504 /
King. Drama p. 89 / King. Story p. 105 /
Robinson. Nommo p. 480 / Selected
BAA p. 196 / Writers Dr 80 p. 863
Mims, Harley, 1925-
Poet
Watts Wr p. 119
Mitchell, Arthur W., 1883-
Lawyer, congressman, orator
Boulware. Oratory p. 151-53 / Who Col
Am 42 p. 368
Mitchell, Henry Heywood, 1919-
Clergyman, educator, author
Bio Dr Min 75 p. 356-57 / Who Blk Am
77 p. 634
Mitchell, John, Jr., 1863-
Newspaper editor/publisher, teacher
Haley. Ency p. 206-207 / Penn. Press
p. 183-87 / Who Col Am 29 p. 269
Mitchell, Leroy E., Jr.
Short story writer
Blk Am Wr 2: 549
Mitchell, Loften, 1919-
Playwright, novelist, critic
Adoff. Blk on p. 233 / Afro-Am Ency
6: 1672-73 / Blk Am Wr 2: 549 /
Childress. Scenes p. 150-51 / Con Auth

Mitchell, Loften (cont'd) ...
81-84: 393-94 / Con Drama 73 p.
548-50 / Con Drama 77 p. 563-65 /
Dr Perf Arts 78 p. 256-57 / Ency
Blk Am p. 564 / King. Drama p. 575 /
Living BAA p. 111 / Negro Alm 71 p.
688 por / Negro Alm 76 p. 734 por /
Notable Names p. 992 / Selected BAA
p. 196-97 / Who Am 80, 2: 2337 /
Writers Dr 80 p. 868 / Writers Dr 82
p. 662
Mixon, W. H., 1859-
Clergyman, editor
Penn. Press p. 201-202 por
Mkalimoto, Ernie, 1942-
Poet
Major. Poet p. 151
Molette, Barbara Jean, 1940-
Playwright
Blk Am Wr 2: 551 / Nat Play Dr p.
217 por / Selected BAA p. 197-98 /
Who Blk Am 77 p. 637
Molette, Carlton W., II, 1939-
Playwright
Blk Am Wr 2: 551-52 / Selected BAA
p. 198-99 / Who Blk Am 77 p. 637-38
Monroe, Reginald, 1938-
Living BAA p. 111
Moody, Anne (Mrs. Austin Straus), 1940-
Autobiographer
Alexander. Young p. 84-102 / David.
Living p. 249-61 / David. Roots p. 68
Moore, Alice Ruth. *See* Dunbar-Nelson, Alice
Ruth Moore
Moore, Carman Leroy, 1936-
Composer, music critic, biographer
Abdul. Enter p. 94-101 / AmSCAP 80 p.
354 / Con Auth 61-64: 380 / Dr Perf
Arts 78 p. 258-59 / Living BAA p.
112 / Who Blk Am 77 p. 640
Moore, David (Amus Mor)
Teacher of art, poet
King. Spirits p. 248
Moore, Richard B.
Lecturer, historian
Afro-Am Ency 6: 1686
Moore, William H. A.
Poet
Johnson. Book p. 85
Mor, Amus. *See* Moore, David
Moreland, Charles King, Jr., 1945-
Poet, editor
Shuman. Galaxy p. 367
Moreland, Wayne, 1948-
Magazine editor, writer, poet
Adoff. Poet p. 531

Morgan, J. H., 1843-
   Minister
      Culp. Twen p. 382-83 il
Morris, Charles Stachell, II, 1899-
   Educator, clergyman, lecturer, orator
      Boulware. Oratory p. 132-33
Morris, Elias C., 1855-1922
   Minister, editor
      Afro-Am Ency 6: 1692-93 / Brawley.
      Builders p. 201-202 / Culp. Twen p.
      258-59 il
Morris, John T.
   Editor
      Penn. Press p. 295-98
Morrison, Aloysius O.
      Scally. Catholic p. 84-85
Morrison, C(harles) T(heodore), 1936
      Living BAA p. 112
Morrison, Toni (Choe Anthony Wofford),
1931-
   Editor, novelist, essayist
      Afro-Am Novel p. 127 / Blk Am Wr 2:
      555-56 / Blk Plots p. 272-73 / Con Auth
      29-32: 473 / Dict Lit Biog 6: 243-47
      por / Ency Blk Am p. 569 / Living
      BAA p. 112-13 / Selected BAA p. 199 por
Morrison, William Lorenzo
   Poet
      Murphy. Ebony p. 109
Morrow, E(verett) Frederic, 1909-
   Lawyer, writer on Negroes in government,
   diarist
      Afro-Am Ency 6: 1695-96 por / Ebony
      Success 1: 229 por / Living BAA p.
      113 / Negro Alm 71 p. 272 / Negro Alm
      76 p. 353, phot p. 354 / Selected BAA
      p. 199-200 por / Who Blk Am 77 p. 651
Morse, Evangeline F., 1914-
      Living BAA p. 113
Morse, George Chester, 1904-
   Poet, essayist
      Cuney. Linc p. 70
Morton, Ferdinand (Jelly Roll), 1885-1941
   Pianist, narrator, autobiographer
      Afro-Am Ency 6: 1697-98 / Negro Alm
      71 p. 810, por p. 811 / Negro Alm 76
      p. 886 / Webster Am Biog p. 743-44
Moseley, Matilda
   Autobiographer
      Jenness. Twelve p. 20-34
Moses, Gilbert, 1942-
   Film director, journalist, playwright
      Blk Am Wr 2: 556 por / Dr Perf Arts
      78, p. 266 / Notable Names p. 1004 /
      Who Theatre 77 p. 957-58

Moses, Louise J.
   Librarian, essayist
      Josey. Blk Librn p. 137-41 / Who Blk
      Am 77 p. 653
Mosley, Joseph M., Jr., 1935-
   Major. Poet p. 152
Motley, Willard, 1912-1965
   Novelist
      Afro-Am Ency 6: 1701-1702 / Afro-Am
      Novel p. 130 / Am Auth & Bks 72
      p. 445 / Am Novel p. 314 por / Blk
      Am Wr 2: 557-58 / Blk Plots p. 273 /
      Hughes. Best p. 504 / Negro Alm 71
      p. 688-89 / Negro Alm 76 p. 735 /
      Reader's Ency 62 p. 768-69 / Selected
      BAA p. 200-201 / Twen CA Sup p.
      693-94 por
Moton, Cora Ball
   Poet
      Bontemps. Golden p. 213-14
Moton, Robert Russa, 1867-1940
   Educator, autobiographer
      Afro-Am Ency 6: 1702 por / Am Auth &
      Bks 72 p. 445 / Brawley. Builders p.
      212-18 / Brawley. Caravan p. 746 / Ency
      Blk Am p. 582 / Hammond. Van p. 16-34
      por / Ovington. Portraits p. 64-77 /
      Reader's Ency 62 p. 769 / Selected
      BAA p. 201 por / Who Col Am 29
      p. 275 por / Who Col Am 33 p. 312-13
      por / Who Col Am 40 p. 383-84 por /
      Who Col Race p. 202 / Woodson.
      Orators p. 573
El Muhajir. *See* Jackmon, Marvin X
Mulet, Paul. *See* Rivers, Louis
Muller-Thyn, Thomas, 1948-
   Writer of short stories
      Coombs. What p. 207-208
Mumford, Samuel T., 1906-
      Living BAA p. 114
Mungin, Horace, 1941-
   Poet
      Adoff. Blk out p. 80 / Blk Am Wr 2:
      560 / Robinson. Nommo p. 481
Murphy (Campbell), Beatrice, 1908-
   Editor, poet, columnist
      Afro-Am Ency 6: 1706 / Blk Am Wr 2:
      560-61 / Bontemps. Golden p. 214 /
      Broadside Auth p. 86-87 / Con Auth
      53-56: 429 / Hughes. Poet p. 617-18 /
      Living BAA p. 114 / Murphy. N. Voices
      p. 113 / Scally. Catholic p. 85-86 /
      Selected BAA p. 203 / Who Blk Am
      77 p. 657

Murray, Albert L., 1916-
Novelist, short story writer, critic
Afro-Am Ency 6: 1708 / Afro-Am Novel
p. 134 / Blk Am Wr 2: 561-62 por /
Blk Plots p. 273 / Con Auth 49-52: 393 /
Emanuel. Dark p. 374-75 / Hill. Anger
p. 216 / Living BAA p. 115 / Margolies.
Read p. 360 / Selected BAA p. 204 por /
Who Blk Am 77 p. 658 / Writers Dr
80 p. 897

Murray, James Patrick, 1946-
Journalist, drama critic, editor
Con Auth 45-52: 393 / Dr Perf Arts
78 p. 268 / Living BAA p. 115-16 /
Who Am 78, 2: 2350 / Who Blk Am 77
p. 659

Murray, Pauli, 1910-
Educator, lawyer, writer, poet, priest
Adoff. Poet p. 531 / Afro-Am Ency 6:
1710 / Am Women Wr 3: 241-43 /
Bontemps. American 63 p. 192 / Bon-
temps. American 74 p. 224 / Diamonstein.
Open p. 289-94 / Ebony Success 1:
233 por / Ency Blk Am p. 584 / Hughes.
Poet p. 618 / Selected BAA p. 205 /
Who Blk Am 77 p. 659

Murray, Walter I., 1910-
Educator, writer on education of
disadvantaged
Living BAA p. 116-17

Murrell, William
Journalist
Penn. Press p. 138-40

Murry, Philip H., 1842-
Phrenologist, editor, educator
Afro-Am Ency 6: 1710-11 / Simmons.
Men p. 43-46

Muse, Clarence E., 1889-
Actor, playwright, director
Dr Perf Arts 78 p. 269 / Negro Alm
76 p. 836

Myers, George A., 1895-1930
Businessman, writer of published letters
Davis. Mem p. 30-31

Myers, Walter D(ean), 1937-
Editor, writer of short stories and books
for children and young people, lecturer,
essayist
Blk Am Wr 2: 563 / Blk Plots p. 273 /
Con Auth 33-36: 592-93 / Coombs. What
p. 208 / Living BAA p. 117 / Selected
BAA p. 205-206

Myles, Glenn, 1933-
Illustrator, poet
Afro-Am Art p. 209 / Blk Am Wr 2:
564 / Miller. Dices p. 142

Nash, Theodore Edward Delafayette, 1881-
Novelist
Who Col Am 42 p. 383

Nazel, Joseph, Jr., 1944-
Novelist, short story writer
Blk Am Wr 2: 564

Neal, Gaston, 1934-
Poet
Jones. Fire p. 666

Neal, Larry (Lawrence P. Neal), 1937-
Poet, editor, essayist
Alhamisi. Arts p. 124 / Bontemps.
American 74 p. 224 / Broadside Auth
p. 88 / Chapman. New p. 305 / Con
Poets 75 p. 1109 / Davis. Cav p. 797 /
Jones. Fire p. 666 / Jordan. Soul p.
142 / King. Spirits p. 248 / Living
BAA p. 117 / Major. Poet p. 152 /
Selected BAA p. 206 / Who Blk Am 77
p. 664 / Writers Dr 76 p. 776 / Writers
Dr 80 p. 906 / Writers Dr 82 p. 689

Nell, William Cooper, 1816-1874
Historian, journalist
Am Auth & Bks 72 p. 455 / Blk Plots
p. 275 / Chittenden. Profiles p. 3-18 /
Ency Blk Am p. 636 / Historical N Bio
p. 104 / Negro Alm 71 p. 689 / Negro
Alm 76 p. 735 / Reader's Ency 62 p.
788 / Selected BAA p. 207 / Sterling.
Speak p. 378-79 / Thorpe. Hist p. 36-37

Nelson, Alice Ruth Moore. *See* Dunbar-
Nelson, Alice Ruth Moore

Nelson, David
Poet
King. Spirits p. 248

Nelson, Richard
Editor
Penn. Press p. 274-78

Newsome, (Mary) Effie Lee, 1885-1923
Librarian, children's poet
Adoff. Poet p. 532 / Blk Am Wr 2:
566 / Bontemps. American 63 p. 192 /
Bontemps. American 74 p. 224 /
Bontemps. Golden p. 214-15 / Cullen.
Carol p. 55 / Hughes. Poet p. 618 /
Rollins. Famous p. 56-59 / Selected
BAA p. 207-208 / Who Col Am 33 p.
318 / Who Col Am 37 p. 390 / Who
Col Am 40 p. 389

Newton, Huey Percy, 1942-
Civil rights activist, author
Afro-Am Ency 7: 1899-1900 phot / Bio
Hist p. 376-79 / Cur Biog Yrbk 73 p.
307-310 por / Haskins. Profiles p. 161-84 /
Negro Alm 71 p. 240-41 / Negro Alm

Olumbo. *See* Cunningham, James

O'Meally, Bob
  Poet
    Cele p. 264

O'Neal, Frederick (Douglass), 1905-
  Actor, director, author
    Dr Perf Arts 78 p. 279 / Lincoln Lib
    Arts 2: 690

O'Neal, Regina Louise Solomon
    Broadside Auth p. 91-92 / Who Blk Am
    77 p. 680

Orford, Ray B., 1935-
  Writer
    Broadside Auth p. 92

O'Rourke, Magdalene
  Librarian, essayist
    Josey. Blk Librn p. 247-52

Ottley, Roi Vincent, 1906-1960
  Novelist, journalist, editor, biographer
    Blk Plots p. 278 / Cur Biog Yrbk 44
    p. 566-67

Overby, Beatris Fitzgerald Hammond
  Poet
    Murphy. N Voices p. 118-19

Owen, Chandler, 1909-1967
  Editor, labor leader
    Blk Plots p. 278

Owens, Albert Franklin
  Journalist
    Afro-Am Ency 7: 1962-63

Owens, Daniel W(alter), 1948-
  Playwright, poet
    Afro-Am Ency 7: 1963 / Blk Am Wr 2:
    574-75 / Murphy. Today p. 81 / Nat
    Play Dr p. 233 por

Owens, Jesse, 1913-
  Athlete, autobiographer
    Afro-Am Ency 7: 1966 / David. Living
    p. 130-42 / Selected BAA p. 211-12 por

Owens, John Henry
  Minister, poet
    Murphy. Ebony p. 111

Owens, Maude Irwin, 1900-
  Illustrator, painter
    Afro-Am Art p. 214

Oyamo. *See* Gordon, Charles Franklin

Page, Daphne Diane
  Poet
    Henderson. Under p. 391

Page, Iman Edward, 1853-1935
  Educator, orator
    Ency Blk Am p. 659 / Katz. West p.
    253 por / Simmons. Men p. 315-20 il /
    Who Col Race 1: 209-210

Paige, Myles Anderson
    Scally. Catholic p. 86-87

Painter, Nell Irvin, 1942-
  Educator, historian, biographer
    Con Auth 65-68: 449

Palmer, Vernon U., 1930-
  Poet
    Blk Am Wr 2: 576

Parker, Gladys Marie
  Poet, short story writer, columnist
    Murphy. Ebony p. 112

Parker, Pat(ricia), 1944-
  Poet, short story writer
    Con Auth 57-60: 441 / Miller. Dices
    p. 141

Parks, David, 1944-
  Author of published diary
    Alexander. Young p. 122-37 por / Con
    Auth 25-28R: 538 / David. Soldier p.
    203-214

Parks, Gordon (Alexander Buchanan), 1912-
  Photographer, movie director, novelist, poet
  illustrator, autobiographer
    Adoff. Blk on p. 233-34 / Afro-Am Art
    p. 216 / Auth News 2: 215 por / Bio
    Hist p. 381-84 / Blk Am Wr 2: 577 /
    Blk Lit HS p. 161-62 / Blk Plots p.
    278-79 / Con Auth 41-44R: 533-34 /
    Cur Biog Yrbk 68 p. 300-332 por /
    David. Growing p. 177-85 / Ebony
    Success 1: 240 por / Ebony Success 2:
    178-83 il / Ency Blk Am p. 664 por /
    Great Negroes 69 p. 205 il / Living
    BAA p. 121-22 / Negro Alm 71 p. 867 /
    Negro Alm 76 p. 836-37 por / Selected
    BAA p. 212-13 / Something ATA 8: 148
    por / Who Am 78, 2: 2502 / Who Blk
    Am 77 p. 691 / Writers Dr 80 p. 954 /
    Writers Dr 82 p. 725

Parris, Guichard, 1903-
  Linguist, educator, editor, translator
    Scally. Catholic p. 88-89

Parrish, Dorothy C.
  Poet
    Afro-Am Ency 7: 1983

Partee, William E., 1860-
  Essayist
    Culp. Twen p. 308-309 il

Paschal, Andrew G., 1907-
  Lecturer, cousnelor, essayist
    Living BAA p. 122

Patterson, Charles, 1914-
  Poet, playwright
    Jones. Fire p. 666 / Major. Poet p. 152

penny, rob. *See* Kilonfe, Oba
Perdue, Robert Eugene, 1940-
Historian
Ency Blk Am p. 668-69 / Who Blk Am
77 p. 703
Perkins, A(rchie) E(benezer), 1879-
Biographer
Who Col Am 33 p. 333 / Who Col Am
37 p. 407 / Who Col Am 40 p. 407 /
Who Col Am 42 p. 403 / Who Col Race
p. 100-101
Perry, Christopher J., 1854-1921
Journalist, editor
Penn. Press p. 145-48
Perry, Julianne D., 1952-
Poet
Adoff. Poet p. 532 / Blk Am Wr 2:
588 / Broadside Auth p. 94
Perry, Margaret, 1933-
Librarian, short story writer, biographer
Bio Dr Librns 70 p. 857 / Blk Am Wr 2:
588 / Con Auth 89-92: 400 / Dr Am
Schol 74, 2: 488 / Dr Am Schol 78,
2: 530 / Handbk Librns p. 164 / Josey.
What p. 306 / Living BAA p. 123 / Who
Blk Am 77 p. 706
Perry, Richard H., 1944-
Novelist, short story writer, teacher
Blk Am Wr 2: 588 / Selected BAA p.
215
Perry, Robert N., Jr.
Songwriter, poet
Murphy. Ebony p. 114
Perry, Rufus L(ewis), 1872-
Minister, ethnologist, editor
Afro-Am Ency 7: 2009-2010 il / Simmons.
Men p. 425-29 / Who Col Race p. 215
Peters, Eugene Raymond, 1933-
Editor, poet, playwright, writer of tele-
vision script, publisher
Blk Am Wr 2: 585-87 / Ebony Success
1: 245 por / Selected BAA p. 215-16 /
Who Blk Am 77 p. 707 / Young, M. Lead
p. 33-36 por
Peterson, Butler Harrison
Essayist
Culp. Twen p. 236-37 il
Peterson, Josephine, 1950-
Poet
Blk Am Wr 2: 589
Peterson, Louis S., 1922-
Playwright, actor
Blk Am Wr 2: 589 / Dr Perf Arts
78 p. 289 / Ford. Insights p. 247 /
Notable Names p. 1043

Petry, Ann (Lane), 1911-
Novelist, short story writer, children's author
Afro-Am Ency 7: 2017, por p. 2018 /
Am Auth & Bks 72 p. 498 / Am Women
Wr 3: 377-79 Auth Bk YP 64 p. 196 /
Auth Bk YP 71 p. 408 / Barksdale.
Writers p. 762-63 / Blk Am Wr 2:
589-90 / Blk Plots p. 280 / Bone. Novel
p. 180-81 / Chapman. Blk V p. 161 /
Con Auth NR-4: 478-80 / Con Novel 76
p. 1082 / Davis. Cav p. 500 / Davis.
Dark p. 193 / Historical N Bio p.
235-36 por / Int Auth & Wr 77 p. 804 /
Living BAA p. 124 / Negro Alm 71
p. 689 / Negro Alm 76 p. 736 / Noble.
Beautiful p. 175-77 / Richardson. Great
56 p. 150-62 il / Richardson. Great 76
p. 150-57 il / Selected BAA p. 216-17
por / Something ATA 5: 148 por / Third
Bk p. 223-24 por / Twen CA Sup 55
p. 776 por / Twen CCW p. 993-94 /
Whitlow. Lit p. 117 / Who Blk Am 77
p. 709 / Writers Dr 80 p. 974
Pettiford, William Reuben, 1849-1914
Minister, essayist
Culp. Twen p. 468-69 / Simmons. Men
p. 305-309 il
Petty, Sarah Dudley (Mrs. Charles Calvin
Petty)
Organization leader, essayist
Culp. Twen p. 182-83 il / Dannett.
Profiles 1: 302-303 il
Pfister, Arthur Joseph, 1949-
Poet, novelist, short story writer
Blk Am Wr 2: 591 / Broadside Auth
p. 94-95 / Con Am Auth 45-48: 438 /
Coombs. Speak p. 246 / King. Spirits
p. 248-49
Pharr, Robert Deanne, 1916-
Novelist, short story writer
Afro-Am Novel p. 136 / Blk Am Wr 2:
592 / Chapman. New p. 60 / Con Drama
49-52: 426 / Living BAA p. 125 / Selected
BAA p. 217 / Southern Wr p. 349-50 /
Whitlow. Lit p. 165
Phelps, Mary Rice
Teacher, essayist
Haley. Ency p. 112-14 por
Phillips, Billie Ann McKindra, 1925-
Teacher, writer on early childhood education
Living BAA p. 125 / Selected BAA p.
217-18
Phillips, Charles Henry, 1858-
Clergyman, writer of church history,
autobiographer

Phillips, Charles Henry (cont'd) ...
Who Col Am 33 p. 337 / Who Col Am
37 p. 412 / Who Col Am 40 p. 412 /
Who Col Am 42 p. 408
Phillips, Frank Lamont, 1953-
Poet
Blk Am Wr 2: 592-93 / Bontemps.
American 74 p. 225 / Cele p. 264
Phinazee, Annette Lewis (Hoage)
Library school dean, writer on librarianship
Bio Dr Librns 70 p. 865 / Who Blk Am
77 p. 712
Pickens, William, 1881-1954
Educator, autobiographer
Afro-Am Ency 7: 2027 / Barton. Witness
p. 24-27 / Blk Am Wr 2: 593-94 / Brown.
Caravan p. 753 / Cromwell. Read p. 369 /
David. Defiance p. 55-61 / Fauset. Free-
dom p. 190 / Historical N Bio p. 236-37
il / Long. Writing 1: 257 / Reader's Ency
62 p. 879 / Selected BAA p. 218 / Who
Col Am 29 p. 293 / Who Col Am 33 p.
337 / Who Col Am 37 p. 415, por p. 417 /
Who Col Am 40 p. 415 / Who Col Am 42
p. 411 / Who Col Am 50 p. 416 / Who
Was 3: 686-87 / Woodson. Orators p. 531
Pinkett, Harold T(homas), 1914-
Historian, archivist
Con Auth 29-32R: 528-29 / Ency Blk Am
p. 677 / Who Blk Am 77 p. 716 / Writers
Dr 80 p. 982
Pinkney, Alphonso, 1929-
Professor of sociology, author
Con Auth 25-28R: 558 / Living BAA
p. 125-26
Pinkney, Jerry, 1939-
Illustrator, designer
Afro-Am Art p. 222 / Illus Ch Bks 57
p. 158
Pinson, Ira David, 1922-
Author, poet
Living BAA p. 126
Pitcher, Oliver, 1924-
Poet, playwright, actor
Adoff. Poet p. 532 / Afro-Am Ency
7: 2032 / Bontemps. American 63 p. 193 /
Bontemps. American 74 p. 225 / Davis.
Cav p. 773 / Hughes. New p. 124 / King.
Drama p. 243 / Selected BAA p. 218
Pittman, Sample Noel, 1927-
Educator
Living BAA p. 126-27 / Who Blk Am 77
p.•717-18
Pitts, Herbert Lee, 1949-
Poet
Coombs. Speak p. 246-47

Pitts, Lucia Mae
Playwright, poet
Murphy. Ebony p. 117 / Murphy. N
Voices p. 128
Plato, Ann
Poet
Blk Am Wr 2: 596-97 / Loewenberg.
Wom p. 174-80 / Robinson. Poets p.
113-14 / Selected BAA p. 219
Plumpp, Sterling D(ominic), 1940-
Editor, teacher
Adoff. Poet p. 533 / Blk Am Wr 2:
596 / Broadside Auth p. 95 / Cele p.
265 / Con Auth 45-48: 446 / Living
BAA p. 127 / Selected BAA p. 219 /
Who Blk Am 77 p. 720
Poinsett, Alex(ander) C., 1926-
Editor, journalist, author
Ebony Success 1: 250 por / Living BAA
p. 127 / Selected BAA 219-20 / Who Blk
Am 77 p. 720
Poitier, Sidney, 1924-
Actor, director, autobiographer
Afro-Am Ency 7: 2047-49 por / Bio Hist
p. 386-88 / Dr Perf Arts 78 p. 292-93 /
Ebony Success 2: 192-97 il / Rollins.
Enter p. 81-86, por p. 12 / Who Am 80,
2: 2654 / Who Blk Am 77 p. 720-21 /
Who Theatre 77 p. 1026
Polite, Allen
Poet
Hughes. New p. 124
Polite, Carlene Hatcher, 1932-
Novelist, dancer, teacher
Afro-Am Novel p. 138 / Au Speaks p.
123-26 / Con Auth 23-24R: 686 / Living
BAA p. 127-28 / Robinson. Nommo p.
482 / Selected BAA p. 220-21 por
Poole, Tom, 1938-
Poet
Adoff. Blk out p. 81 / Blk Am Wr 2:
597 / Major. Poet p. 152
Popel, Esther A. W.
Poet, essayist
Cromwell. Read p. 369
Porter, Dorothy B(urnett), 1905-
Librarian, curator, black studies bibliog-
rapher, writer on black librarianship
Blk Am Wr 2: 598 / Blk Plots p. 282 /
Ebony Success 1: 251 por / Ency Blk Am
p. 696-97 / Living BAA p. 128 / Selected
BAA p. 221 / Who Blk Am 77 p. 723
Porter, George Washington, 1849-
Autobiographer, poet
Blk Am Wr 2: 598

Porter, Timothy L., 1946-
Poet
Blk Am Wr 2: 599 / Coombs. Speak
p. 247
Poston, Ted R., 1906-1974
Editor, short story writer, essayist,
autobiographer
Adoff. Blk on p. 234 / Blk Am Wr 2:
599 / Brown. Caravan p. 96 / David.
Defiance p. 129-30 / Hughes. Best p.
505
Potter, R. K. *See* Yates, Josephine Silone
Poussaint, Alvin Francis, 1934-
Psychiatrist, author, essayist
Cur Biog Yrbk 73 p. 333-35 / Ebony
Success 1: 253 por / Ebony Success 2:
202-205 il / Living BAA p. 129 /
Metcalf. Up p. 234-60 / Negro Alm 76
p. 1033 / Who Blk Am 77 p. 725
Powe, Blossom, 1929-
Poet, short story writer
Watts Wr p. [201]
Powell, Adam Clayton, 1865-1953
Clergyman, novelist, autobiographer
Afro-Am Ency 7: 2109-2110 il / Am
Auth & Bks 72 p. 511 / Blk Am Wr 2:
600 / Ency Blk Am p. 702-703 por /
Great Negroes 69 p. 105 / Historical N
Bio p. 237-38 por Richardson. Great
56 p. 200-210 il / Who Col Am 29 p.
295 / Who Col Am 33 p. 343 por / Who
Col Am 37 p. 420 / Who Col Am 40
p. 420 / Who Col Am 42 p. 419 por /
Who Col Am 50 p. 422-23 por / Who
Col Race p. 222 / Young, M. Lead p.
102-104 por
Powell, Adam Clayton, Jr., 1908-1972
Congressman, clergyman, orator, author
Afro-Am Ency 7: 2106-2107 il / Am
Auth & Bks 72 p. 512 / Bio Hist p.
388-91 / Blk Lit HS p. 162 / Boulware.
Oratory p. 169 / Christopher. Congress
p. 194-208 / Con Auth 33-36R: 644 /
Ency Am Biog p. 878-79 / Haskins.
Profiles p. 31-60 / Historical N Bio
p. 238-39 por / Negro Handbk 66 p.
411 / O'Neill. Speeches p. 192-93 /
Selected BAA p. 222 por / Webster Am
Biog p. 841-42 / Young. Since 1940 p.
55-56, 63-65
Powell, Gloria J., 1936-
Psychiatrist, author
Who Blk Am 77 p. 726 / Williams. Wom
p. 180

Powell, William I.
Poet
Murphy. Ebony p. 122
Powell, William J.
U.S. Army officer, aviator, autobiographer
Barton. Witness p. 49-51
Prescott, Patrick B., Jr., 1890-
Jurist, orator, short story writer
Boulware. Oratory p. 162-65
Preston, Eugene Antony (Tony Preston), 1952-
Playwright
Who Blk Am 77 p. 728
Prestwidge, Kathleen J., 1927-
Educator, author
Living BAA p. 129
Prettyman, Quandra. *See* Stadler, Quandra
Prettyman
Prevost, Maurice Ernest, 1907-
Poet
Scally. Catholic p. 92
Price, Joseph C., 1854-1893
Educator, minister, orator
Brawley. Builders p. 205-206 / Paths
p. 179 por / Simmons. Men p. 528-31 il /
Woodson. Orators p. 488
Pride, Armistead S., 1906-
Professor of journalism, author
Who Blk Am 77 p. 730 / Who Col
Am 50 p. 424-25 por
Priestley, Alma Mary
Medical social worker, poet, writer of short
stories
Scally. Catholic p. 94
Priestley, Eric John, 1943-
Poet, short story writer, novelist
Blk Am Wr 2: 601 / Coombs. Speak
p. 247 / Coombs. What p. 208-209
Prince, Lucy Terry. *See* Terry (Prince), Lucy
Pritchard, Norman Henry, II, 1939-
Poet, short story writer
Adoff. Poet p. 533 / Blk Am Wr 2:
602 / Blk Plots p. 282-83 / Chapman.
New p. 319-20 / Living BAA p. 129-30 /
Major. Poet p. 153 / Selected BAA p.
222-23
Proctor, Henry Hugh, 1868-1933
Minister, autobiographer
Culp. Twen p. 316-17 il / Jenness.
Twelve p. 53-68 / Who Col Am 27 p.
163 / Who Col Am 33 p. 347-48 /
Who Col Race p. 224 / Who Was 1:
998
Proctor, Samuel Dewitt, 1921-
Educator, clergyman, author
Bio Dr Min 75 p. 415-16 / Ebony
Success 1: 355 por / Living BAA p.

Proctor, Samuel Dewitt (cont'd) ...
130 / Negro Handbk 66 p. 411 / Who
Blk Am 77 p. 731-32
Puckett, Garland Henderson, 1917-
Attorney, novelist
Who Blk Am 77 p. 733
Pugh, Charles, 1948-
Novelist, storyteller, historian
Con Auth 81-84: 455
Pulliam, Helen, 1945-
Poet
Broadside Auth p. 96
Purcell, Isaac Lawrence, 1857-
Essayist
Culp. Twen p. 104-105 il
Purvis, Robert, 1810-1898
Abolitionsit, writer
Afro-Am Ency 7: 2128 il / Barksdale.
Writers p. 140-42 / Historical N Bio
p. 110 / Nat Cyclo 1: 413 il / Sterling.
Speak p. 379, il p. 265
Putnam, Georgiana Frances, 1839-1914
Teacher, writer
Brown. Homespun p. 135-40 / Dannett.
Profiles 1: 111

Quarles, Benjamin A(rthur), 1904-
Historian, educator
Afro-Am Ency 7: 2133-34 il / Con Auth
2-R: 154-55 / Dr Am Schol 78, 1: 550 /
Ebony Success 1: 256 por / Ency Blk Am
p. 710 por / Living BAA p. 130-31 /
Selected BAA p. 223-24 / Something ATA
12: 166 por / Thorpe. Hist p. 179-80 /
Who Am 78, 2: 2637 / Who Blk Am 77
p. 735
Quigless, Helen Gordon, 1944-
Poet
Afro-Am Ency 7: 2136 / Blk Am Wr 2:
605 / Broadside Auth p. 96 / Living
BAA p. 131 / Major. Poet p. 153 /
Murphy. Today p. 93

Ragland, J. Farley, 1904-
Clergyman, poet, teacher of science
Blk Am Wr 2: 605 / Murphy. Ebony
p. 123 / Murphy. N Voices p. 134
Rainey, Joseph H., 1832-1887
Public official, congressman, orator
Bio Dr Am Cong 61 p. 1493 / Christo-
pher. Congress p. 25 / Dict Am Biog
35, 15: 327-28 / Dict Am Biog 63, 8-1:

Rainey, Joseph H. (cont'd) ...
327-28 / Historical N Bio p. 112 por /
Negro Alm 76 p. 328 / Woodson. Orators
p. 300
Ramsey, Leroy L., 1923-
Novelist, essayist
Blk Am Wr 2: 606
Randall, Ann Knight, 1942-
Librarian, educator
Bio Dr Librns 70 p. 895 / Josey. What
p. 306 / Who Blk Am 77 p. 738
Randall, Dudley (Felker), 1914-
Publisher, librarian, poet, literary critic
Adoff. Blk out p. 81 / Adoff. Poet p.
533 / Alhamisi. Arts p. 111 / Bio Dr
Librns 70 p. 896 / Blk Am Wr 2: 607 /
Bontemps. American 74 p. 225 / Broad-
side Auth p. 97-98 / Cele p. 265 / Chap-
man. Blk V p. 468 / Chapman. New p.
322 / Con Auth 25-28: 577-78 / Con Poets
70 p. 893 / Con Poets 75 p. 1234-36 /
Davis. Cav p. 744 / Ebony Success 1:
257 por / Emanuel. Dark p. 488-89 /
Ency Blk Am p. 727 / Ford. Insights
p. 317 / Handbk Librns p. 162-63 /
Hayden. Kal p. 130 / Hughes. New p.
124 / Hughes. Poet p. 620 / Living
BAA p. 131-32 / Major. Poet p. 153 /
Selected BAA p. 224-26 / Turner. Voices
p. 272 / Who Blk Am 77 p. 738 /
Writers Dr 76 p. 874 / Writers Dr 80
p. 1019 / Writers Dr 82 p. 773
Randall, James A(ndrews), Jr., 1938-
Journalist, editor, poet
Blk Am Wr 2: 609-610 por / Broadside
Auth p. 98
Randall, James P., 1943-
Teacher, poet, short story writer, essayist
Broadside Auth p. 99
Randall, Jon Clayton, 1942-
Poet
Blk Am Wr 2: 610-11 / Broadside Auth
p. 99
Randolph, Asa Philip, 1889-1979
Labor leader, editor, author
Afro-Am Ency 7: 2164-65 il / Bio Hist
p. 393-95 / Blk Lead / Blk Lit HS
p. 162-63 / Boulware. Oratory p.
118-23 / Con Auth 85-88: 488 / Cur
Biog Yrbk 40 p. 671-73 por / David.
Defiance p. 92-101 / Ebony Success 1:
257 por / Ency Am Biog p. 888-89 /
Flynn. Achieve p. 235-48 / Gayle. Bond
p. 150 / Great Negroes 69 p. 121 il /

Randolph, Asa Philip (cont'd) ...
Historical N Bio p. 240-41 / Negro
Handbk 66 p. 412 / O'Neill. Speeches
p. 112-13 / Pol Profiles: Eisenhower
p. 495-96 / Pol Profiles: Johnson p.
488-90 / Pol Profiles: Kennedy p. 417-19 /
Pol Profiles: Truman p. 450-51 / Richard-
son. Great 56 p. 236-46 il / Richardson.
Great 76 p. 195-205 por / Selected BAA
p. 226-27 por / Sterne. Dream p. 21-43 /
Webster Am Biog p. 855-56 / Who Blk
Am 77 p. 738 / Who Col Am 33 p.
349 / Who Col Am 37 p. 429 por /
Who Col Am 40 p. 426, por p. 431 /
Who Col Am 42 p. 425, por p. 427 /
Young, M. Lead p. 23-26 por
Ransom, Reverly C., 1861-
Minister, editor, orator
Penn. Press p. 148
Who Col Am 33 p. 350 / Who Col
Am 37 p. 43 / Who Col Am 40 p.
430 / Who Col Am 42 p. 426 / Who
Col Race p. 225-26
Raphael, Lennox, 1940-
Playwright, poet, short story writer
Major. Poet p. 153
Rapier, James T., 1840-
Public official, orator
Bio Dr Am Cong 61 p. 1499 / Woodson.
Orators p. 338
Rashidd, Amir, 1943-
Poet
Major. Poet p. 153
Rashidd, Niema
Poet
Major. Poet p. 153
Raullerson, Calvin H., 1920-
Essayist, poet
Cuney. Linc p. 70
Ravelomanantsoa, Glen Anthony, 1948-
Journalist, playwright, actor
Blk Am Wr 2: 612
Raven, John, 1936-
Poet, reviewer
Blk Am Wr 2: 613 / Broadside Auth
p. 100
Ray, Henrietta C(ordelia), 1850-1916
Poet
Blk Am Wr 2: 613 / Brown. Homespun
p. 171-75 / Robinson. Poets p. 136 /
Selected BAA p. 227 / Sherman. Invisible
p. 129-31 / White. Verse p. 151

Razaf(keriefo), Andrea Paul, 1895-1973
Poet, playwright, composer
AmSCAP 80 p. 411 / Blk Am Wr 2:
613-14 / Con Auth 41-44: 499 (obit) / Ker-
lin. Poets 23 p. 277 / Kerlin. Poets 35
p. 343
Reason, Arthur W.
Poet
Dreer. Am Lit p. 59
Reason, Charles L(ewis), 1818-1898
Educator, poet, essayist
Afro-Am Ency 2: 2170-72 il / Blk Am Wr
2: 614 / Brawley. Early p. 250-52 / Histor-
ical N Bio p. 114 il / Kerlin. Poets 23
p. 277 / Kerlin. Poets 35 p. 344 /
Sherman. Invisible p. 27-32 / Simmons.
Men p. 799-801 / White. Verse p. 43
Reddick, Lawrence Dunbar, 1910-
Educator, editor, curator, children's author,
historian, librarian
Am Auth & Bks 72 p. 529 / Con Auth
61-64: 445-46 / Ebony Success 1: 259
por / Ency Blk Am p. 728 / Thorpe.
Hist p. 182 / Who Blk Am 77 p. 743-44 /
Who Col Am 42 p. 429-30
Redding, Jay Saunders, 1906-
Novelist, educator, critic, writer, editor
Am Auth & Bks 72 p. 529 / Barton.
Witness p. 238-253 / Blk Am Wr 2:
615-16 / Con Auth 1-4R: 788 / Cur Biog
Yrbk 69 p. 355-57 por / David. Growing
p. 225-30 / Ebony Success 1: 260 por /
Hill. Anger p. 216 / Living BAA p. 132 /
North Car Auth p. 97-98 / Twen CA Sup
55 p. 817-18 por / Who Col Am 42 p.
429-30
Reddy, T. J., 1945-
Playwright, artist, poet, editor
Blk Am Wr 2: 618 / Con Auth 45-48:
462-63 / Owen. Poet p. 158 / Shuman.
Galaxy p. 377
Redmond, Charles Lenox, 1810-1873
Abolitionist, orator
Afro-Am Ency 8: 2201-2204 / Bormann.
Fore p. 165 / Gayle. Bond p. 165 /
Sterling. Speak p. 380 / Woodson.
Orators p. 125-28
Redmond, Eugene Benjamin, 1937-
Professor of English, poet, critic
Adoff. Poet p. 533 / Afro-Am Ency 8:
2190 / Blk Am Wr 2: 618-20 / Blk Plots
p. 287 / Cele p. 265 / Chapman. New
p. 325 / Con Auth 25-28: 602 / Con
Auth 25-28R: 582-83 / Living BAA p.

Redmond, Eugene Benjamin (cont'd) ...
132-33 / Selected BAA p. 228-29 /
Shuman. Galaxy p. 381 / Writers Dr
76 p. 882 / Writers Dr 80 p. 1028 /
Writers Dr 82 p. 779-80

Redmond, L. C., Jr. (Obi Antarah), 1943-
Novelist
Blk Am Wr 1: 35

Redmond, Sarah Parker, 1815-?
Abolitionist, lecturer, pamphleteer
Afro-Am Ency 8: 2204 / Dannett. Profiles 1: 112-13 / Notable Am Wom 3:
136-37

Reed, Clarence
Poet, political activist, photographer
Jones. Fire p. 667 / King. Spirits p. 250

Reed, Ishmael (Scott), 1938-
Novelist, poet
Adoff. Poet p. 533-34 / Afro-Am Ency
p. 2190-91 por / Afro-Am Novel p. 140 /
Am Auth & Bks 72 p. 529 / Blk Am
Wr 2: 623 / Blk Plots p. 287 / Cele p.
265 / Chapman. New p. 329 / Con Auth
23-24: 348 / Con Auth 21-24R: 714-15 /
Con Novel 75 p. 1152-54 / Con Poets 70
p. 904-905 / Con Poets 75 p. 1254 /
Con Poets 80 p. 1248-50 / Dict Lit Biog
2: 417-22 por / Dict Lit Biog 5-2:
180-84 por / Ford. Insights p. 304 /
Hughes. Poet p. 620 / Jordan. Soul p.
143 / Living BAA p. 133 / Major. Poet
p. 154 / Miller. Dices p. 142 / Negro
Alm 76 p. 737 / Robinson. Nommo p.
483 / Selected BAA p. 229-30 / Southern
Wr p. 377-79 / Whitlow. Lit p. 154 /
Wor Auth 70-75 p. 679-82 / Writers Dr
76 p. 883 / Writers Dr 80 p. 1029 /
Writers Dr 82 p. 780

Reedburg, Robert
Poet
Afro-Am Ency 8: 2193-94

Reese, Sarah Carolyn
Teacher, writer
Blk Am Wr 2: 625 / Broadside Auth p.
101 / Hughes. Poet p. 620

Reeves, Donald, 1952-
News reporter, autobiographer, orator
Blk Am Wr 2: 625-26 por / Con Auth
37-40R: 453-54

Reid, Inez Smith, 1937-
Educator, lawyer, author
Con Auth 49-52: 448 / Living BAA p.
133 / Who Am 78, 2: 2685 / Who Blk
Am 77 p. 748

Reid, Ira De A(ugustine), 1901-1968
Sociologist, educator, writer
Brown. Caravan p. 1017 / Cur Biog
Yrbk 46 p. 503-505 por / Cur Biog Yrbk
68 p. 461 / Selected BAA p. 230-31 /
Who Col Am 42 p. 443

Reilly, J. Terrence, 1945-
Playwright
Blk Am Wr 2: 627

Render, Sylvia Lyons, 1913-
Professor of English, writer on Afro-
American literature
Con Auth 41-44R: 567-68 / Living BAA
p. 134

Revels, Hiram Rhoades, 1822-1901
U.S. senator, orator, editor
Afro-Am Ency 8: 2208-2210 il / Bio Dr
Am Cong 61 p. 1510 / Great Negroes
69 p. 48 il / Paths p. 181 por / Simmons.
Men p. 948-50 / Webster Am Biog p.
867 / Who Was HR; 509 / Woodson.
Orators p. 285

Reynolds, Barbara Ann, 1942-
Journalist, teacher, poet, biographer
Con Auth 73-76: 526-27 / Selected BAA
p. 231 / Who Blk Am 77 p. 750

Reynolds, Louis Bernard, 1917-
Minister, author, editor
Bio Dr Min 75 p. 426 / Con Auth 41-44:
570 / Who Blk Am 77 p. 750

Rhodes, Hari, 1932-
Novelist
Con Auth 17-20: 666 / Who Blk Am 77
p. 752

Ribman, Ronald (Burt), 1932-
Dramatist
Con Auth 21-22R: 722-23 / Writers Dr
80 p. 1038

Rice, Albert, 1903-
Poet
Cullen. Carol p. 176-77 / Kerlin. Poets
35 p. 344

Richards, Edward
Poet
Murphy. Ebony p. 125

Richards, Fannie M., 1840-1923
Teacher
Afro-Am Ency 8: 2226-27 il / Historical
N Bio p. 116-17 il

Richards, Nathan A.
Poet
Henderson. Under p. 392

Richardson, Arthur St. George, 1863-
Educator, essayist
Culp. Twen p. 330-31 il / Who Col Race
1: 230

Richardson, James Nathanial (Nat Richards), 1942-
Novelist
Con Auth 53-56: 484
Richardson, Nola M., 1936-
Poet
Blk Am Wr 2: 628-29 / Con Auth 57-60: 478 / Selected BAA p. 231-32
Richardson, Willis, 1889?-
Playwright, critic
Barksdale. Writers p. 638-39 / Blk Am Wr 2: 629 / Blk Plots p. 288 / Cromwell. Read p. 369 / Dr Perf Arts 78 p. 310 / Dreer. Am Lit p. 284 / Lincoln Lib Arts 2: 720 / Scally. Catholic p. 95-96 / Selected BAA p. 232 / Who Col Am 29 p. 308 / Who Col Am 33 p. 359 / Who Col Am 37 p. 438 / Who Col Am 40 p. 438 / Who Col Am 42 p. 435
Riley, Clayton, 1933-
Educator, journalist, playwright
Dr Perf Arts 78 p. 310-11 / Ebony Success 1: 264 por / Who Blk Am 77 p. 758
Riley, Constantia E.
Poet
Murphy. Ebony p. 126
Riley, Lawrence Calvin, 1947-
Broadside Auth p. 102
Rivers, Clarence Joseph, 1931-
Priest, composer, playwright, TV script writer
Con Auth 77-80: 455 / Who Blk Am 77 p. 760
Rivers, Conrad Kent, 1933-1967
Poet
Adoff. Blk on p. 81 / Adoff. Poet p. 534 / Afro-Am Ency 8: 2240 / Blk Am Wr 2: 631 / Blk Plots p. 288-89 / Bontemps. American 63 p. 193 / Bontemps. American 74 p. 225 / Broadside Auth p. 102 / Cele p. 266 / Ency Blk Am p. 732 / Hayden. Kal p. 204 / Hughes. Best p. 505 / Hughes. New p. 124 / Hughes. Poet p. 620 / Major. Poet p. 154 / Selected BAA p. 232-33
Rivers, Louis (Paul Mulet, pseud), 1922-
Drama instructor, playwright
Blk Am Wr 2: 632-33 por / Dr Perf Arts 78 p. 311-12 / Nat Play Dr p. 260 por
Roberson, Charles Edwin, 1939-
Poet, lecturer
Blk Am Wr 2: 634-35 por / Chapman. New p. 334 / Con Auth 77-80: 456

Roberson, Ed. *See* Roberson, Charles Edwin
Roberts, James, 1753-?
Soldier, narrator of experiences
David. Soldier p. 17-30
Roberts, James Deotis, 1927-
Clergyman, educator, author
Bio Dr Min 65 p. 308 / Bio Dr Min 75 p. 432 / Who Blk Am 77 p. 762 / Young. Since 1940 p. 143-44
Roberts, Joseph Jenkins, 1809-1876
Public official, essayist, orator
Dict Am Biog 35, 16: 10 / Dict Am Biog 63, 8-2: 10-11 / Who Was HR: 518
Roberts, Walter Adolphe, 1886-1965
Journalist, poet, novelist
Hughes. Poet p. 621
Robertson, Hugh A.
Film editor, author
Ebony Success 3: 148 por
Robeson, Eslanda (Cardoza) Goode, 1896-1965
Anthropologist, lecturer, writer, biographer
Brown. Caravan p. 815 / Cur Biog Yrbk 45 p. 505-507 / Gayle. Bond p. 150 / Notable Names 4: 583-86 / Selected BAA p. 234-35
Robeson, Paul Leroy Bustill, 1898-1976
Actor, singer, civil rights activist, author of published addresses
Afro-Am Ency 8: 2244-45 il / Brown. Caravan p. 815-19 / Cur Biog Yrbk 76 p. 345-48 por / Dr Perf Arts 78 p. 313-14 / NYT Obit 2: 160-62 il / Ovington. Portraits p. 205-215 / Pol Profiles: Eisenhower p. 516-17 / Pol Profiles: Truman p. 468-69 / Richardson. Great 76 p. 61-71 por / Rogers. World p. 512-20 por / Rollins. Enter p. 95-100 por / Webster Am Biog p. 880 / Who Col Am 37 p. 445 por / Who Col Am 40 p. 444 por / Who Col Am 42 p. 441, por p. 437
Robinson, Carrie C.
Librarian
Josey. Blk Librn p. 275-83
Robinson, Ed, 1939-
Poet
Hughes. Poet p. 620-21
Robinson, Etholia Arthur
Social worker, poet
Murphy. Ebony p. 127
Robinson, Florine, 1920-
Educator, author
Living BAA p. 135-36

Robinson, George T(homas), 1854-
Lawyer, newspaper editor
    Culp. Twen p. 108-109 por / Haley.
    Ency p. 620-21 por
Robinson, (Jackie) John Roosevelt, 1919-1972
Athlete, autobiographer
    Cur Biog Yrbk 47, p. 544-46 por / Flynn.
    Achieve p. 121-37 / NYT Obit 2: 163-65 il
Robinson, Lewis Green, 1929-
Civil rights organizer
    Living BAA p. 136
Robinson, Louie, Jr., 1926-
Free-lance writer, editor, author
    Who Blk Am 77 p. 769
Robinson, Magnus L., 1852-
Editor, writer
    Penn. Press p. 150-54
Robinson, Matt(hew), 1937-
Producer, writer, poet, children's
author
    Con Auth 45-48: 481 / Who Blk Am
    77 p. 770
Robinson, Ophelia
Poet
    Dreer. Am Lit p. 51
Robinson, R. G., 1873-
Educator, essayist
    Culp. Twen p. 302-303 por
Robinson, Robert L., 1946-
Free-lance writer
    Broadside Auth p. 102
Robinson, T. L., 1946-
Poet
    Coombs. Speak p. 247
Robinson, William Henry, Jr., 1922-
Educator, author
    Dr Am Schol 78, 2: 573 / Living BAA
    p. 136-37 / Selected BAA p. 235 /
    Who Blk Am 77 p. 773
Rock, John S., 1825-1866
Physician, abolitionist, orator
    Sterling. Speak p. 380
Rodgers, Carolyn M(arie) (Imani)
Poet, teacher, editor
    Adoff. Poet p. 534 / Afro-Am Ency 8:
    2262 / Alhamisi. Arts p. 108 / Broadside
    Auth p. 103 / Cele p. 266 / Con Poets
    75 p. 1293 / Con Poets 80 p. 1281-82 /
    Coombs. Speak p. 247-48 / King. Spirits
    p. 250 / Living BAA p. 137 / Long.
    Writing 2: 775 / Selected BAA p. 236 /
    Writers Dr 76 p. 907 / Writers Dr 80
    p. 1055 / Writers Dr 82 p. 800

Rogers, Alex C., 1876-1930
Playwright, songwriter, poet
    Johnson. Book p. 158
Rogers, Benjamin Howard, 1949-
    Broadside Auth p. 103-104
Rogers, Elymas Payson, 1814-1861
Abolitionist, minister, poet
    Blk Am Wr 2: 637 / Robinson. Poets
    p. 60 / Sherman. Invisible p. 21-24
Rogers, Joel Augustus, 1883-1966
Historian, journalist, novelist
    Afro-Am Ency 8: 2265 / Blk Am Wr 2:
    638-39 / Blk Plots p. 289 / Brown.
    Caravan p. 173 / Ency Blk Am p. 735 /
    Negro Alm 71 p. 691 / Negro Alm 76 p.
    737 / Selected BAA p. 236-37 / Thorpe.
    Hist p. 152-53 / Who Col Am 40 p.
    449 / Who Col Am 42 p. 445 por / Who
    Col Am 50 p. 446-47
Roker, Myntora J.
Poet
    Blk Am Wr 2: 639 / Murphy. N Voices
    p. 136
Rollins, Bryant, 1937-
Novelist, journalist, poet, playwright
    Blk Am Wr 2: 639-40 / Con Auth 49-52:
    464-65 / Living BAA p. 137-38
Rollins, Charlemae Hill, 1897-1979
Librarian, author of books for children
    ALA Yrbk (80) 5: 228 por / Auth Bk
    YP 64 p. 216 / Auth Bk YP 71 p. 440 /
    Blk Am Wr 2: 638-40 / Con Auth 11-12:
    349 / Ency Am Biog p. 735 / Living
    BAA p. 138-39 / More Books p. 299-302
    por / Rollins. Famous p. 96 / Rollins.
    They p. 166 / Selected BAA p. 237-38
    por / Something ATA 3: 175-76 por
Roman, Charles Victor, 1864-1934
Physician, orator, writer on race and
medicine
    Who Col Am 33 p. 368 / Woodson.
    Orators p. 643
Romero, Emanuel Augustus, 1887-
Essayist, book reviewer
    Scally. Catholic p. 98-99
Rooks, Charles Shelby, 1924-
Theologian, author
    Young. Since 1940 p. 97-98, 103-107 /
    Who Blk Am 77 p. 777
Roper, Moses, 1816?-?
Narrator of life story
    Afro-Am Ency 8: 2266-73 il / Barksdale.
    Writers p. 209 / Blk Am Wr 2: 641 /
    Robinson. Prose p. 115-21

Salgado, Lionel, 1928-
Teacher, poet
Shuman. Galaxy p. 397
Sanamu. *See* Kennedy, Vallejo Ryan
Sanchez, Sonia (Knight), 1934-
Poet, playwright
Adoff. Blk out p. 81 / Adoff. Poet
p. 535 / Alhamisi. Arts p. 132 /
Broadside Auth p. 105-106 por / Cele p.
266 / Chapman. New p. 336-37 / Chester.
Rising p. 238 / Con Auth 33-36R: 691 /
Con Poets 76 p. 1329 / Con Poets 80
p. 1323-25 / Crowell CAP p. 276-77 /
Davis. Cav p. 811 / Dr Perf Arts 78
p. 324 / Jones. Fire p. 667 / Jordan.
Soul p. 143 / King. Spirits p. 250 /
Living BAA p. 142 / Major. Poet p.
154 / Negro Alm 76 p. 737 / Robinson.
Nommo p. 483 / Selected BAA p. 241-42
por / Something ATA 22: 214-15 por /
Southern Wr p. 395-96 / Turner. Voices
p. 272 / Writers Dr 76 p. 939-40 /
Writers Dr 80 p. 1092 / Writers Dr
82 p. 826-27
Sanders, Stanley, 1942-
Autobiographer
Chapman. Blk V p. 347
Sarver, Ruth E. J. (Mrs. Marcellus Jacobs)
Journalist, poet
Murphy. Ebony p. 128
Saunders, Doris E(vans), 1921-
Librarian, columnist, editor, author
Con Auth 77-80: 473 / Ebony Success 1:
274 por / Who Am 80, 2: 2902 / Who
Blk Am 77 p. 791
Saunders, Prince, 1775-1839
Public official, author of published addresses
Dict Am Biog 35, 16: 382 / Dict Am
Biog 63, 8-2: 382 / Historical N Bio
p. 31-32 / Who Was H: 464-65 /
Who Was HR: 536
Saunders, Ruby Constance X, 1939-
Teacher of chemistry, playwright, poet
Blk Am Wr 2: 648 / Coombs. Speak
p. 248
Savage, W(illiam) Sherman, 1890-
Historian, educator
Con Auth 69-72: 512 / Ency Blk Am
p. 741 / Thorpe. Hist p. 175
Saxon, Alvin A., Jr. (Ojenki), 1947-
Poet
Blk Am Wr 2: 571-72 / Watts Wr p. 59
Sayers, Gale, 1943-
Professional athlete, writer on football
Ebony Success 1: 275 por

Scarborough, William Sanders, 1852-1925
Educator, essayist
Afro-Am Ency 8: 2315-16 por / Brawley.
Builders p. 204 / Cromwell. Read p. 369 /
Culp. Twen p. 414-15 il / Great Negroes
69 p. 134 il / Historical N Bio p. 122
il / Simmons. Men p. 269-75 il / Who
Col Race p. 237
Schomburg, Arthur Alfonso, 1874-1938
Essayist, bibliophile, historian
Afro-Am Ency 8: 2317-18 / Am Auth &
Bks 72 p. 564 / Ency Blk Am p. 742-43 /
Great Negroes 69 p. 140 il / Rogers.
World p. 449-53 / Thorpe. Hist p.
145-46 / Who Col Race p. 237
Schuyler, George S(amuel), 1895-1977
Journalist, novelist, critic, autobiographer,
short story writer
Afro-Am Ency 8: 2319 / Am Auth & Bks
72 p. 566 / Blk Am Wr 2: 648-49 /
Blk Plots p. 291 / Bone. Novel p. 89-90 /
Brown. Caravan p. 86 / Davis. Dark p.
104-105 / Ebony Success 1: 275 por /
Long. Writing 2: 457 / Negro Alm 71 p.
692 / Negro Alm 76 p. 737-38 / Selected
BAA p. 242-43 por / Whitlow. Lit p.
96-97 / Who Col Am 33 p. 375 / Who
Col Am 37 p. 460 / Who Col Am 40
p. 456, 459 / Who Col Am 42 p.
454-55 / Who Col Am 50 p. 454-55 por
Schuyler, Philippa Duke, 1932-1967
Concert pianist, composer, author,
autobiographer
Afro-Am Ency 8: 2319 / AmSCAP 66 p.
653 / AmSCAP 80 p. 449 / Con Auth
5-6: 373 / Dr Perf Arts 78 p. 327 /
Lincoln Lib Arts 2: 736 / Negro Alm
71 p. 784-85 / Negro Alm 76 p. 859-60
Scott, Calvin
Poet
Haslam. Forgot p. 383
Scott, Emmett Jay, 1873-1957
Administrator, author, orator
Afro-Am Ency 8: 2321 por / Am Auth
& Bks 72 p. 567 / Ency Am Biog p.
974-75 / Ency Blk Am p. 748 / Who
Col Am 33 p. 375 / Who Col Am 40
p. 459 / Who Col Am 42 p. 455 por
p. 457 / Who Col Am 50 p. 456 / Who
Was 3: 767 / Woodson. Orators p.
607-608
Scott, J. Irving E(lias), 1901-
Educator, author
Con Auth 73-76: 561 / Who Blk Am
77 p. 795

Scott, John S., 1937-
Poet, playwright
Nat Play Dr p. 279 por / Who Blk Am
77 p. 795-96
Scott, Johnie Harold, 1946-
Playwright, writer of TV documentaries, poet
Blk Am Wr 2: 650, por p. 651 / Con
Auth 33-36R: 703-704 / Coombs. Speak
p. 248 / Major. Poet p. 154
Scott, Nathan A(lexander), Jr., 1925-
Theologian, literary critic, author
Afro-Am Ency 8: 2323 / Bio Dr Min 76
p. 449 / Blk Am Wr 2: 651-53 por / Con
Auth NR-5: 479-80 / Davis. Cav p.
820 / Dr Am Schol 74, 4: 560 / Dr Am
Schol 78, 4: 423 / Ebony Success 1:
276 por / Ency Blk Am p. 748 / Emanuel.
Dark p. 537-38 / Ency Am Biog p. 748 /
Living BAA p. 143 / Negro Alm 76
p. 738 / Selected BAA p. 244-46 / Who
Blk Am 77 p. 796 / Writers Dr 76
p. 957-58 / Writers Dr 80 p. 1112 /
Writers Dr 82 p. 841
Scott, Seret, 1947-
Actress, playwright
Blk Am Wr 2: 656
Scott, Sharon, 1951-
Poet
Blk Am Wr 2: 656
Scott-Heron, Gil, 1949-
Musician, poet, novelist
Afro-Am Novel p. 151 / AmSCAP 80
p. 452 / Blk Am Wr 2: 656-57 / Blk
Plots p. 292 / Con Auth 45-48: 509 /
Dr Perf Arts 78 p. 329 / Living BAA
p. 143-44 / Selected BAA p. 246 / Who
Blk Am 77 p. 798
Scruggs, Lucie Johnson, 1864-
Teacher, author
Scruggs. Wom p. 331-37
Seale, Robert George (Bobby), 1936-
Political activist
David. Living p. 310-17 / Ebony Success
1: 277 por / Negro Alm 71 p. 239-40 il /
Negro Alm 76 p. 233-34 il / Pol Profiles:
Nixon p. 585-86 / Who Blk Am 77 p. 798
Sebree, Charles, 1914-
Playwright, theater designer, illustrator
Afro-Am Artists p. 251-52 / Dr Perf
Arts 78 p. 329-30 / Negro Alm 76 p. 774
Séjour, Victor, 1817-1874
Dramatist, poet
Afro-Am Ency 8: 2331 / Bio Dict S Auth
p. 392 / Blk Am Wr 2: 657 / Dict
Am Biog 35, 16: 565-66 / Dict Am Biog

Séjour, Victor (cont'd) ...
63, 8-2: 565-66 / Dr Perf Arts 78 p.
330 / Historical N Bio p. 122-23 / Selected
BAA p. 246-47 / Who Was H: 474 /
Who Was HR: 545
Sellers, Thomas Peyton, III, 1949-
Poet, novelist
Broadside Auth p. 106-107
Senna, Carl, 1944-
Writer, poet, editor
Blk Am Wr 2: 659 / Con Auth NR-4:
526 / Shuman. Galaxy p. 164
Settle, Josiah T. "Joe," 1850-
Public official, orator
Afro-Am Ency 8: 2334 por / Haley.
Ency p. 42-49 / Historical N Bio p.
123-24 / Simmons. Men p. 365
Sexton, Wendell P., 1928-
Blk Am Wr 2: 659-660
Shabazz, K. Sayif M. *See* Geary, Bruce
Shackleford, Theodore Henry, 1888-1923
Poet
Johnson. Book p. 209
Shackleford, William Henry
Clergyman, writer, poet
Who Col Am 42 p. 460
Shadd, Mary Ann. *See* Cary, Mary Ann Shadd
Shaed, Dorothy Lee Louise
Writer, poet
Murphy. N Voices p. 136
Shaik, Lily Anne La Salle
Poet
Scally. Catholic p. 105
Shange, Ntozakek (Paulette Williams), 1948-
Playwright, poet, dancer
Con Auth 85-88: 534-35 / Cur Biog Yrbk
78 p. 380-83 por / Dr Perf Arts 78
p. 331 / Nat Play Dr p. 283 por /
Selected BAA p. 248 / Who Blk Am 77
p. 803
Shango, Chaka Aku. *See* Coleman, Horace
W(endell), Jr.
Sharpe, Saundra, 1942-
Actress, author, poet
Blk Am Wr 2: 661 / Con Auth 45-48:
514 / Coombs. Speak p. 248-49 / Dr
Perf Arts 78 p. 331 / Living BAA p.
144 / Who Blk Am 77 p. 803
Shaw, Letty M., 1926-
Novelist
Blk Am Wr 2: 662
Shaw, Spencer G(ilbert), 1916-
Librarian, educator
Josey. Blk Librn p. 142-70 / Who Blk Am
77 p. 805

Shearer, John
  Photographer, author of children's book
    Auth Bk YP Sup 79 p. 248
Sheba. See Early, Jacqueline
Shelton, Ruth Ada Gaines, 1872-
  Playwright
    Who Col Am 33 p. 383 / Who Col Am
    40 p. 565 / Who Col Am 42 p. 461
Shepp, Archie (Vernon), 1934-
  Musician, playwright
    Blk Am Wr 2: 662 / King. Drama p. 33 /
    Who Blk Am 77 p. 807
Sherman, Jimmie, 1944-
  Playwright, poet
    Watts Wr p. 79
Shine, Ted, 1936-
  Playwright, teacher, editor
    Blk Am Wr 2: 663 / Blk Plots p. 293 /
    Childress. Scenes p. 151 / Con Auth
    77-80: 492-93 / Dr Perf Arts 78 p. 333 /
    Selected BAA p. 249
Shipp, Jesse A., 1859-1934
  Playwright, actor
    Dr Perf Arts 78 p. 333-34
Shockley, Ann Allen, 1925-
  Librarian, writer
    Afro-Am Ency p. 753 / Bio Dr Librns 70
    p. 1000 / Bk Am Wr 2: 664 / Con
    Auth 49-52: 493-94 / Handbk Librns
    p. 163-64 / Josey. Blk Librn p. 225-34 /
    Living BAA p. 144-45 / Selected BAA p.
    249 / Who Blk Am 77 p. 810 / Writers
    Dr 80 p. 1136
Shorter, Susie Isabella Lankford, 1859-1912
  Poet, journalist
    Brown. Homespun p. 205-207, por opp. p.
    182 / Majors. Wom p. 143-44 / Scruggs.
    Wom p. 162-64
Silver, Edward S(ilvera), 1906-1937
  Physician, poet
    Blk Am Wr 2: 665 / Cullen. Carol p.
    213-14 / Cuney. Linc p. 71 / Hughes.
    Poet p. 621 / Kerlin. Poets 35 p. 344
Simmons, Barbara
  Poet
    Jones. Fire p. 667
Simmons, Dan, 1923-
  Teacher, poet
    Blk Am Wr 2: 665 / Coombs. Speak
    p. 249
Simmons, Gloria (Mitchell), 1932-
  Librarian, editor
    Bio Dr Librns 70 p. 1007 / Con Auth
    37-40R: 500 / Living BAA p. 145

Simmons, Herbert A(lfred), 1929-
  Novelist, playwright, poet
    Con Auth 3: 187 / Living BAA p. 146 /
    Major. Poet p. 155 / Selected BAA p.
    249-50
Simmons, Judy Dothard, 1944-
  Poet, writer
    Blk Am Wr 2: 668 / Broadside Auth p.
    108 / Cele p. 267 / Henderson. Under
    p. 393
Simmons, William J., 1849-1890
  Clergyman, educator, author, editor
    Afro-Am Ency 8: 2346 por / Brawley.
    Builders p. 200-201 / Great Negroes 69
    p. 135 il / Simmons. Men p. 5-19
Simone, Nina (Eunice Kathleen Waymon),
  1933-
  Singer, pianist, composer, autobiographer
    Afro-Am Ency 8: 2347 / Cur Biog Yrbk
    68 p. 365-68 por / Dr Perf Arts 78
    p. 338-39 / Negro Alm 76 p. 841 /
    Paths p. 186 por / Who Blk Am 77 p.
    816
Simpson, O(renthal) J(ames), 1947-
  Professional athlete, actor, autobiographer
    Con Auth 103: 467 / Cur Biog Yrbk 69
    p. 400-402 por / Dr Perf Arts 78 p.
    339 / Who Am 80, 2: 3049 / Who Blk
    Am 77 p. 815
Skeeter, Sharyn Jeanne
  Poet
    Blk Am Wr 2: 670 / Exum. Keep p.
    287 / Who Blk Am 77 p. 820
Small, Robert Van Dyke, 1924-
  Educator, author
    Living BAA p. 146-47
Smallwood, Will
  Poet
    Murphy. Ebony p. 129
Smart, Alice McGee
  Poet
    Dreer. Am Lit p. 63
Smith, Al(vin), 1933-
  Painter, illustrator
    Afro-Am Art p. 260-61 / Illus Bks YP
    70 p. 115 / Illus Bks YP 75 p. 155 /
    Illus Ch Bks 57 p. 177 / Who Blk Am
    77 p. 824
Smith (Jemand), Amanda Berry, 1837-1915
  Evangelist, autobiographer
    Dannett. Profiles 1: 146-50 il / Miller.
    Ten p. 41-46 / Notable Am Wom 3:
    304-305 / Who Col Race p. 246

Smith, Arthur L(ee), Jr. (Molefi Kete Asante), 1942-
Educator, poet, editor, writer
Con Auth 33-36R: 48-49 / Living BAA p. 147 / Selected BAA p. 250-52 por / Who Blk Am 77 p. 26 / Writers Dr 80 p. 41 /
Smith, James Edgar
Social worker, poet
Murphy. Ebony p. 130
Smith, Jessie Carney
Library administrator, writer on librarianship
Bio Dr Librns 70 p. 1023 / Con Auth 89-92: 485 / Josey. Blk Librn p. 191-204 / Living BAA p. 147-48 / Who Blk Am 77 p. 830-31
Smith, Jules Wynn
Poet, singer, actor
Murphy. Ebony p. 131
Smith, Lucy
Poet
Hughes. New p. 125
Smith, Lucy Wilmot, ca. 1870-
Editor
Scruggs. Wom p. 165-71
Smith, Milton (Mbende), 1946-
Poet
Broadside Auth p. 86
Smythe, Hugh H(eyne), 1913-1977
Researcher in race relations, diplomat, author
Con Auth 9-12R: 848-49 / Con Auth 69-72: 542 (obit) / Living BAA p. 148-49
Smythe, Mabel M(urphy), 1918-
Professor of economics, researcher, freelance writer, author
Con Auth 37-40R: 507-508 / Living BAA p. 149-50 / Who Blk Am 77 p. 838
Snellings, Rol(l)and (Askia Muhammad Touré)
Editor, poet
Adoff. Poet p. 536 / Alhamisi. Arts p. 29 / Broadside Auth p. 118 / Hughes. Poet p. 623-24 / Jones. Fire p. 668 / King. Spirits p. 252 / Selected BAA p. 267-68
Snowden, Frank Martin, Jr., 1911-
Professor of classics
Ebony Success 1: 287 por / Living BAA p. 150-51 / Who Am 80, 2: 3101
Southern, Eileen Jackson, 1920-
Music educator, historian, editor
Con Auth 37-40R: 513 / Living BAA p. 151 / Selected BAA p. 253-54 por / Who Blk Am 77 p. 841

Spellman, A(lfred) B., 1934-
Poet, jazz critic, historian
Adoff. Poet p. 535 / Blk Am Wr 2: 678 / Con Poets 70 p. 1038 / Hughes. New p. 124-25 / Jones. Fire p. 668 / Major. Poet p. 155 / Miller. Dices p. 139 / Selected BAA p. 254
Spencer, Anne Scales, 1882-1976
Librarian, poet
Adoff. Poet p. 535 / Blk Am Wr 2: 678-79 / Bontemps. American 63 p. 193 / Bontemps. American 74 p. 225 / Brown. Caravan p. 351 / Cullen. Carol p. 47 / Dreer. Am Lit p. 47 / Handbk Librns p. 160-61 / Hayden. Kal p. 14 / Hughes. Poet p. 622 / Johnson. Book p. 213 / Kerlin. Poets 23 p. 278 / Kerlin. Poets 35 p. 344 / Selected BAA p. 254-55 por / Southern Wr p. 421-22
Stadler, Quandra Prettyman (Quandra Prettyman), 1933-
Poet
Adoff. Blk out p. 81 / Adoff. Poet p. 533 / Selected BAA p. 255 / Who Blk Am 77 p. 846
Stanford, Theodore
Newspaper editor, poet
Murphy. Ebony p. 132
Staples, Robert E(ugene), 1942-
Sociologist, author, editor
Living BAA p. 151-52 / Selected BAA p. 255 / Who Blk Am 77 p. 848
Stateman, Norman Hills
Poet
Murphy. Ebony p. 133
Steptoe, John (Lewis), 1950-
Illustrator, author of children's books
Afro-Am Art p. 268 / Blk Am Wr 2: 680 / Con Auth 49-52: 522 / Con Auth NR-3: 516 / Fourth Bk p. 321-22 por / Illus Bks YP 75 p. 159 / Illus Ch Bks 67 p. 161 / Living BAA p. 152 / Selected BAA p. 256 por / Something ATA 8: 197-98 il / Twen CCW p. 1168-69
Stevens, Sandra, 1950-
Poet
Shuman. Galaxy p. 401
Stiles, Thelma Jackson, 1939-
Playwright
Blk Am Wr 2: 681-82 por
Still, James, 1812-
Physician, autobiographer
Blk Am Wr 2: 682-83

Still, William, 1821-1902
  Abolitionist, historian
    Afro-Am Ency 9: 2569-70 / Alli Sup 2:
    1391 / Blk Am Wr 2: 683 / Bontemps.
    American 74 p. 223 / Brown. Caravan
    p. 784-85 / Davis. Cav p. 125-26 /
    Dict Am Biog 36, 18: 22-23 / Dict Am
    Biog 64, 9-2: 22-23 / Ency Blk Am
    p. 809 / Great Negroes 69 p. 31 il /
    Historical N Bio p. 127 por / Negro Alm
    76 p. 738 / Selected BAA p. 256 /
    Simmons. Men p. 149-61 / Sterling. Speak
    p. 381 / Thorpe. Hist p. 43 / Who Was
    1: 1187
Stone, Charles Sumner (Chuck Stone), 1924-
  Novelist, essayist
    Afro-Am Novel p. 154 / Blk Am Wr 2:
    684-85 / Living BAA p. 152-53 / Who
    Blk Am 77 p. 856
Stroud, Welvin (Dust), 1937-
  Poet
    Blk Am Wr 1: 258
Sublette, Walter (S. W. Edwards), 1940-
  Playwright, novelist, poet
    Blk Am Wr 2: 686
Sutherland, Christopher, 1932-
  Poet
    Blk Am Wr 2: 687
Swancy, Andre D., 1935-
  Poet
    Blk Am Wr 2: 687

Talbert, Mary Burnett (Mrs. William A.
  Talbert), 1862-1923
  Teacher, lecturer, writer
    Brown. Homespun p. 217-19 / Culp.
    Twen p. 16-17 por / Dannett. Profiles 1:
    316-17 / Historical N Bio p. 127-28 /
    Who Col Race p. 258
Talley, Thomas Washington
  Teacher, writer
    Culp. Twen p. 338-39 il / Who Col Race
    p. 258
Tanner, B(enjamin) Tucker, 1935-1923
  Bishop, historian, editor, journalist
    Afro-Am Ency 9: 2588-89 por / Alli Sup
    2: 1417 / Bruce. Sketches p. 87-91 /
    Northrop. College p. 31-33 / Simmons.
    Men p. 705-708 por / Thorpe. Hist
    p. 154-55 / Who Col Race p. 258
Tanner, Henry Ossawa, 1859-1937
  Painter, illustrator, editor
    Afro-Am Art p. 272-75 / Afro-Am Ency

Tanner, Henry Ossawa (cont'd) ...
    9: 2589-90 / Bio Hist p. 420-22 / Dict
    Am Biog 58, 22 Sup 2: 648-49 / Negro
    Alm 76 p. 761 por / Rogers. World
    p. 454-61 / Who Col Am 27 p. 196 /
    Who Was 1: 1215
Tarry, Ellen, 1906-
  Journalist, autobiographer, writer for
  young people
    Afro-Am Ency 9: 2591 / Auth Bk YP 71
    p. 501 / Books Are p. 280-82 por /
    Con Auth 73-76: 598 / Dannett. Pro-
    files 2: 247-54 / David. Living p.
    172-93 / Lerner. Wom p. 296-97 / Scally.
    Catholic p. 108-110 / Selected BAA p.
    258 por / Something ATA 16: 250-56
    por / Who Blk Am 77 p. 867
Tate, Bennie L.
  Librarian
    Josey. What p. 306-307
Tate, Eleanora E., 1948-
  Poet, children's author
    Broadside Auth p. 112 por / Blk Am Wr
    2: 689
Tate, Merze W(esley), 1903-
  Historian, writer on politics
    Con Auth 17-18R: 721 / Ency Blk Am
    p. 814 / Living BAA p. 154-55 / Selected
    BAA p. 258-59 / Who Blk Am 77 p.
    868 / Who Col Am 40 p. 496, 499 /
    Who Col Am 42 p. 499 / Writers Dr
    80 p. 1222
Tate, Neal
  Music educator, playwright
    Blk Am Wr 2: 690
Taylor, Alrutheus Ambush, 1892-1950
  Educator, historian
    Dreer. Lit p. 100 / Ency Blk Am p. 814 /
    Thorpe. Hist p. 178-79 / Who Col Am 40
    p. 499
Taylor, Arnold H., 1929-
  Educator, historian
    Con Auth 33-36R: 727 / Who Blk Am 77
    p. 869
Taylor, Cledie (Collins), 1926-
  Illustrator, writer
    Broadside Auth p. 113 por / Who Blk
    Am 77 p. 870
Taylor, Clyde R(ussell), 1931-
  Teacher, poet, critic
    Con Auth 45-48: 573 / Selected BAA
    p. 259-60
Taylor, Della B(rown), 1922-
  Ceramist, poet, educator, art critic
    Afro-Am Art p. 277 / Who Blk Am 77
    p. 870

Taylor, Isabella McClellan
Poet
Murphy. Ebony p. 134
Taylor, Jeanne A., 1934-
Prose writer
Chapman. New p. 173 / Watts Wr p. [67]
Taylor, Margaret. *See* Burroughs, Margaret Taylor Goss
Taylor, Marshall W., 1878-
Bicyclist, autobiographer
Barton. Witness p. 45-48
Taylor, Marshall William, 1846-1887
Clergyman, editor, writer on race and religion, biographer
Alli Sup 2: 1421 / Bio Dict S Auth p. 427 / Dict Am Biog 36, 18: 337-38 / Dict Am Biog 64, 9-2: 337-38 / Ohio Auth p. 620 / Penn. Press p. 227 / Simmons. Men p. 662-63
Taylor, Prentiss, Jr., 1951-
Poet, journalist
Blk Am Wr 2: 691 / Broadside Auth p. 114
Taylor, Susie (Baker) King, 1848?-
Teacher, nurse, autobiographer
Blk Pioneers 1 / Dannett. Profiles 1: 166-73 il / Lerner. Wom p. 99 / Loewenberg. Wom p. 89-94
Taylor, William Edward (Billy), 1921-
Pianist, composer, writer on jazz
Cur Biog Yrbk 80 p. 398-401 por / Ebony Success 1: 300 por / Who Am 78, 2: 3200
Teabeau, Hazel McDaniel
Educator, poet, essayist, short story writer
Scally. Catholic p. 111-13
Teague, Robert (Bob Teague), 1929-
Journalist, short story writer, author of books for young people
Afro-Am Ency 9: 2604 / Auth Bk YP Sup 79 p. 271 / David. Living p. 292-99 / Dr Perf Arts 78 p. 355 / Flynn. Achieve p. 182-88 / Selected BAA p. 260 / Who Blk Am 77 p. 875
Teer, Barbara Ann, 1937
Actor, dancer, director, essayist
Blk Am Wr 2: 691 / Dr Perf Arts 78 p. 355-56 / Notable Names p. 1175 / Who Blk Am 77 p. 875
Temple, Herbert, 1919-
Painter, illustrator
Afro-Am Art p. 278 / Ebony Success 1: 300 por / Who Blk Am 77 p. 875

Terrell, Mary Eliza Church, 1863-1954
Educator, civil rights activist, orator, author
Afro-Am Ency 9: 2608-2609 / Barton. Witness p. 68-69 / Bio Hist p. 422-25 / Blk Pioneers 2 / Boulware. Oratory p. 102-103 / Culp. Twen p. 172-73 / Cur Biog Yrbk 42 p. 827-30 por / Cur Biog Yrbk 54 p. 602 / Dannett. Profiles 1: 207-11 il / David. Living p. 143-52 / Ency Blk Am p. 815 por / Great Negroes 69 p. 119 il / Historical N Bio p. 251 / Lerner. Wom p. 206 / Nat Cyclo 52: 524-25 / Noble. Beautiful p. 136-37 / Notable Am Wom Mod p. 678-80 / Sign Am Wom p. 54 il / Sterling. Fore p. 118-57 / Sterling. Lift p. 55-81 il / Who Am 42 p. 2158 / Who Col Am 29 p. 357, por p. 352 / Who Col Am 33 p. 415 por / Who Col Am 37 p. 509, por p. 417 / Who Col Am 40 p. 502, por p. 507 / Williams. Wom p. 181
Terrell, Robert L(ouis), 1943-
Poet, essayist
Con Auth 41-44R: 692-93 / Coombs. Speak p. 249 / Who Blk Am 77 p. 876
Terry (Prince), Lucy, 1730-1821
Storyteller, poet
Afro-Am Ency 9: 2611 / Blk Am Wr 2: 691-93 / Dannett. Profiles 1: 30-31 / Hughes. Poet p. 622 / Katz. West p. 59-63 / Negro Alm 76 p. 738-53 / Robinson. Poets p. 3-4 / Selected BAA p. 260-61
Thelwell, Michael (Mike Thelwell), 1938-
Novelist, poet, short story writer, educator
Chapman. New p. 132 / Blk Am Wr 2: 693 / Hughes. Best p. 505
Thierry, Camille, 1814-1875
Businessman, poet
Blk Am Wr 2: 693 / Dict Am Biog 36, 18: 417 / Dict Am Biog 64, 9-2: 417 / Who Was H: 525 / Who Was HR: 597
Thigpen, William A(nthony), Jr., 1948-1971
Writer
Broadside Auth p. 114 / Blk Am Wr 2: 694
Thomas, Beverly, 1948-
Teacher, writer
Broadside Auth p. 114
Thomas, Charles Columbus
Educator, poet
Blk Am Wr 2: 694-95 por / Coombs. Speak p. 249-50 / Ebony Success 1: 302 por

Thomas, David Gatewood
Organization official, poet
Murphy, Ebony p. 137
Thomas, Joyce Carol
Poet
Cele p. 267
Thomas, Lillian May, 1857-
Editor, journalist
Scruggs. Wom p. 235-40
Thomas, Lorenzo, 1944-
Poet, editor, translator
Adoff. Poet p. 535 / Blk Am Wr 2:
696 / Chapman. New p. 342 / Jones.
Fire p. 669 / Living BAA p. 155 /
Selected BAA p. 261
Thomas, Richard W(alter), 1939-
Poet
Adoff. Poet p. 536 / Blk Am Wr 2:
696-97 / Broadside Auth p. 114-15 /
Hughes. Poet p. 623 / Jones. Fire p.
669 / King. Spirits p. 251 / Shuman.
Galaxy p. 402 / Shuman. Nine p. 186
Thomas, Roscoe A., 1928-
Teacher
Living BAA p. 155
Thomas, Will, 1905-
Novelist, short story writer, autobiographer
Blk Am Wr 2: 697 / David. Growing
p. 39-56
Thompson, Aaron Bedford, 1883-1929
Poet, publisher
Dabney. Cin p. 318 / Ohio Auth p. 629
Sherman. Invisible p. 207-208
Thompson, Carolyn, 1944
Artist, writer
Broadside Auth p. 155 por
Thompson, Clara Ann
Elocutionist, writer
Dabney. Cin p. 320
Thompson, Clarissa M(innie)
Essayist, novelist
Haley. Ency p. 566-70 por
Thompson, Donnis H(azel), 1934-
Educator, writer on women's sports
Living BAA p. 156 / Who Blk Am 77
p. 885
Thompson, Eloise Bibb, 1878-1927
Poet, short story writer, playwright,
journalist, lecturer
Blk Am Wr 1: 74 / Scally. Catholic
p. 114-15 / Sherman. Invisible p. 204-
205 / Who Col Race p. 262
Thompson, Era Bell, 1911-
Editor, author, critic
Blk Plots p. 304 / David. Roots p. 186 /

Thompson, Era Bell (cont'd) ...
Ency Blk Am p. 816 / Living BAA p.
156 / Selected BAA p. 261-62 / Who Blk
Am 77 p. 885
Thompson, Garland Lee, 1938-
Poet, playwright
Blk Am Wr 2: 698 / Dr Perf Arts 78
p. 357
Thompson, James W., 1935-
Dancer, editor, writer of poetry and short
stories
Adoff. Poet p. 536 / Blk Am Wr 2: 699 /
Broadside Auth p. 116 / Coombs. Speak
p. 250 / King. Spirits p. 251-52 / King.
Story p. 255 / Living BAA p. 157 /
Selected BAA p. 262
Thompson, Julius Eric, 1946-
Poet
Living BAA p. 157
Thompson, Larry, 1950-
Magazine editor, playwright, poet
Adoff. Blk out p. 81 / Adoff. Poet p.
536 / Blk Am Wr 2: 699
Thompson, Mozelle, ?-1970
Painter, illustrator
Afro-Am Art p. 280 / Illus Bks YP 75
p. 165
Thompson, Patrick H.
Clergyman, historian, educator
Thorpe. Hist p. 159-60
Thompson, Pricilla Jane
Poet
Dabney. Cin p. 319
Thompson, Richardson W., 1865-
Journalist
Culp. Twen p. 350-51 il / Who Col
Race p. 263
Thornhill, Lionel Oscar, 1897-
Short story writer, novelist
Blk Am Wr 2: 700 / Living BAA p.
157
Thorpe, Earl(ie) E(ndris), 1924-
Educator, historian
Blk Am Ency p. 817 / Con Auth 61-64:
558 / Living BAA p. 157-58 / Selected
BAA p. 263 / Who Blk Am 77 p. 890
Thurman, Howard, 1900-1981
Theologian, author
Afro-Am Ency 9: 2626-27 por / Bio Dr
Min 75 p. 502-503 / Brown. Caravan p.
685-86 / Boulware. Orators p. 184 /
Con Auth 97-100: 534-35 / Ebony Success
1: 304 por / Ency Blk Am p. 817 / Great
Negroes p. 106 il / Historical N Bio p.

Thurman, Howard (cont'd) ...
  251-52 il / Jenness. Twelve p. 145-60 /
  Living BAA p. 158-59 / Negro Alm 71 p.
  693 / Negro Alm 76 p. 739 / Negro
  Handbk 66 p. 414 / Selected BAA p.
  263 por / Who Am 78 p. 3241 / Who
  Blk Am 77 p. 891 / Young. Since 1940
  p. 46-47, 53-54
Thurman, Wallace, 1902-1934
  Novelist, playwright, short story writer,
  critic, editor
    Afro-Am Ency 9: 2627 / Am Auth & Bks
    72 p. 640 / Barksdale. Writers p. 604-
    606 / Blk Am Wr 2: 701-702 / Brown.
    Caravan p. 220 / Davis. Dark p. 108-109 /
    Dr Perf Arts 78 p. 358 / Reader's Ency
    62 p. 1138 / Selected BAA p. 265
Tilghman, A. L.
  Journalist, poet
    Penn. Press p. 401-405 por / Scruggs.
    Wom p. 211-16
Tillman, Kate D. Chapman, 1870-
  Poet
    Scruggs. Wom p. 203-206
Tinsley, Tomi Carolyn
  Poet
    Murphy. Ebony p. 140
Tobias, Channing H., 1882-
  Clergyman, orator
    Boulware. Orators. p. 192-94 / Who
    Col Am 33 p. 425-26 / Who Col Am
    37 p. 521 / Who Col Am 40 p. 514,
    517
Todd, Beverly, 1946-
  Actress, playwright
    Dr Perf Arts 78 p. 358-59
Tolson, Melvin Beaunorus, 1890-1966
  Poet, playwright, professor of English
    Adams. Auth p. 40 / Adoff. Poet p.
    536 / Afro-Am Ency 9: 2635 / Barksdale.
    Writers p. 668-70 / Blk Am Wr 2: 703-
    705 / Blk Plots p. 305-306 / Bontemps.
    American 63 p. 193 / Bontemps. American
    74 p. 225-26 / Bontemps. Golden p.
    215 / Broadside Auth p. 116-17 / Brown.
    Caravan p. 398 / Chapman. Blk V p.
    386-87 / Con Auth 89-92: 518 / Cuney.
    Linc p. 71 / Davis. Cav p. 364 / Davis.
    Dark p. 167-68 / Emanuel. Dark p.
    471-72 / Ford. Insights p. 100 / Haslam.
    Forgot p. 275 / Hayden. Kal p. 56-57 /
    Hill. Anger p. 217 / Hughes. Poet p.
    623 / Kerlin. Poets 35 p. 346 / Long.
    Writing 2: 535 / Murphy. N Voices p.

Tolson, Melvin Beaunorus (cont'd) ...
  149-50 / Negro Alm 71 p. 693-94 / Negro
  Alm 76 p. 739 / Poets p. 1011-13 /
  Robinson. Nommo p. 484 / Selected BAA
  p. 265-66 / Southern Wr p. 457-59 /
  Wor Auth 50-70 p. 1432-34 por
Toomer, Jean (Nathan Eugene Toomer),
1894-1967
  Poet, novelist, playwright, short story writer
    Adoff. Poet p. 536 / Afro-Am Ency 9:
    2636 / Am Auth & Bks 72 p. 644 /
    Barksdale. Writers p. 500-502 / Blk Am
    Wr 2: 706-707 / Blk Plots p. 306 /
    Bone. Novel p. 81-82 / Bontemps.
    American 63 p. 193 / Bontemps. American
    74 p. 226 / Bontemps. Harlem p. 51-62 /
    Broadside Auth p. 117-18 / Brown. Cara-
    van p. 41-42 / Chapman. Blk V p. 63 /
    Con Auth 85-88: 590-91 / Cullen. Carol
    p. 93-94 / Davis. Cav p. 285 / Davis.
    Dark p. 44-45 / Dreer. Am Lit p. 79 /
    Emanuel. Dark p. 95-98 / Ford. Insights
    p. 150 / Hayden. Kal p. 50 / Hughes.
    Best p. 505 / Hughes. Poet p. 623 /
    Kendricks. Voices p. 208 / Kerlin. Poets
    35 p. 344 / Locke. Four p. 31 / Long.
    Writing 2: 393-94 / Margolies. Read p.
    360 / Negro Alm 71 p. 694 / Negro
    Alm 76 p. 739-40 por / Selected BAA p.
    266-67 por / Sign Am Auth p. 61 /
    Southern Wr p. 459-60 / Wagner. Poets p.
    260-64 / Whitlow. Lit p. 80-83 / Who Am
    17, p. 1932-33 / Who Col Am 37 p.
    604 / Who Col Am 40 p. 604 / Who Col
    Am 42 p. 605 / Wor Auth 50-70, p.
    1135-37
Toppin, Edgar A(llan), 1928-
  Professor of history, author
    Con Auth 21-22R: 882 / Ency Blk Am p.
    818 / Living BAA p. 159-60 / Selected
    BAA p. 267 / Who Blk Am 77 p. 897
Totper, R. K. (pseud). *See* Yates, Josephine
Silone
Totten, Herman, 1938-
  Librarian, educator
    Bio Dr Librns 70 p. 1100 / Josey. Blk
    Librn p. 216-24 / Josey. What p. 307 /
    Who Blk Am 77 p. 897
Touré, Askia Muhammad. *See* Snellings,
Rol(l)and
Townsend, Willard Saxby, 1895-1957
  Labor union leader, orator
    Boulware. Oratory p. 123-27 / Negro Alm
    71 p. 405 / Who Was 3: 860

Townsend, William Bolden, 1854-
Editor, publisher, politician
Penn. Press p. 312-14
Trotter, James Monroe, 1844-1912
Public official, publisher, author
Afro-Am Ency 9: 2646 por / Great
Negroes 69 p. 54 il / Greene. Defenders
p. 94 por / Simmons. Men p. 587-94 il
Trotter, William Monroe, 1872-1934
Publisher, civil rights activist
Afro-Am Ency 9: 2646-48 / Bennett.
Pioneers p. 220-30 por / Blk Plots
p. 306 / Ency Am Biog p. 1103 / His-
torical N Bio p. 254-55 / Long. Writing
1: 193-94 / Rogers. World p. 399-405 /
Selected BAA p. 268-69 por / Who Col
Am 33 p. 428, 431
Troup, Cornelius V., 1902-
Association executive, poet, educator
Blk Am Wr 2: 713-14 por / Con Auth
9-10: 452 / Con Auth P-1: 633 / Murphy.
Ebony p. 144 / Murphy. N Voices p.
153 / Troup. Geor p. x-xiii / Who Blk
Am 77 p. 901
Troupe, Quincy, 1943-
Teacher, poet, novelist, editor
Adoff. Poet p. 536-37 / Blk Am Wr 2:
714-15 / Cele p. 267 / Chapman. New
p. 346-47 / Coombs. Speak p. 250-51 /
King. Spirits p. 252 / Major. Poet p.
156 / Selected BAA p. 269
Truth, Sojourner (Isabella Baumfree), ca.
1797-1883
Abolitionist, lecturer, narrator of experiences
Afro-Am Ency 9: 2648-50 / Bennett.
Pioneers p. 114-28 il / Bio Hist p. 425-
27 / Brawley. Builders p. 73-79 / Dannett.
Profiles 1: 94-101 il / David. Defiance p.
29-33 / Davis. Cav p. 78-79 / Ency Am
Biog p. 1107-1108 / Great Negroes 69 p.
33 il / Historical N Bio p. 130-31 il /
Lerner. Wom p. 370-72 / Negro Alm 71 p.
886, il p. 190 / Negro Alm 76 p. 247, por
p. 246 / Notable Am Wom 3: 479-81 /
Sign Am Wom p. 14 il / Webster Am
Biog p. 1054
Tsuffis, Mary Lee
Librarian
Bio Dr Librns 70 p. 1107 / Josey. Blk
Librn p. 237-46 / Who Blk Am 77 p.
901
Turner, Beth
Playwright
Nat Play Dr p. 318 por

Turner, Darwin T., 1931-
Professor of English, poet, literary critic
Blk Am Wr 2: 716 / Blk Plots p. 307
Chapman. Blk V p. 677 / Chapman. New
p. 499 / Con Auth 21-22: 890-91 / Con
Auth 21-24R: 890-91 / Con Drama 73 p.
925 / Hughes. Poet p. 624 / Living
BAA p. 160 / Major. Poet p. 156 /
Selected BAA p. 270-71 / Shuman. Galaxy
p. 407 / Turner. Voices p. 2, 273-74 /
Who Blk Am 77 p. 904 / Writers Dr
76 p. 1120 / Writers Dr 80 p. 1261 /
Writers Dr 82 p. 953
Turner, Doris (LinYatta), 1950-
Broadside Auth p. 77
Turner, Douglas. *See* Ward, Douglas Turner
Turner, Ezra W.
Educator, poet
Dreer. Am Lit p. 76
Turner, Henry McNeal, 1834-1914
Clergyman, Journalist, orator
Afro-Am Ency 9: 2659-60 por / Culp.
Twen p. 42-43 por / Ency Blk Am p.
820 por / Great Negroes 69 p. 103 il /
Greene. Defenders p. 94-95 por / Haley.
Ency p. 35-38 por / Northrop. College
p. 29-30 por / Penn. Press p. 356-60 /
Robinson. Prose p. 24-25 / Simmons. Men
p. 566-76 / Who Col Race p. 268 /
Young. 1755 p. 140-41, 149-50
Turner, John Adolph
Poet
Dreer. Am Lit p. 58
Turner, Lorenzo Dow, 1914-
Professor of English, linguist
Selected BAA p. 272 / Who Col Am 33
p. 432 / Who Col Am 40 p. 522 /
Who Col Am 42 p. 525
Turner, Lucy Mae
Murphy. N. Voices p. 157
Turner, Mae Caesar, 1889-
Living BAA p. 161
Turner, Mary G., 1917-
Living BAA p. 161
Turner, Nat, 1800-1831
Slave revolt leader, narrator
Afro-Am Ency 9: 2661-69 por, il /
Barksdale. Writers p. 161-63 / Bennett.
Pioneers p. 83-97 / Bio Hist p. 431-33 /
David. Living p. 200-215 / Ency Am
Biog p. 1112-13 / Ency Blk Am p. 821 /
Great Negroes 69 p. 30 il / Historical
N Bio p. 134 / Robinson. Prose p. 67 /
Rogers. World p. 325-31 / Rollins. They
p. 132-37 / Webster Am Biog p. 1057 /
Young. 1755 p. 52-60

Vivian, Octavia Geans, 1928-
Biographer
   Living BAA p. 163 / Who Blk Am 77
   p. 914
Vroman, Mary Elizabeth, 1923-1967
Novelist, poet, writer of short stories and
screenplays
   Afro-Am Ency 9: 2726 / Afro-Am Novel
   p. 160 / Blk Am Wr 2: 725 / Blk Plots
   p. 309 / Hughes. Best p. 506 / Selected
   BAA p. 275

Wakefield, Jacques (Abayome Oji)
Poet
   Coombs. Speak p. 251
Walcott, Brenda, 1938-
Playwright
   Blk Am Wr 2: 726
Walcott, Ronald, 1946-
Teacher of English, literary critic
   Selected BAA p. 275-76 por
Walden, (Alfred) Islay, 1847-1884
Teacher, minister, poet
   Blk Am Wr 2: 726-27 / Sherman.
   Invisible p. 104-106 / White. Verse p.
   234-35
Walker, Alice Malsencor, 1944-
Writer, poet
   Adoff. Poet p. 537 / Au Speaks p.
   167-68 / Blk Am Wr 2: 727-28 por /
   Blk Plots p. 310 / Broadside Auth p. 119 /
   Con Auth 37-40R: 524 / Dict Lit Biog
   6: 350-58 por / King. Story p. 133 /
   Living BAA p. 163 / Selected BAA p.
   276-77 / Who Blk Am 77 p. 916
Walker, David, 1785-1830
   Afro-Am Ency 9: 2731-32 / Barksdale.
   Writers p. 151-53 / Bennett. Pioneers p.
   69-80 / Blk Am Wr 2: 729 / Brawley.
   Early p. 123-24 / Brown. Caravan p. 587 /
   Davis. Cav p. 42-43 / Ency Blk Am p.
   830 / Great Negroes 69 p. 29 / Historical
   N Bio p. 137-38 / Long. Writing 1: 25 /
   Negro Alm 71 p. 694 / Negro Alm 76
   p. 729 / Peters. Ebony p. 21-22 / Robin-
   son. Prose p. 51-52 / Selected BAA p.
   277-78 / Turner. Voices p. 274 / Web-
   ster Am Biog p. 1084 / Young. 1755 p.
   41-51
Walker, Ernestine, 1926-
Historian, essayist
   Ency Blk Am p. 830 / Who Blk Am 77
   p. 917

Walker, Evan K.
Writer of short stories, playwright
   Coombs. What p. 209 / King. Story p. 47
Walker, H. L., 1859-
   Culp. Twen p. 342-43 il
Walker, John L., 1850-1907
Lawyer, journalist, editor
   Penn. Press p. 188-94
Walker, Joseph A., 1935-
Playwright, actor, director
   Con Auth 89-92: 544 / Dr Perf Arts 78,
   p. 372 / King. Drama p. 349 / Notable
   Names p. 1202 / Writers Dr 80 p.
   1292 / Writers Dr 82 p. 975
Walker (Alexander), Margaret Abigail
Poet, novelist
   Blk Am Wr 2: 731-32 / Bontemps. Amer-
   ican 63 p. 193 / Bontemps. American
   74 p. 226 / Broadside Auth p. 120 / Cele
   p. 268 / Chapman. Blk V p. 458 /
   Chapman. New p. 202-203 / Con Auth
   73-76: 626 / Con Novel 76 p. 1424 /
   Con Poets 70 p. 1136-37 / Con Poets
   75 p. 1613 / Con Poets 80 p. 158-59 /
   Crowell CAP p. 319-22 / Cur Biog Yrbk
   42 p. 799-801 por / Ebony Success 1:
   6 por / Emanuel. Dark p. 493-94 / Ency
   Blk Am p. 97 / Living BAA p. 164 /
   Long. Writing 2: 519 / Noble. Beautiful
   p. 177-79 / Profiles Blk Ach 402-246 /
   Selected BAA p. 278-79 por / Who Am
   78, 2: 3361 / Writers Dr 82 p. 975
Walker, Thomas H(amilton) B(eb), 1873-
Clergyman, novelist, historian, orator, editor
   Who Col Am 42 p. 535 / Who Col Race
   p. 274-75
Walker, Victor Steven, 1947-
Writer of short stories
   Chapman. New p. 189-90
Walker, William A.
Poet
   Blk Am Wr 2: 734
Wallace, Michele, 1952-
Poet, journalist
   Exum. Keep p. 288
Wallace, Ruby Ann. *See* Dee, Ruby
Waller, Owen Meredith, 1868-
Minister
   Culp. Twen p. 362-63 il
Walls, William Jacob, 1885-1975
Clergyman, editor
   Afro-Am Ency 5: 2738 / Con Auth
   81-84: 591-92

Walrond, Eric, 1898-1966
Journalist, short story writer
Afro-Am Ency 9: 2738-39 / Barksdale.
Writers p. 598-99 / Blk Am Wr 2: 735 /
Blk Plots p. 309-310 / Emanuel. Dark p.
p. 124-25 / Hughes. Best p. 506 / Negro
Alm 76 p. 741 / Selected BAA p. 279 /
Who Col Am 40 p. 604 / Who Col Am
42 p. 605
Walters, Alexander, 1858-1917
Clergyman, orator, autobiographer
Dict Am Biog 36, 19: 398-99 / Dict Am
Biog 64, 10-1: 398-99 / Northrop. College
p. 30-31 / Simmons. Men p. 220-23 por /
Who Was 1: 1295 / Woodson. Orators p.
554
Walters, Mary Dawson (Mrs. Vincent Walters),
1923-
Library administrator
Ebony Success 1: 319 por / Josey. What
p. 307 / Negro Alm 76 p. 1017 / Who
Blk Am 77 p. 923
Walton, Hanes, Jr., 1942-
Professor of political science, writer on
poetry and politics
Con Auth 41-44: 663 / Con Auth 41-44R:
747 / Ency Blk Am p. 831-32 / Living
BAA p. 164 / Selected BAA p. 280
Walton, Lester A., 1881-
Playwright, journalist
Afro-Am Ency 9: 2739-40
Walton, Ortiz (Montaigne), 1933-
Sociologist, free-lance writer, musician
Con Auth 45-48: 614 / Living BAA p.
164-65 / Selected BAA p. 280-81 / Who
Blk Am 77 p. 924 / Writers Dr 80 p.
1296-97
Wamble, Thelma, 1916-
Novelist
Blk Am Wr 2: 736 / Living BAA p.
165
Wangara, Harun Kofi. *See* Lawrence,
Harold G.
Wangara, Malaika Ayo. *See* Lawrence, Joyce
Whitsitt
Ward, Douglas Turner, 1930-
Actor, playwright, drama critic
Blk Plots p. 311 / Con Auth 81-84:
593-94 / Con Drama 73 p. 786-89 / Con
Drama 77 p. 821-23 / Cur Biog Yrbk
76 p. 417-21 por / Dict Lit Biog 7-2:
300-304 por / Dr Perf Arts 78 p. 376 /
Ency Blk Am p. 832 / King. Drama
p. 229 / Living BAA p. 165-66 / Notable

Ward, Douglas Turner (cont'd) ...
Names p. 1205-1206 / Oliver. Drama p.
317-18 / Selected BAA p. 281 / Who Am
80, 2: 3430 / Who Blk Am 77 p. 925 /
Who Theatre 77 p. 1222 / Wor Auth 70-75
p. 850-52 por / Writers Dr 76 p. 1120 /
Writers Dr 80 p. 1297 / Writers Dr 82
p. 978
Ward, Jerry W., Jr., 1943-
Professor of English, poet, critic, editor
Dr Am Schol 78, 2: 708
Ward, Richard, 1915-1979
Actor, playwright, television script writer
Dr Perf Arts 78 p. 375
Ward, Samuel Ringgold, 1817-1864?
Autobiographer, orator
Afro-Am Ency 9: 2741 por / Brown.
Caravan p. 622 / Dict Am Biog 36, 19:
404 / Dict Am Biog 64, 10-1: 404 /
Historical N Bio p. 140 il / Long.
Writing 1: 87 / Negro Alm 76 p. 741 /
Selected BAA p. 282 / Who Was H: 561 /
Who Was HR: 633 / Woodson. Orators
p. 193 / Young. 1755 p. 98-99, 107-109
Ward, Theodore, 1902-
Playwright, teacher, actor
Brown. Caravan p. 561 / Childress. Scenes
p. 151 / Dr Perf Arts 78 p. 376 / Negro
Alm 76 p. 843-44 / Selected BAA p.
282-83 / Who Blk Am 77 p. 926
Ward, Wally, 1950-
Poet
Coombs. Speak p. 241
Waring, Cuney, 1906-
Poet
Johnson. Book p. 283
Waring, Laura Wheeler, 1887-1948
Painter, illustrator, educator
Afro-Am Art p. 293 / Ency Blk Am p.
832 / Negro Alm 76 p. 767
Warren, Alyce (Mrs. Michael P. Pringle),
1940-
Teacher
Blk Am Wr 2: 739 / Living BAA p. 166
Warren, Lloyd
Actor, poet
Murphy. Ebony p. 150
Washington, Booker T(aliaferro), 1856-1915
Educator, autobiographer, orator
Afro-Am Ency 9: 2746-61 il / Am Auth &
Bks 72 p. 675 / Barton. Witness p. 3-17 /
Bio Hist p. 437-41 / Blk Am Wr 2:
739-40 / Boulware. Orators p. 39-53 /
Brawley. Builders p. 147-57 por / Brawley.

Washington, Booker T(aliaferro) (cont'd) ...
Lit p. 59-63 / Cromwell. Read p. 370 /
David. Growing p. 111-26 / Davis. South
p. 862 / Dreer. Am Lit p. 121 / Ency
Am Biog p. 1153-55 / Ford. Insights
p. 14-15 / Gayle. Bond p. 150-51 / Great
Negroes 69 p. 136-37 il / Haley. Ency
p. 84-87 por / Hammond. Van p. 16-34
por / Long. Writing 1: 131-33 / Miller.
Ten p. 47-53 / Negro Alm 71 p. 295-96
por / Negro Alm 76 p. 248-49 / Nat
Cyclo 7: 363-64 il / Northrop. College
p. 60-62 / O'Neill. Speeches p. 72-73 /
Reader's Ency 62 p. 1197-98 por / Robin-
son. Prose p. 93 / Rogers. World p.
383-98 / Rollins. They p. 141-42 / Selected
BAA p. 283 por / Southern Wr p.
473-74 / Sterling. Lift p. 1-26 il / Thorpe.
Hist p. 59-61 / Young, M. Lead p. 15-17
por
Washington, Dell
Poet
Coombs. Speak p. 251
Washington, Hazel L.
Poet
Murphy. Ebony p. 151
Washington, Joseph R., Jr., 1930-
Minister, professor of religion, historian
Con Auth 11-12: 433-34 / Living BAA p.
166 / Selected p. 284-85 / Who Blk Am
77 p. 930-31
Washington, Josephine Turpin, 1861-1949
Teacher, columnist, poet
Dannett. Profiles 1: 320-21 il / Penn.
Press p. 393-96 / Scruggs. Wom p. 89-93
Washington, Raymond, 1942-
Blk Am Wr 2: 742 / Living BAA p. 167
Waters, Ethel, 1900-
Actress, singer, autobiographer
Afro-Am Ency 9: 2771, 2772 por / Bio
Hist p. 441-44 / Blk Lit HS p. 165-66 /
Con Auth 73-76: 630-31 / Con Auth
81-84: 594 / Cur Biog Yrbk 41 p.
899-901 por / Cur Biog Yrbk 51 p. 644-47
por / David. Growing p. 156-76 / Dr
Perf Arts 78 p. 381-82 / Great Negroes
69 p. 168 il / Historical N Bio p.
256-57 por / King. Famous p. 97-101 /
Lincoln Lib Arts 2: 792 / Negro Alm 76
p. 844 / Noble. Beautiful p. 240-42 /
Notable Names p. 1210 / Sign Am Wom
p. 77 il / Webster Am Biog p. 1100
Watkins, Gordon R., 1930-
Actor, playwright, filmscript writer, poet
Blk Am Wr 2: 743-44 / Con Auth 37-40R:
592-93 / Nat Play Dr p. 327 por

Watkins, Lucian B., 1879-1921
Poet
Blk Am Wr 2: 744 / Johnson. Book
p. 211 / Kendricks. Voices p. 198 / Kerlin.
Poets 23 p. 278 / Kerlin. Poets 35 p.
345
Watkins, Mel (Franklin Jefferson Jackson),
1940-
Journalist, author
Con Auth 89-92: 550
Watkins, Sylvestre C(ornelius), 1911-
Business executive, editor, writer on black
literature
Who Blk Am 77 p. 934
Watson, Evelyn
Teacher, poet
Dreer. Am lit p. 78
Watson, Harmon C., 1943-
Playwright
Blk Am Wr 2: 744 / Ford. Insights p.
289
Watson, Roberta Bruce, 1911-
Novelist
Blk Am Wr 2: 744-45
Watt, Ann Stewart
Librarian
Josey. What p. 307
Waymon, Eunice Kathleen. See Simone, Nina
Weatherly, Tom, 1942-
Poet
Adoff. Poets p. 537 / Blk Am Wr 2:
745 / Chapman. New p. 351-52 / Con
Auth 45-48: 621
Weaver, Eleanor
Poet
Murphy. N Voices p. 161
Weaver, Robert C(lifton), 1907-
Economist, author
Afro-Am Ency 9: 2780 il / Bio Hist
p. 444-46 / Con Auth 11-12R: 435-36 /
Great Negroes 69 p. 132 il / Historical
N Bio p. 257-58 por / Negro Alm 71 p.
44-45 por / Negro Alm 76 p. 358 / Negro
Handbk 66 p. 416 / Selected BAA p.
287 por / Webster Am Biog p. 1105-1106 /
Who Am 80, 1: 3451-52 / Who Blk Am
77 p. 939 / Young, M. Lead p. 53-55 il
Webb, Charles Lewis, 1918-
Novelist, teacher
Blk Am Wr 2: 746-47 por
Webb, Frank J.
Novelist
Robinson. Prose p. xvi (footnote) / Whit-
low. Lit p. 46-47

Whitfield, James M., 1822-1878
Poet
Barksdale. Writers p. 222-23 / Blk Am Wr
2: 764-65 / Brawley. Early p. 228 /
Robinson. Poets p. 39 / Sherman. Invis-
ible p. 42-46 / Whitlow. Lit p. 33-34
Whitlow, W. Edward
Educator
Afro-Am Ency 9: 2806-2807
Whitman, Albery Allson, 1851-1902
Poet
Barksdale. Writers p. 446-47 / Blk Am Wr
2: 765 / Blk Plots p. 312-313 / Brown.
Caravan p. 297 / Ency Blk Am p. 854 /
Kerlin. Poets 35 p. 345 / Robinson. Poets
p. 203 / Selected BAA p. 294 / Sherman.
Invisible p. 112-16 / Southern Wr p.
486-87 / White. Verse p. 50
Whitsitt, Joyce E. *See* Lawrence, Joyce
Whitsitt
Wideman, John E(dgar), 1941-
Teacher, novelist, short story writer, poet
Afro-Am Novel p. 168 / Blk Am Wr 2:
766-67 / Blk Plots p. 313 / Living BAA
p. 170 / Selected BAA p. 294-95 / Who
Blk Am 77 p. 955
Wiggins, Jefferson, 1929-
Living BAA p. 170
Wilder, James Randall
Culp. Twen p. 210-11 por
Wilkes, Laura Eliza, 1871-
Teacher, historian
Thorpe. Hist p. 150
Wilkins, Patricia (Mandulo)
Playwright
Blk Am Wr 1: 118 / Nat Play Dr p.
333 por
Wilkins, Roy, 1901-1981
Organization official, writer of published
speeches
Afro-Am Ency 9: 2812-14 / Bio Hist p.
459-61 / Ebony Success 1: 329 por /
Ency Am Biog p. 1202-1203 / Fax.
Leaders p. 65-79 / Metcalf. Profiles p.
85-111 / Negro Handbk 66 p. 417 /
Pol Profiles: Eisenhower p. 642-43 / Pol
Profiles: Johnson p. 648-50 / Pol Pro-
files: Kennedy p. 538-40 / Pol Profiles:
Nixon p. 669-70 / Young, M. Lead p.
20-23 por
Wilkinson, Doris Y., 1938-
Educator
Con Auth 29-33R: 752-53 / Living BAA
p. 170-71 / Who Blk Am 77 p. 959-60

Willerford, Frederick P., 1930-
Librarian, administrator
Bio Dr Librns 70 p. 1183 / Josey.
Blk Librn p. 205-215 / Who Blk Am 77
p. 960
Williams, Ann. *See* Dee, Ruby
Williams, Arthur D., 1895-
Army chaplain, theologian, author, poet,
playwright
Bio Dr Min 65 p. 385
Williams, Chancellor, 1902-
Historian, novelist
Innis. Profiles p. 90-91 / Selected BAA
p. 295
Williams, Collen
Dreer. Am Lit p. 242
Williams, Daniel Barclay, 1861-
Editor, journalist
Penn. Press p. 340-44
Williams, Daniel T., 1937-
Archivist, author
Living BAA p. 171
Williams, Dick Anthony, 1938-
Actor, playwright, director, producer
Dr Perf Arts 78 p. 392-93 / Who Blk
Am 77 p. 964-65 / Who Theatre 77 p.
1254
Williams, Edward C., 1871-1929
Educator, scholar, librarian, writer of short
stories and poems
Davis. Mem p. 40-41 por
Williams, Edward G., 1929-
Poet, novelist, short story writer
Blk Am Wr 2: 769-770 por / Con Auth
29-32R: 754 / Shuman. Galaxy p. 171
Williams, Edward W.
Clergyman, poet
Blk Am Wr 2: 769
Williams, Ella V. Chase, ca. 1860-
Teacher, editor
Scruggs. Wom p. 95-97
Williams, Ethel L., 1909-
Librarian, author
Con Auth 37-40R: 619 / Ency Blk Am
p. 858 / Living BAA p. 171 / Selected
BAA p. 295 / Who Blk Am 77 p. 966
Williams, Fannie Barrier (Mrs. S. Laing
Williams), 1855-1944
Teacher, club organizer, autobiographer
Dannett. Profiles 1: 326-27 il / David.
Defiance p. 73-81 / Haley. Ency p. 147
por / Lerner. Wom p. 164-65 / Loewen-
berg. Wom p. 263-64 / Northrop. College
p. 107-108 / Notable Am Wom 3: 620-22

Williams, G. Bernel, 1893-
Teacher
Living BAA p. 171-72
Williams, George Washington, 1849-1891
Journalist, historian, clergyman, novelist,
poet
Barksdale. Writers p. 257-60 / Blk Am Wr
2: 772-73 / Brown. Caravan p. 863 /
Davis. Cav p. 142 / Ency Blk Am p.
858 por / Greene. Defenders p. 99-100
por / Historical N Bio p. 144-45 il /
Kendricks. Voices p. 126 / Selected BAA
p. 296 / Simmons. Men p. 371-83 por /
Thorpe. Hist p. 46-55 / Who Was 1:
654
Williams, Henry Roger, 1869-1921
Poet
Blk Am Wr 2: 773
Williams, Jamye Coleman, 1918-
Educator, editor
Living BAA p. 172 / Who Blk Am 77
p. 970
Williams, John A(lfred), 1925-
Novelist, journalist, editor, biographer,
autobiographer, historian
Adoff. Blk on p. 235 / Afro-Am Ency
10: 2829 / Afro-Am Novel p. 172 /
Au Speaks p. 181-83 / Blk Am Wr 2:
773 / Blk Plots p. 313 / Con Auth
53-56: 585-86 / Con Novel 76 p. 1494 /
David. Soldier p. 179-89 / Dict Lit Biog
2: 537-42 por / Emanuel. Dark p. 392-93 /
Ency Blk Am p. 858 / Ford. Insights p.
341 / Hughes. Best p. 507 / King. Story
p. 107 / Living BAA p. 172-73 / Major.
Poet p. 156 / Margolies. Read p. 360-61 /
Selected BAA p. 296-97 / Sign Am Auth
p. 77 / Southern Wr p. 493-94 / Whitlow.
Lit p. 179-80 / Wor Auth 50-70, p. 1550-52
por / Writers Dr 76 p. 1158 / Writers
Dr 80 p. 1341 / Writers Dr 82 p. 1012
Williams, John B. L., 1853-
Minister
Culp. Twen p. 120-21 il
Williams, June Vanleer
Journalist, actress, playwright
Nat Play Dr p. 333 por
Williams, Lance A.
Editor, teacher, essayist, poet
Selected BAA p. 297-98
Williams, Lucy Ariel. *See* Holloway, (Lucy)
Ariel Williams
Williams, McDonald, 1917-
Educator
Living BAA p. 173 / Who Blk Am 77 p.
973

Williams, Mance A.
Poet
Hughes. New p. 125
Williams, Maxine A., 1911-
Priest, poet
Scally. Catholic p. 125
Williams, Ora (Ruby), 1926-
Bibliographer, teacher of English
Con Auth 73-76: 644 / Selected BAA p.
298-99 por
Williams, Oscar, 1939-
Director, producer, writer
Dr Perf Arts 78 p. 395
Williams, Paulette L. *See* Shange, Ntozake
Williams, Peter, 1786-1823
Minister, orator
Brawley. Early p. 100-101 / Sterling.
Speak p. 382-83 / Woodson. Orators
p. 32
Williams, Sandra Beth (Auransia), 1948-
Actor, playwright, poet
Blk Am Wr 2: 776-78 por
Williams, Sherley Anne (Shirley Williams),
1944-
Teacher of English, poet, playwright, writer
of television scripts
Con Auth 73-76: 645
Williams, Virginia W.
Journalist, editor, poet, reading specialist
Shuman. Galaxy p. 425 / Who Blk Am 77
p. 976-77
Williamson, Craig, 1943-
Con Auth 29-32: 756
Williamson, Harvey M., 1908-
Educator, writer of short stories, poet
Blk Am Wr 2: 778
Williamson, John H., 1844-
Public official, editor
Penn. Press p. 180-83
Willie, Charles V., 1927-
Professor of education and urban studies
Con Auth 41-44: 690-91 / Living BAA
p. 173-74 / Selected BAA p. 299 / Who
Blk Am 77 p. 978
Willis, John Ralph, 1938-
Educator
Living BAA p. 174
Wilson, Alice T., 1908-
Nurse, writer of screenplay and poetry
Blk Am Wr 2: 778-79
Wilson, Art
Poet
Coombs. Speak p. 252
Wilson, August, 1945-
Poet
Adoff. Poet p. 537

Wright, Sarah E(lizabeth) (Mrs. Joseph G. Kaye), 1929-
  Poet, novelist, critic
    Adoff. Poet p. 538 / Afro-Am Novel p. 187 / Blk Am Wr 2: 791 / Blk Plots p. 314-15 / Con Auth 37-40: 574 / Con Auth 37-40R: 637-38 / Exum. Keep p. 288 / Hughes. Poet p. 626 / Living BAA p. 176-77 / Selected BAA p. 304-305 / Whitlow. Lit p. 162
Wright, Theodore Sedgewick, 1797-1847
  Minister, abolitionist, orator
    Afro-Am Ency 10: 2866 / Barksdale. Writers p. 127-28 / Historical N Bio p. 148 / Kendricks. Voices p. 59 / Sterling. Speak p. 383 / Woodson. Orators p. 85-86
Wyche, Marvin, Jr., 1951-
  Poet, minister
    Bontemps. American 74 p. 226

Yarborough, Camille, 1938-
  Singer, dance instructor, poet
    Blk Am Wr 2: 792-93 por
Yates, Ella Gaines, 1927-
  Librarian, writer on librarianship
    Bio Dr Librns 70 p. 1213 / Josey. What p. 308 / Who Blk Am 77 p. 1001
Yates, Josephine Silone (R. K. Potter; R. K. Totper), 1852-1912
  Educator, poet, essayist
    Afro-Am Ency 10: 2872 / Brown. Home-spun p. 178-81 / Culp. Twen p. 20-21 por / Dannett. Profiles 1: 332-33 il / Scruggs. Wom p. 40-47
Yerby, Frank (Garvin), 1916-
  Novelist, short story writer
    Afro-Am Ency 10: 2873-74 / Afro-Am Novel p. 189 / Am Auth & Bks 72 p. 715 / Blk Am Wr 2: 793 / Blk Plots p. 315 / Bontemps. American 74 p. 227 / Con Auth 11-12: 466-67 / Con Novel 72 p. 1416 / Con Novel 76 p. 1550 / Cur Biog Yrbk 46 p. 672-74 por / Ency Blk Am p. 871 / Historical N Bio p. 267-68 / Hughes. Best p. 507 / Hughes. Poet p. 626 / Int Auth & Wr 77 p. 1118 / Living BAA p. 177 / Longman CT p. 588 / Novelists 79 p. 1331-32 / Penguin Am Lit p. 277 / Selected BAA p. 305-306 / Sign Am Auth p. 77 / Southern Wr p. 510-11 / Twen CA Sup 55 p. 1115-16 por / Webster Am Biog p. 1169 /

Yerby, Frank (Garvin) (cont'd) ...
    Who Am 80, 2: 3611 / Who Blk Am 77 p. 1001 / Writers Dr 76 p. 1189 / Writers Dr 80 p. 1376
Yette, Samuel F(rederick), 1929-
  Journalist, author
    Con Auth 102: 542
Young, Al(bert James), 1939-
  Novelist, poet, writer of short stories
    Afro-Am Novel p. 194 / Blk Am Wr 2: 795-97 por / Blk Plots p. 316 / Cele p. 268 / Chapman. New p. 146 / Con Auth 29-32: 701 / Con Auth 29-32R: 776 / Con Novel 76 p. 177 / Con Poets 70 p. 1206 / Coombs. Speak p. 252 / Living BAA p. 177-78 / Major. Poet p. 156 / Miller. Dices p. 137 / Reader's Adviser 74, 1: 339-40 / Selected BAA p. 307 por / Writers Dr 80 p. 1378 / Writers Dr 82 p. 1039
Young, Alexander
  Poet
    Murphy. Ebony p. 160
Young, Andrew Sturgeon Nash (A. S. "Doc" Young), 1924-
  Editor, journalist, author
    Dr Perf Arts 78 p. 406 / Ebony Success 1: 340 por / Living BAA p. 178
Young, Bernice Elizabeth, 1931-
  Biographer, writer of children's books
    Auth Bk YP Sup 79 p. 297 / Con Auth 37-40R: 643-44 / Selected BAA p. 308 / Writers Dr 80 p. 1378 / Writers Dr 82 p. 1039
Young, Charles A., 1864-1922
  US Army officer, author, poet
    Bio Hist p. 479-81 / Brawley. Builders p. 167-72 / Greene. Defenders p. 158-63 por
Young, Henry J., 1943-
  Theologian, researcher, editor, author
    Who Blk Am 77 p. 1004
Young, Nathan B(enjamin), 1862-
  Educator, writer on Negro education
    Culp. Twen p. 124-25 por / Who Col Race p. 296
Young, Whitney M(oore), Jr., 1921-1971
  Organization official, writer on civil rights
    Bio Hist p. 482-83 / Con Auth 13-14: 489 / Con Auth P-1: 695 / Ency Am Biog p. 1239-40 / Fax. Leaders p. 33-47 / Great Negroes 69 p. 123 il / Historical N Bio p. 268-69 por / Metcalf. Profiles p. 307-333 / Negro Handbk 66 p. 418 / Selected

Young, Whitney M(oore), Jr. (cont'd) ...
    BAA p. 309-310 por / Webster Am Biog
    p. 1171-72
Yvonne (Chism-Peace)
  Poet
    Cele p. 268

Zuber, Ron
  Poet, playwright
    King. Drama p. 429

Indexed Collections by Title

ALA Yearbook. Vols. 1-6. American Library Association, 1976-1981 (ALA Yrbk)

ASCAP Biographical Dictionary of Composers, Authors and Publishers, The. 1966 ed. Compiled and edited by the Lynn Farnol Group, Inc. ASCAP, c1966 (AmSCAP 66)

-ASCAP Biographical Dictionary. 4th ed. Compiled by Jaques Cattell Press. Bowker, 1980 (-AmSCAP 80)

Afro-American Artists. Theressa D. Cederholm, comp. Trustees of the Boston Public Library, 1973 (Afro-Am Art)

Afro-American Authors. William Adams. Houghton Mifflin, 1972 (Adams. Auth)

Afro-American Encyclopedia. 10 vols. Educational Book Publishers, 1974 (Afro-Am Ency)

Afro- American Encyclopedia. James T. Haley, comp. Nashville, 1885 (Haley. Ency)

Afro-American Novel, 1965-1975, The. Helen R. Houston. Whitston, 1977 (Afro-Am Novel)

Afro-American Press and Its Editors, The. Irvin Garland Penn. Willey, 1891 (Penn. Press)

Afro-American Voices, 1960's-1970's. Ralph Kendricks and Claudette Levitt. Oxford Book Co., 1970 (Kendricks. Voices)

Afro-American Writing. 2 vols. Richard A. Long and Eugenia W. Collier, eds. New York University Press, 1972 (Long. Writing)

American Authors and Books. 3rd rev. ed. W. J. Burke and Will D. Howe. Revised by Irving Weiss and Anne Weiss. Crown, 1972 (Am Auth & Bks)

American Authors, 1600-1900. Stanley J. Kunitz and Howard Haycraft, eds. H. W. Wilson, 1939 (Am Auth)

American Black Women in the Arts and Social Sciences: A Bibliographic Survey. Rev. edition. Ora Williams. Scarecrow, 1978 (Williams. Wom)

American Literature by Negro Authors. Herman Dreer. Macmillan, 1950 (Dreer. Am Lit)

American Negro Poetry. Arna Bontemps, ed. Hill and Wang, 1963 (Bontemps. American 63)

American Negro Poetry. Rev. ed. Arna Bontemps, ed. Hill and Wang, 1974 (Bontemps. American 74)

American Novelists of Today. Harry R. Warfel. Greenwood Press, 1976 (Am Novel)

American Women Writers. Vols. 1-3. Lina Mainiero, ed. Ungar, 1979-1981 (Am Wom Wr)

America's Black Congressmen. Maurine Christopher. Crowell, 1971 (Christopher. Congress)

Anger and Beyond: The Negro Writer in the United States. 1st ed. Herbert Hill, ed. Harper & Row, 1966 (Hill. Anger)

Anthology of Magazine Verse for 1926. William Stanley Braithwaite, ed. Brimmer, 1926 (Anth Mag Verse)

Anthology of Verse by American Negroes, An. Newman Ivey White. Durham, NC: Trinity College Press, 1924 (White. Verse)

Author Speaks: Selected "PW" Interviews, 1967-1976, The. *Publishers Weekly* editors and contributors. Bowker, 1977 (Au Speaks)

Authors and Illustrators of Children's Books. Miriam Hoffman and Eva Samuels. Bowker, 1972 (Auth & Ill)

Authors in the News. Vols. 1 and 2. Barbara Mykoruk, ed. Gale Research Co., 1976, 1977 (Auth News)

Authors of Books for Young People. 1st Supplement. Martha E. Ward and Dorothy A. Marquardt. Scarecrow, 1967 (Auth Bk YP 67)

Authors of Books for Young People. 2nd ed. Martha E. Ward and Dorothy A. Marquardt. Scarecrow, 1971 (Auth Bk YP 71)

Authors of Books for Young People. Supplement to the 2nd ed. Martha E. Ward and Dorothy A. Marquardt. Scarecrow, 1979 (Auth Bk YP Sup 79)

Beautiful, Also, Are the Souls of My Black Sisters: A History of the Black Woman in America. Jeanne L. Noble. Prentice-Hall, 1978 (Noble. Beautiful)

Best Short Stories by Negro Writers, The. Langston Hughes, ed. Little, Brown, 1967 (Hughes. Best)

Bid the Vassal Soar. Phillis Richmond. Howard University Press, 1975 (Richmond. Bid)

Biographical Dictionary of Librarians in the United States, A. 5th ed. Lee Ash, ed., American Library Association, 1979 (Bio Dr Librns)

Biographical Directory of Negro Ministers. Ethel L. Williams. Scarecrow, 1965 (Bio Dr Min 65)

Biographical Directory of Negro Ministers. 3rd ed. Ethel L. Williams. G. K. Hall, 1975 (Bio Dr Min 75)

Biographical Dictionary of Southern Authors. Lucian L. Knight. Gale Research Co., 1978. Reprint of the 1929 ed. (Bio Dict S Auth)

Biographical Directory of the American Congress, 1774-1961. GPO, 1961 (Bio Dr Am Cong)

Biographical History of Blacks in America since 1528. Edgar A. Toppin. McKay, 1971 (Bio Hist)

Biographical Sketches and Interesting Anecdotes of Persons of Color. 2nd ed. Abigail F. Mott. Day, 1837 (Mott. Bio)

*Black American Leaders. Margaret B. Young. Watts, 1969 (*Young, M. Lead)

Black American Literature. Roger Whitlow. Hall, 1973 (Whitlow. Lit)

Black American Writers, Past and Present. 2 vols. Theressa Gunnel Rush, Carol Fairbanks Myers and Esther Spring Arata. Scarecrow, 1975 (Blk Am Wr)

Black Arts. Ahmed Alhamisi and Harun Kofi Wangara, eds. Black Arts Publications, 1969 (Alhamisi. Arts)

Black Authors (6 filmstrips) Brunswick; Miller-Brody, 1976 (Blk Auth)

Black Defenders of America, 1775-1973. Robert Ewell Green. Johnson Publishing Co., 1974 (Greene. Defenders)

Black Defiance: Black Profiles in Courage. Jay David. Morrow, 1972 (David. Defiance)

Black Drama Anthology. Woodie King and Ron Miller, eds. Columbia University Press, c1972 (King. Drama)

Black Fire. LeRoi Jones and Larry Neal. Morrow, 1968 (Jones. Fire)

*Black Foremothers: Three Lives. Dorothy Sterling. Feminist Press, c1979 (*Sterling. Fore)

Black Historians, a Critique. Earl E. Thorpe. Morrow, 1969 (Thorpe. Hist)

Black Insights: Significant Literature by Black Americans — 1790 to the Present. Nick Aaron Ford, ed. Ginn, 1971 (Ford. Insights)

Black Leaders of the Centuries. S. Okechukwu Mezu and Ram Desai. Black Academy Press [n.d.] (Mezu. Leaders)

Black Leaders of the Twentieth Century. (Filmstrips, cassettes) Miami, FL: International Book Corp., 1969 (Blk Lead)

Black Leadership in American History. Thomas T. Lyons. Addison-Wesley, c1971 (Lyons. Leader)

Black Librarian in America, The. E. J. Josey, ed. Scarecrow, 1970 (Josey. Blk Librn)

"Black Librarians as Creative Writers," by Ann A. Shockley. In *Handbook of Black Librarianship*, compiled and edited by E. J. Josey and Ann A. Shockley, p. 160-66. Libraries Unlimited, 1977 (Handbk Librans)

Black Literature for High School Students. Barbara Stanford and Karima Amin. National Council of Teachers of English, 1978 (Blk Lit HS)

Black on Black: Commentaries by Negro Americans. Arnold Adoff, ed. Macmillan, 1968 (Adoff. Blk on)

*Black out Loud: An Anthology of Modern Poems by Black Americans. Arnold Adoff, ed. Macmillan, 1970 (*Adoff. Blk out)

Black Pioneers in American History. Vols. 1 and 2 (Record or cassette) Jonathan Katz, ed. Caedmon (Blk Pioneers)

Black Plots and Black Characters. Robert L. Southgate. Gaylord Professional Publications, 1979 (Blk Plots)

Black Writers of America: A Comprehensive Anthology. Richard Barksdale and Keneth Kinnamon. Macmillan, 1972 (Barksdale. Writers)

Bondage, Freedom and Beyond: The Prose of Black Americans. Addison Gayle, Jr. Doubleday, 1971 (Gayle. Bond)

Book of American Negro Poetry, The. James Weldon Johnson. Harcourt, Brace, 1931 (Johnson. Book)

Books Are by People: Interviews with 104 Authors and Illustrators of Books for Young Children. Lee Bennett Hopkins. Citation Press, 1974 (Books Are)

Broadside Authors and Illustrators: An Illustrated Biographical Dictionary. Leaonead Bailey, comp. Broadside Press, 1974 (Broadside Auth)

*Brothers and Sisters: Modern Stories by Black Americans. Arnold Adoff, ed. Macmillan, 1970 (*Adoff. Brothers)

Caroling Dusk: An Anthology of Verse by Negro Poets. Countee Cullen, ed. Harper, 1927 (Cullen. Carol)

Cavalcade: Negro American Writing from 1760 to the Present. Arthur P. Davis and Saunders Redding, eds. Houghton Mifflin, 1971 (Davis. Cav)

Celebrations: A New Anthology of Black American Poetry. Arnold Adoff, comp. Follett, 1977 (Cele)

Chamber's Biographical Dictionary. Revised ed. J. O. Thorne, ed. Chamber, 1969 (Chamber)

Cincinnati's Colored Citizens. Wendell P. Dabney. Negro Universities Press, 1926 (Dabney. Cin)

College of Life, The. Henry D. Northrop. Originally published in 1895. Menemosyne, 1969 (Northrop. College)

Contemporary American Authors: A Critical Survey of 219 Bio-Bibliographies. Fred Benjamin Millett. Harcourt, 1940 (Con Am Auth)

-Contemporary Authors: A Bio-Bibliographical Guide to Current Authors and Their Works. Vols. 1-103. Gale Research Co., 1962-1982 (-Con Auth)

-Contemporary Authors, First Revision Vols. 17-44. Gale Research Co., 1965-1979 (-Con Auth ... R)

-Contemporary Authors New Revision Series. Vols. 1-4. Gale Research Co., 1962-1981 (-Con Auth NR)

Contemporary Authors, Permanent Series. Vols. 1 and 2. Gale Research Co., 1975, 1978 (Con Auth P)

Contemporary Black Drama. Clinton F. Oliver and Stephanie Sills, ed. Scribner's Sons, 1971 (Oliver. Drama)

Contemporary Black Leaders. Elton C. Fax. Dodd, Mead, 1970 (Fax. Leaders)

Contemporary Dramatists. James Vinson, ed. St. Martin's Press, c1973 (Con Drama 73)

Contemporary Dramatists. 2nd ed. James Vinson and D. L. Kirpatrick, eds. St. Martin's Press, 1977 (Con Drama 77)

Contemporary Novelists. James Vinson, ed. St. Martin's Press, c1972 (Con Novel 72)

Contemporary Novelists. 2nd ed. James Vinson, ed.; D. L. Kirpatrick, associate ed. St. Martin's Press, c1976 (Con Novel 76)

Contemporary Poetry of North Carolina. Guy Owen and Mary C. Williams, eds. Blair, 1977 (Owen. Poet)

Contemporary Poets. Rosalie Murphy and James Vinson, eds. St. Martin's Press, 1970 (Con Poets 70)

Contemporary Poets. 2nd ed. James Vinson, ed.; D. L. Kirpatrick, associate ed. St. Martin's Press, 1975 (Con Poets 75)

Contemporary Poets. 3rd ed. James Vinson, ed.; D. L. Kirpatrick, associate ed. St. Martin's Press, 1980 (Con Poets 80)

Crowell's Handbook of Contemporary American Poetry. Karl Malkoff. Crowell, c1973 (Crowell CAP)

Crowell's Handbook of Contemporary Drama. Michael Anderson and others. Crowell, c1971 (Crowell CD)

-Current Biography Yearbook. H. W. Wilson, 1940-1980 (-Cur Biog Yrbk)

Dark Symphony: Negro Literature in America. James A. Emanuel and Theodore Goss, eds. Free Press, 1968 (Emanuel. Dark)

Dices or Black Bones. Adam D. Miller, ed. Houghton Mifflin. 1970 (Miller. Dices)

-Dictionary of American Biography. Prepared under the auspices of the American Council of Learned Societies. Scribner's Sons. Original edition, vols. 1-20, 1928-1937; Subscription edition, vols. 1-11, 1944-1958. (-Dict Am Biog)

-Dictionary of American Biography, Supplement. Vols. 1-5. Scribner's Sons, 1944-1977 (-Dict Am Biog Sup)

Dictionary of Literary Biography. Vols. 1-8. Gale Research Co., 1978-1981 (Dict Lit Biog)

Dictionary of Literary Biography Yearbook: 1980. Gale Research Co., c1981 (Dict Lit Biog Yrbk)

-Directory of American Scholars. Bowker, 1969, 1974, 1978 (-Dr Am Schol)

Directory of Blacks in the Performing Arts. Edward Mapp. Scarecrow, 1978 (Dr Perf Arts)

Distinguished Negro Georgians. Cornelius V. Troup. Dallas: Royal, 1962 (Troup. Geor)

Dramatists. James Vinson, ed. St. Martin's Press, 1979 (Dramatists)

Early Black American Poets. William H. Robinson, Jr. Wm. C. Brown, c1971 (Robinson. Poets)

Early Black American Prose. William H. Robinson, Jr. Wm. C. Brown, c1971 (Robinson. Prose)

Early Negro American Writers. Benjamin Brawley. University of North Carolina Press, 1935 (Brawley. Early)

*Ebony Book of Black Achievement, The. Margaret Peters. Johnson Publishing Co., 1970 (*Peters. Ebony)

Ebony Rhythm: An Anthology of Contemporary Verse. Beatrice M. Murphy, ed. Books for Libraries, 1968 (Murphy. Ebony)

Ebony Success Library, The. 3 vols. Editors of Ebony. Southwestern Co. by arrangement with Johnson Publishing Co., 1973 (Ebony Success)

Encyclopedia of American Biography. John A. Garraty, ed. Harper & Row, 1974 (Ency Am Biog)

Encyclopedia of Black America. W. Augustus Low and Virgil A. Clift, eds. McGraw-Hill, 1981 (Ency Blk Am)

*Famous American Negro Poets. Charlemae H. Rollins. Dodd, Mead, c1965 (*Rollins. Famous)

Famous Black Entertainers of Today. Raoul Abdul. Mead, c1974 (Abdul. Enter)

*Famous Negro Entertainers of Stage, Screen, and TV. Charlemae H. Rollins. Dodd, Mead, 1967 (*Rollins. Enter)

For Freedom: A Biographical Story of the American Negro. Arthur Huff Fauset. Franklin, 1927 (Fauset. Freedom)

Forerunners of Black Power: The Rhetoric of Abolition. Ernest G. Bormann. Prentice-Hall, 1971 (Bormann. Fore)

Forgotten Pages of American Literature. Gerald W. Haslam. Houghton Mifflin, 1970 (Haslam. Forgot)

Four Negro Poets. Alain Locke, ed. Simon & Schuster, 1927 (Locke. Four)

*Four Took Freedom. Philip Sterling and Rayford Logan. Doubleday, c1967 (*Sterling. Four)

Fourth Book of Junior Authors and Illustrators. Doris De Montreville and Elizabeth D. Crawford, eds. H. W. Wilson, 1978 (Fourth Bk)

From the Ashes: Voices of Watts. Budd Schulberg, ed. New American Library, c1967 (Watts Wr)

From the Dark Tower: Afro-American Writers, 1900-1950. Arthur P. Davis. Howard University Press, 1974 (Davis. Dark)

Galaxy of Black Writing. A. R. Baird Shuman. Moore, 1968 (Shuman. Galaxy)

*Golden Slippers: An Anthology of Negro Poetry for Young Readers. Arna Bontemps. Harper & Row, 1941 (*Bontemps. Golden)

Great American Negroes. Ben Richardson. Revised by William A. Fahey. Crowell, c1956 (Richardson. Great 56)

Great Black Americans. 2nd rev. ed. Formerly titled Great American Negroes. Ben Richardson and William A. Fahey. Crowell, c1976 (Richardson. Great 76)

Great Negroes, Past and Present. 3rd ed. Russell Adams L. Afro-American Publishing Co., 1969 (Great Negroes)

Great Slave Narratives. Arna Bontemps, comp. Beacon, c1969 (Bontemps. Great)

Growing up Black. Jay David. Morrow, 1968 (David. Growing)

Guide to American Literature from Emily Dickinson to the Present. James T. Callow and Robert J. Reilly. Barnes & Noble, 1977 (Guide Am Lit)

Harlem Renaissance Remembered, The. Arna Bontemps. Dodd, Mead, c1972 (Bontemps. Harlem)

Historical Negro Biographies. Wilhelmena S. Robinson. Publishers Co., 1967 (Historical N Bio)

Homespun Heroines and Other Women of Distinction. Hallie Q. Brown, comp. Aldine, c1926 (Brown. Homespun)

*I Have a Dream. Emma Sterne. Knopf, c1965 (*Sterne. Dream)

Illustrators of Books for Young People. Martha E. Ward and Dorothy A. Marquardt. Scarecrow, 1970 (Illus Bks YP 70)

Illustrators of Books for Young People. 2nd ed. Martha E. Ward and Dorothy A. Marquardt. Scarecrow, 1975 (Illus Bks YP 75)

Illustrators of Children's Books, 1957-1966. Lee Kingman, Joanna Foster and Ruth Giles Lontoft, comps. Horn Book, 1968 (Illus Ch Bks 57)

Illustrators of Children's Books, 1967-1976. Lee Kingman, Grace Allen Hogarth and Harriet Quimby, comps. Horn Book, 1978 (Illus Ch Bks 67)

In the Vanguard of a Race. L. H. Hammond. Council of Women for Home Missionaries & the Missionary Education Movement of the United States and Canada, 1922 (Hammond. Van)

International Authors and Writers Who's Who. 8th ed. Adrian Gaster, ed. International Biographical Centre, 1977 (Int Auth & Wr)

Invisible Poets: Afro-Americans of the Nineteenth Century. Joan A. Sherman. University of Illinois Press, 1974 (Sherman. Invisible)

Kaleidoscope: Poems by American Negro Poets. Robert Hayden, ed. Harcourt, Brace & World, 1967 (Hayden. Kal)

Keeping the Faith: Writings by Contemporary Black American Women. Pat Crutchfield Exum. Fawcett, c1974 (Exum. Keep)

*Lift Every Voice. Dorothy Sterling and Benjamin Quarles. Doubleday, Zenith Books, 1965 (*Sterling. Lift)

Lincoln Library of the Arts, II. Frontier, 1973 (Lincoln Lib Arts)

Lincoln University Poets: Centennial Anthology, 1854-1954. Waring Cuney, Langston Hughes, and Bruce McM. Wright. Fine Editions Press, 1954 (Cuney. Linc)

Living Black American Authors: A Biographical Dictionary. Ann Allen Shockley and Sue P. Chandler. Bowker, 1973 (Living BAA)

Living Black in White America. Jay David and Elaine Crane. Morrow, 1971 (David. Living)

Longman Companion to Twentieth Century Literature. Alfred C. Ward. Longman Group, c1970 (Longman CT)

McGraw-Hill Encyclopedia of World Drama. 4 vols. McGraw-Hill, 1972 (McGraw Ency WD)

Major Black Religious Leaders, 1755-1940. Henry J. Young. Abingdon, c1977 (Young. 1755)

Major Black Religious Leaders since Nineteen Forty. Henry J. Young. Abingdon, 1979 (Young. Since 1940)

Memorable Negroes in Cleveland's Past. Russell H. Davis. Western Reserve Historical Society, 1969 (Davis. Mem)

Men of Mark. William J. Simmons. Johnson Publishing Co., 1970. Reprint of 1887 ed. (Simmons. Men)

More Books by More People. Lee Bennett Hopkins. Citation Press, 1974 (More Books)

More Junior Authors. Muriel Fuller, ed. H. W. Wilson, 1963 (More Jun Auth)

Narratives of Colored Americans. Abigail F. Mott and M. S. Wood, comps. W. Wood, 1877 (Mott. Nar)

-National Cyclopaedia of American Biography. James T. White, 1891 (-Nat Cyclo)

National Playwrights Directory. Phyllis J. Kaye, ed. O'Neill Theater Center, 1977 (Nat Play Dr)

Native Sons Reader, A. Edward Margolies, ed. Lippincott, 1970 (Margolies. Read)

Negro Almanac, The. 2nd ed. Harry A. Ploski and Ernest Kaiser, comps. Bellwether, c1971 (Negro Alm 71)

Negro Almanac, The: A Reference Work on Afro-Americans, 1776 Bicentennial Edition. Harry A. Ploski and Warren Marr, II, comps. Bellwether c1976 (Negro Alm 76)

Negro Builders and Heroes. Benjamin Brawley. University of North Carolina Press, 1937 (Brawley. Builders)

Negro Caravan, The. Sterling A. Brown, Arthur P. Davis, and Ulysses Lee, eds. Dryden, 1941 (Brown. Caravan)

Negro Catholic Writers, 1900-1943: A Bio-Bibliography. Sister Mary Anthony Scally. Romig, 1945 (Scally. Catholic)

Negro Handbook, The. Editors of Ebony. Johnson Publishing Co., 1966 (Negro Handbk)

Negro in Literature and Art in the United States, The. Benjamin Brawley. Duffield, 1930. Reprint. Scholarly Press, 1972 (Brawley. Lit)

Negro Novel in America, The. Rev. ed. Robert A. Bone. Yale University Press, 1965 (Bone. Novel)

Negro Orators and Their Orations. Carter Goodwin Woodson. Associated Publishers, 1925 (Woodson. Orators)

Negro Poets and Their Poems. Robert T. Kerlin. Associated Publishers, c1923 (Kerlin. Poets 23)

Negro Poets and Their Poems. 3rd ed. Robert T. Kerlin. Associated Publishers, c1935 (Kerlin. Poets 35)

Negro Trail Blazers of California, The. Delilah L. Beasley. Los Angeles, 1919 (Beasley. Trail)

Negro Voices: An Anthology of Contemporary Verse. Beatrice M. Murphy, ed. Harrison, c1938 (Murphy. N Voices)

Negroes of Achievement in Modern America. James J. Flynn. Dodd, Mead, 1970 (Flynn. Achieve)

New Black Poetry, The. Clarence Major, ed. International Publishers, 1969 (Major. Poet)

New Black Voices: An Anthology of Contemporary Afro-American Literature. Abraham Chapman, ed. New American Library, c1972 (Chapman. New)

New Negro Poets, U.S.A., The. Langston Hughes. Indiana University Press, 1964 (Hughes. New)

New York Times Obituaries Index, 1969-1978. Vol. 2. The New York Times, 1980 (NYT Obit)

Nine Black Poets. R. Baird Shuman, ed. Moore, 1968 (Shuman. Nine)

Nommo: An Anthology of Modern Black African and Black American Literature. William H. Robinson, Jr., ed. Macmillan, c1972 (Robinson. Nommo)

North Carolina Authors: A Selective Handbook. Joint Committee of the North Carolina English Teachers Association and the North Carolina Library Association. University of North Carolina Library, 1952 (North Car Auth)

Notable American Women: Modern Period: A Biographical Dictionary. Barbara Sicherman and others, eds. Belknap Press, 1980 (Notable Am Wom Mod)

Notable American Women, 1607-1950: A Biographical Dictionary. 3 vols. Edward T. James and others, eds. Belknap Press, 1971. (Notable Am Wom)

Notable Names in the American Theatre. White, 1976 (Notable Names)

Noted American Negro Women, Their Triumphs and Activities. M. A. Majors. Donohue and Heneberry, 1893 (Majors. Wom)

Novelists and Prose Writers. James Vinson and D. L. Kirpatrick, eds. St. Martin's Press, 1979 (Novelists)

Ohio Authors and Their Books ..., 1796-1950. William Coyle. World, 1962 (Ohio Auth)

Open Secrets: Ninety-four Women in Touch with Our Time. Barbaralee Diamonstein. Viking, 1972 (Diamonstein. Open)

Oratory of Negro Leaders: 1900-1968, The. Marcus H. Boulware. Negro Universities Press, 1969 (Boulware. Oratory)

Oxford Companion to American Literature. 4th ed. Oxford University Press, 1965 (Oxford Am 65)

Paths toward Freedom: A Biographical History of Blacks and Indians in North Carolina by Blacks and Indians. North Carolina State University, Center for Urban Affairs, c1976 (Paths)

Penguin Companion to American Literature. Malcolm Bradbury, Eric Mottram, and Jean Franco, eds. McGraw-Hill, c1971 (Penguin Am Lit)

*Pioneers in Print: Adventures in Courage. Alice Fleming. Reilly & Lee, 1971 (*Fleming. Pioneers)

Pioneers in Protest. Lerone Bennett, Jr. Johnson Publishing Co., 1968 (Bennett. Pioneers)

Poetry of Black America, The. Arnold Adoff, ed. Harper & Row, 197 (Adoff. Poet)

Poetry of the Negro, 1746-1949, The: An Anthology. Langston Hughes, ed. Garden City, 1949 (Hughes. Poet)

Poets. James Vinson and D. L. Kirpatrick, eds. St. Martin's Press, 1970 (Poets)

Political Profiles. Nelson Lichtenstein and Eleanora W. Schoenbaum, eds. Facts on File, Inc., 1976-1979 (Pol Profiles)

Portraits in Color. Mary White Ovington. Viking, 1927 (Ovington. Portraits)

Profiles in Black: Biographical Sketches of 100 Living Black Unsung Heroes. Doris Funnye Innis and Julian Wu, eds. CORE Publications, 1976 (Innis. Profiles)

*Profiles in Black and White: Stories of Men and Women Who Fought against Slavery. Elizabeth F. Chittenden. Scribner's Sons, 1973 (*Chittenden. Profiles)

Profiles in Black Power. James Haskins. Doubleday, 1972 (Haskins. Profiles)

Profiles in Literature: Tom and Muriel Feelings. (Videotape) Temple University, 1971 (Profiles Lit)

Profiles of Black Achievement. (Filmstrip, disc, cassette) Guidance Associates, 1973-1976 (Profiles Blk Ach)

Profiles of Negro Womanhood. 2 vols. Sylvia G. L. Dannett. Educational Heritage, 1964, 1966 (Dannett. Profiles)

Reader's Adviser, The: A Layman's Guide to Literature. 12th ed. Vol. 1: The Best in American and British Fiction, Poetry, Essays, Literary Biography, Bibliography, and Reference. Sarah L. Prakken, ed. Bowker, 1974 (Reader's Adviser)

Reader's Encyclopedia of American Literature, The. Max J. Herzbert and the staff of the Thomas Y. Crowell Co., c1962 (Reader's Ency)

Readings from Negro Authors for Schools and Colleges. Otelia Cromwell. Harcourt, Brace, 1931 (Cromwell. Read)

Rising Tides: 20th Century American Poets. Laura Chester and Sharon Barba, eds. Washington Square Press, 1973 (Chester. Rising)

Selected Black American Authors. James A. Page. G. K. Hall, 1977 (Selected BAA)

Short Biographical Sketches of Eminent Negro Men and Women in Europe and the United States. John E. Bruce, comp. Gazette Press, 1910 (Bruce. Sketches)

*Significant American Authors, Poets, and Playwrights. Children's Press, 1975 (*Sign Am Auth)

*Significant American Women. Children's Press, 1975 (*Sign Am Wom)

Something about the Author. Vols. 1-25. Gale Research Co., c1971-1981 (Something ATA)

Soulscript: Afro-American Poetry. Jane Jordan, ed. Zenith Books, Doubleday, c1970 (Jordan. Soul)

Southern Writers: A Biographical Dictionary. Robert Bain, Joseph M. Flora, and Louis D. Rubin, Jr., eds. Louisiana State University Press, 1979 (Southern Wr)

Southern Writing, 1585-1920. Richard Beale Davis, C. Hugh Holman, and Louis D. Rubin, Jr., eds. Odyssey, 1970 (Davis. South)

Sparkling Gems of Race Knowledge Worth Reading. James T. Haley, comp. Haley, 1897 (Haley. Spark)

Speak out in Thunder Tones: Letters and Other Writings by Black Northerners, 1787-1867. Dorothy Sterling, ed. Doubleday, 1973 (Sterling. Speak)

Speeches by Black Americans. Daniel J. O'Neill, comp. Dickenson, c1971 (O'Neill. Speeches)

*Stories of Twenty-three Famous Negro Americans. John T. King and Marcet H. King. Steck-Vaughn, 1967 (*King. Famous)

-Supplement to Allibone's Critical Dictionary of British and American Authors, A. 2 vols. John F. Kirk. Lippincott, 1891. Gale Research Co., 1965 (-Alli Sup)

*Ten Slaves Who Became Famous. Basil Miller. Zondervan, 1951 (*Miller. Ten)

*They Showed the Way. Charlemae H. Rollins. Crowell, 1964 (*Rollins. They)

Third Book of Junior Authors. Doris De Motreville and Donna Hill, eds. H. W. Wilson, 1972 (Third Bk)

Today's Negro Voices: An Anthology by Young Negro Poets. Beatrice M. Murphy. Messner, 1970 (Murphy. Today)

Twelve Black Floridians. Leedell W. Neyland. The Florida Agricultural and Mechanical University Foundation, 1970 (Neyland. Flor)

Twelve Negro Americans. Mary Jenness. Friendship, 1938 (Jenness. Twelve)

Twentieth Century Authors: A Biographical Dictionary of Modern Literature. Stanley J. Kunitz and Howard Haycraft. H. W. Wilson, 1942 (Twen CA)

Twentieth Century Authors, First Supplement: A Biographical Dictionary of Modern Literature. Stanley J. Kunitz and Vineta Colby. H. W. Wilson, 1955 (Twen CA Sup)

Twentieth Century Children's Writers. D. L. Kirpatrick, ed. St. Martin's Press, c1978 (Twen CCW)

Twentieth Century Negro Literature; or A Cyclopedia of Thought. Daniel Wallace Culp, ed. Toronto, 1902. Reprint. Arno Press, 1969 (Culp. Twen)

Twenty Black Women: A Profile of Contemporary Black Maryland Women. Frances N. Beckles. Gateway Press, 1978 (Beckles. Twenty)

Understanding the New Black Poetry: Black Poetry, Black Speech and Black Music as Poetic Reference. Stephen E. Henderson, ed. Morrow, 1973 (Henderson. Under)

Up from the Ghetto. Phillip T. Drotning and Wesley W. South. Cowles, 1970 (Drotning. Up)

Up from Within: Today's New Black Leaders. George R. Metcalf. McGraw-Hill, 1971 (Metcalf. Up)

Voices from the Black Experience: African and Afro-American Literature. Darwin T. Turner and others, eds. Ginn, 1972 (Turner. Voices)

We Speak as Liberators: Young Black Poets. Orde Coombs, ed. Dodd, Mead, 1970 (Coombs. Speak)

Webster's American Biographies. Charles Van Doren, ed., Robert McHenry, associate ed. Merriam, 1979 (Webster Am Biog)

What Black Librarians Are Saying. E. J. Josey, ed. Scarecrow, 1972 (Josey. What)

What We Must See: Young Black Storytellers, an Anthology. Orde Coombs, comp. Dodd, Mead, 1971 (Coombs. What)

Who Was Who: Historical Volume, 1607-1896. Marquis, c1963 (Who Was H)

Who Was Who: Historical Volume, 1607-1896. Revised edition, 1967. Marquis, c1967 (Who Was HR)

Who Was Who in America. Vols. 1-6. Marquis, 1942-1976 (Who Was)

Who's Who among Black Americans. 2nd ed., 1977-1978. Who's Who among Black Americans, Inc., 1978 (Who Blk Am)

-Who's Who in America. Vols. 1-41. Marquis, 1899-1980 (-Who Am)

Who's Who in Colored America: A Biographical Dictionary of Notable Living Persons of Negro Descent in America. Who's Who in Colored America Corp., 1927-1950 (Who Col Am)

Who's Who in Colored Louisiana, with Brief Sketches of History and Romance. A. E. Perkins, ed. Louisiana State University Press, 1930 (Who Col Lo)

Who's Who in the Theatre: A Biographical Record of the Contemporary Stage. 16th ed. Ian Herbert, ed. Gale Research Co., 1977 (Who Theatre)

Who's Who in Twentieth Century Literature. Martin Seymour-Smith. Holt, Rinehart and Winston, 1976 (Who Twen)

Who's Who of the Colored Race: A General Biographical Dictionary of Men and Women of African Descent. Frank Lincoln Mather, ed. Chicago, 1915. Gale Research Co., 1976 (Who Col Race)

Witnesses for Freedom: Negro Americans in Autobiography. Rebecca C. Barton. Harper, 1948 (Barton. Witness)

Women Builders. Sadie I. Daniel. Associated Publishers, 1970. Reprint of 1931 ed. (Daniel. Wom)

Women in America: A Guide to Books, 1963-1975. Barbara Haber. G. K. Hall, 1978 (Wom Am)

Women of Distinction: Remarkable in Works and Invincible in Character. Lawson A. Scruggs. Raleigh, NC: Scruggs, 1893 (Scruggs. Wom)

World Authors, 1950-1970: A Companion Volume to Twentieth Century Authors. John Wakeman, ed. H. W. Wilson, 1975 (Wor Auth 50-70)

World Authors, 1970-1975: A Companion Volume to Twentieth Century Authors. John Wakeman, ed. H. W. Wilson, 1980 (Wor Auth 70-75)

World's Great Men of Color. Vol. 2. J. A. Rogers. Collier Books, Macmillan, c1972. Original ed., c1947 (Rogers. World)

Writers Directory, The, 1976-1978. St. Martin's Press, 1976 (Writers Dr 76)

Writers Directory, The, 1980-1982. St. Martin's Press, 1979 (Writers Dr 80)

Writers Directory, The, 1982-1984. St. Martin's Press, 1981 (Writers Dr 82)

*Young and Black in America. Rae Pace Alexander, comp. Random House, c1970 (*Alexander. Young)

*Young Readers' Picturebook of Tar Heel Authors. 5th ed. rev. Richard Walser and Mary Reynolds Peacock. North Carolina Department of Cultural Resources, Division of Archives and History, c1981 (*Walser. Young)